The
PRODIGAL
FATHER

"While lawyers tend to focus on the financial aspect of paternal absence . . . author Mark Bryan proposes a provocative, different approach to the problem."

—PEOPLE

"Bryan has put together an admirable package of anecdote and action to get the men who are among divorce's victims moving to heal themselves and their broken relationships."

—LIBRARY JOURNAL

"This is a timely book; those who are prepared to make the difficult journey back into their estranged children's lives will find much practical assistance here."

—PUBLISHERS WEEKLY

The
PRODIGAL
FATHER

Reuniting Fathers and Their Children

*With a special
section for mothers*

MARK BRYAN

THREE RIVERS PRESS
NEW YORK

The stories in *The Prodigal Father* are true. However, all of the names and geographic details have been changed. Some of the stories are composites. I chose to do this to protect the anonymity of the fathers and families involved. To all of you, thanks.

Published by Three Rivers Press, a division of Crown Publishers, Inc., 201 East 50th Street, New York, New York 10022. Member of the Crown Publishing Group.

Random House, Inc. New York, Toronto, London, Sydney, Auckland
www.randomhouse.com

Originally published in hardcover by Clarkson Potter/Publishers in 1997.

THREE RIVERS PRESS is a trademark of Crown Publishers, Inc.

Printed in the United States of America

Design by Susan DeStaebler

Library of Congress Cataloging-in-Publication Data
Bryan, Mark A.
    Prodigal father: reuniting fathers and their children: with a special section for mothers / Mark Bryan.
        Originally published: New York: Clarkson Potter, 1997.
        Includes bibliographical references and index.
        1. Fatherhood.   2. Parenting.   3. Divorced fathers.   4. Absentee fathers.   I. Title.
HQ756.B79   1998
306.874'2–dc21   98-13497

ISBN 0-609-80203-8

10 9 8 7 6

To my son, Scott, for his courage,
his truth, for having a heart
as big as Texas and for letting
me love him anew

And to my stepdaughter, Domenica,
for teaching me to love another child;
to my father, Jim, and my mother,
Dorothy, for their love and the many
wonderful things they did for me;
to Scott's mother, the first woman I ever
loved, who raised our son when I couldn't;
to Elizabeth and Caroline;
to the people who loved me before I could
love myself

CONTENTS

"The most urgent domestic challenge facing the United States at the close of the twentieth century is the re-creation of fatherhood as a vital social role for men. At stake is nothing less than the success of the American experiment. For unless we reverse the trend of fatherlessness, no other set of accomplishments . . . will succeed in arresting the decline of child well-being and the spread of male violence. To tolerate the trend of fatherlessness is to accept the inevitability of continued societal recession."

—DAVID BLANKENHORN, *FATHERLESS AMERICA*

INTRODUCTION

*It is a wise father that knows
his own child.*

WILLIAM SHAKESPEARE

This book began as a conversation on a train in 1988. I was
traveling on Amtrak from Chicago to Virginia to be reunited
with my son, Scott, whom I had not seen in more than ten
years. During the day-long trip, I sat beside a sociology professor from the University of Wisconsin. We struck up a conversation. I told him about my son and how we had been separated
in the wake of my teenage marriage and divorce. The professor
told me that social scientists were becoming increasingly
alarmed by the negative effects of father absence on children. I
was so nervous about my personal reunion with Scott, I could
barely listen.

"I've always missed my son," I told the professor. "But I was
so confused about fatherhood, I thought he might be better off
without me."

"Father absence has a negative impact on children, and it
is not a small one," ventured the professor. "Your son may have
missed and needed you as much as you missed him."

This was a sobering piece of information. While I had always been haunted by the memory of my son and the shame of having lost contact with him, *I had never let myself acknowledge, or even imagine, that my son might miss me as much as I missed him.*

Just the thought of this possibility jostled something deep inside me. I felt as if a key clicked into place as my heart opened to the idea that children and fathers should be reunited out of *mutual* need and love.

I realized in that instant that I knew many men who suffered from the loss of their children and it had always seemed to me that no one understood how fathers felt about it or why. A writer by trade and temperament, I resolved to document the story of my reunion with Scott and to do what I could to bring other men back to their children. The book you hold in your hands is a distillate of all the understanding I have found and the tools I have used from the beginning of my own reunion, over ten years ago, to the present.

I now believe the absent father is the central, unspoken fact of American life, and children—and their mothers and fathers—are paying a terrible untold emotional, psychological, and spiritual price.

It is not the purpose or within the scope of this book to address all of the well-known diverse and catastrophic social ills the professor discussed with me that day—illiteracy, crime, drugs, loneliness. It is the aim of this book to address the factor that contributes to all of them: families without fathers, fathers without families. As David Blankenhorn wrote in *Fatherless America*: "In virtually all human societies, children's well being depends decisively upon a relatively high level of paternal investment." Unfortunately our society has lost sight of this basic truth. About one-third of all childbirths in the nation now occur outside of marriage; in most of these cases, the space for the father's name is left blank. Fifty percent of divorced fathers see their children only once a year.

Thirty percent of children of divorce have never been inside their fathers' homes.

A father becomes disengaged from his children for many reasons. Some of the most common are anger about the divorce agreement, inability to deal with the mother's anger, the difficulty of becoming a visiting father after having been a live-in father, having grown up without a father, having witnessed domestic violence in the home as a child, depression, alcoholism, pathological narcissism, or a combination of the above. Regardless of the reason for the separation, this book can guide a father back to his children. I hope both men and women will read it.

OUR CULTURAL CONDITIONING

Our society is full of advice on motherhood and homemaking. In every supermarket and drugstore every week, you can see images of women holding their children. *Good Housekeeping, Ladies' Home Journal, Redbook, Working Woman*–the magazine racks are filled with how-to articles addressed to women. It is widely recognized that women are juggling the two roles of nurturer and provider. And what about father?

Men have *Gentleman's Quarterly, Esquire*, the car magazines, and the specialty sports guides. So much for the media in portraying the deep love of fathers for their children. The men's magazines are commonly all about sex, prestige, and money because our culture defines a man by how much money he makes. This is why it is a prevalent fantasy among estranged fathers that they are somehow, someday, going to make enough money or gain enough prestige to return to their children without shame.

The value of a father's love is rarely modeled to men. Instead of father love, what they hear about is their financial responsibility, a message that reinforces the old stereotype of a man being equal to the money he earns.

Father love? Many of the media images disseminated for men are Father's Day–card clichés–duck decoys and sailboats. How many men do you know who go duck hunting or own sailboats? These images address a demographic age group and earning level to which few fathers actually belong. Where are the tool belts, work boots, ties, briefcases, and socks with worn-out heels that are the symbols of a man's real work life? And is fatherhood really about the work he does? Is it about the perks his income offers–wooden ducks and boats?

No. Money isn't all of what fathering is about. Financial support of children is only part of the support we owe our children and want to give them; particular qualities of child rearing that have been shown to be extremely important to the healthy development of children. Yet money is the only part we hear about, the part we are blamed for, judged by.

Still worse, if our culture offers men little honor in their work, unless it pays extravagantly, it offers them less for their genuine parental role. I'm thinking of the men who come home from a day on the road or working construction and roughhouse or play ball with their kids, help them with their homework, listen to their daughter's latest woes with a nasty playmate.

Many men, whose wives work, do share in taking kids to school and back, do help with the grocery shopping, and do perform some of the household chores. The fact is, men have always had to combine work outside the home with fathering. Yet the fathering aspects have rarely been honored.

Today when I meet people and they ask me what I do, I say I'm a writer-teacher who works to reunite fathers with their children. This often strikes an immediate chord. Everyone knows a divorced or a separated father, an abandoned or hurt child, an angry or struggling single mother. Often they are those people themselves.

"You work to reunite fathers and children?"

"Yes."

"You mean you actually help fathers get back together with their kids, even if it has been a long time, or really awful or . . . ?"

"Yes."

"You see, I–" Here they often pause as emotion catches them.

I have learned to wait quietly until the man or the woman in front of me has a chance to gather some courage. Then, after he clears his throat and shuffles his feet for a few moments, with a blend of excitement and skepticism in his voice, he usually asks, "How do you do that?"

The same way *I* learned to do it, I answer.

It's a simple process that allows fathers to honor and heal themselves–and then to heal their relationships with the mothers of their children and then their children. This work requires courage, but remember that courage has as its root the French word *coeur*–"heart." At base, we are talking about acknowledging and healing a nation of broken hearts.

This book is a step-by-step guide for reuniting an absent father with his children, whether the father abandoned the child, was exiled by an angry mother, is still living with the child but is emotionally distant, or is visiting his children after a divorce. The circumstances may vary but the pain of separation is the same. So is the joy of reunion.

The purpose of this book is to tell you true stories of exile and reunion and present the spiritual and behavioral tools that have guided many members of disengaged families toward reconnection.

For a decade now I have assisted fathers, mothers, and children. I will include the stories of many of them to illustrate key concepts. I will also tell my personal story of my loss and later reunion with my son. All of these stories will illustrate one simple unchangeable fact: it doesn't matter who they are, where they live, what their work is, what their bank balance or ethnic background is, all members of father-absent families are on some level hurt and hurting.

You can start, on this page, to change our national language of denial, to help dispel the myth that there are "fatherless children." There is no such thing. They may be absent, dead, or missing in action, but all children have or have had fathers. Fathers may be visiting or living in the house and still be emotionally distant, but so long as the father is alive, labeling children as fatherless serves only to doom any hope of reunion and to encourage feelings of failure instead of solution.

For starters, unfathered children grow up with an idealized or distorted image of their father built from fantasy or misinformation that they may carry as shame their whole lives. The mothers are often angry, sad, or resentful at having to fulfill too many roles. And the fathers aren't content either. They are often lonely, ashamed, and frustrated, alienated from their ancestral line, their legacy, and the drive to provide.

ENDING THE EUPHEMISMS AND EVASION

If a father can say, "My children are without me, I am not a part of their life," then he will have to face up to why he isn't part of their life and discover what is at the root of his absence. If a mother can say, "My son's father never visits him," she can begin to assess her own contribution to that situation. By rejecting the role of victim and the language of euphemism, we begin the dialogue for change.

The courage of fathers who overcome their anger or shame and return to their children never ceases to amaze me. The heart wisdom of these men in taking action and the heart wisdom of the women who support them in their return resonates like the bell of a great cathedral.

I am humbled by the sight of formerly angry single mothers who have quietly come to forgive, honor, and appreciate the men who fathered their children. And I am still astounded by the displays of love and downright courage that I have seen in children of all ages, some of whom have never known their fathers, once they established–or reestablished–a relationship with them. This process is not easy, but it is critical.

REUNION IS BASED ON REALITY

Reunion starts with a decision to face the truth, and that demands a candid assessment of our situation. "I don't see my kids" is an honest statement and one that you can do something about. I have established support groups to help reunite fathers with their children, and I have also worked with mothers and at-risk teens and children who have grown up without at least one of their parents.

If you are a father estranged from your children, a single mother hurt by a man who refuses to parent, or confused by a father who wants to be a parent despite your anger at him, then this book will help.

Fathers, allow yourselves to entertain the idea that it might be possible to restore a loving relationship with your children *no matter how long you have been away from them.* I was finally reunited with my own son after an absence of fourteen years.

Mothers, imagine getting real support–emotional, spiritual, *and* financial–from your former partner. You can both reach a point where you will feel more appreciated and alive. Less burdened by dangerous resentments and fears yourself, you will also be blessed with happier kids.

As most of us unconsciously and uncomfortably know, it is the relationship between the father and the mother that will determine the quantity and quality of the father's visits with his children, regardless of how old the children are. There is never a point when we are too young or too old to know our fathers. Children will be healthier if both parents are part of their identity and support system from the start. Mothers need to find room in their hearts to foster a connection between fathers and children. Fathers must insist upon and live up to their rights as fathers.

I can tell you from years of experience that children suffer from the absence of a father. Henry Friedman at Harvard Medical School says, "What is central to a good outcome of divorce for children is the ability of the father to establish a relationship with them that reflects his personality in a way that is both spontaneous and intimate. For this to occur, fathers must have access to the children and be able to experience everyday life with them."

Charles Ballard, a sociologist working in a Cleveland ghetto, proved that by bringing jobless fathers back into their children's lives, most of the men were subsequently motivated to find jobs and pay support.

Fathers need to reclaim their children not only for the benefit of their own hearts and lives but for the benefit of the children. Ultimately, of course, this benefits society as a whole.

My experience has shown me that when a man returns to his children he is often empowered in many other areas of his life. The simple act of returning can reverse a downward spiral that his disengagement from his children may have helped cause. Shame can trigger successive failures that lead a man further and further from his true self.

I call this book *The Prodigal Father* because the problems of absent fathers in many ways mirror those in the parables of the Prodigal Son found in the Old and New Testaments. In the stories, the younger son, after deserting his people for a decadent life, returns home. When he returns, his father is overjoyed and welcomes him home. Jubilant, the old man puts on a feast to celebrate. But the older brother, the loyal son who toiled dutifully beside his father for the many years his younger brother was missing, is enraged. Wl y is all the attention being lavished on his reprobate brother? What about him, the dutiful one? The elder son's resentment threatens to sabotage the family reunion. Finally, the father steps in to resolve the conflict, but peace does not come without struggle and compromise by everyone in the family.

Most often we view the prodigal son as a wastrel, gar-landed in shame for his disappearance. To my eyes, that is only half the story.

The prodigal son returns home bearing a hard-won gift: he has learned the emptiness of a life built solely on outward achievement and sensual rewards. He has come to realize that the outward victory, the materialistic life, is a lie. The prodigal son has, in the words of the Eagles song, "taken it to the limit," and what he has found at that far boundary is exile not only from his community but from himself, from his soul.

The story of the prodigal son is a story about a different kind of riches than money. The prodigal son did not merely burn through worldly excesses; he saw through worldly excesses. He came home bearing a message: a life lived for external rewards does not work. Home is in the heart. This is why his homecoming is a cause for celebration.

The older son's envy is grounded in the fact that he too, though loyal and dutiful, wonders if he didn't somehow miss out by not going adventuring. His resentment is grounded in the fact that he too feels "not enough." The wisdom of the father lies in his insistence on celebrating the son's return as a return to right witness, to values of the heart.

The world of value is the world of relationships, not appear-ances. Men and women alike must realize that the destruction of the family has been caused by our refusal to cherish each other, to see that we have value other than fiscal value. Our very presence in each other's lives is the greatest gift.

Yet, understandably many single mothers harbor the same resentment felt by the elder son. They need help and support in dismantling that resentment. This book can help them.

If you are an estranged father, this book can help you gain insight into the often difficult dynamics between you and the mother of your children, whether she is your former spouse or not. It can help you learn to respect and honor the enormous contribution she has made to your children while also allowing you to see those you could yet make. It can forge a path toward reunion.

Men need to witness the women they have left behind and honor them. Women need to honor and witness the father who seeks to return. He now knows the value of connection and community. He can offer this hard-earned wisdom as the gift of his return and even celebrate it if we allow our hearts to open to the vulnerable joy of reconnection.

This book is not about accountability. It is not about shame. It is about something different: the celebration of our responsibility. Responsibility means what it says: "response-ability." This book is about our ability as men and women to respond to what we truly know is the deepest call of our human heart.

We are meant to cherish one another. We are meant to know ourselves and each other as sacred, even precious—meaning fine, inestimable, priceless, rare. These words apply to our children, but also to ourselves.

A RETURN TO THE HEART

My goal in presenting this program is twofold: to help you ready yourself for reunion and to show you how to maintain and manage that connection with your child once it has been established. I'm not suggesting that divorced spouses remarry, or try to resume an unhealthy relationship. It is not my intention to tell people how they must live or that they must "stay together for the children." It is my intention to help you rekindle respect for each other and develop the capacity to communicate despite whatever emotional abyss may seem at this time to yawn between you.

During my own years as a prodigal father, my years as a parent and stepparent, and more recently in my work counseling families trying to put their lives back together, I have become keenly aware of a terrible and familiar story from abandoned children and the men who left them.

It is important that you know the essential elements of this story. It always includes emotional pain, whether outwardly acknowledged or not. It always includes confusion about how to set things right. It always includes denial about the degree of the pain and the degree of the confusion. Finally, and significantly, the fathers and children have two things in common no matter what their individual circumstances: one is the fantasy of the reunion; the other is a sense of loss and bewilderment about the separation itself and the wish for a workable route back into each other's lives.

You may not be sure how you feel about reunion at all; you may be confused about whether it is the best thing to do. I will help you examine your feelings and thoughts so that you can come to your own conclusions. To reach your goal you might have to resolve your fights with your ex-wife, seek medical treatment for depression, get clean and sober, find a job, travel to the other side of the country, or all of the above.

Perhaps your child's mother has erected seemingly impenetrable barriers to your return. Together we will work to change that.

This book is meant as a family survival kit for the twenty-first century. It is not a victim book, nor is it a sociological treatise, though I hope social scientists will use it.

As a teacher, my first goal is to break the silence surrounding father-child loss. Men *do* love their children, and the loss of the father role is nothing short of catastrophic for their children's well-being as well as for their own growth.

Secondly, in order to move forward as parents, we have to acknowledge the rights and responsibilities of fatherhood, and help the estranged fathers among us find a way back to the lives and love of their children and therefore themselves. It is impossible to have full self-esteem and therefore self-love if a man is in exile from his children.

Because this book is meant as a vision for the future, I will focus on stories of families reunited. It is my hope that men reading this book will shoulder their responsibilities and claim their authority as parents, noncustodial or not.

Finally I would like to extend a special invitation to those men who, like me, abandoned their rights and obligations to father their children—the "Deadbeat Dads," as they are called by the media; the men I call the Brokenhearted Dads. I hope this book is the beginning of your own journey home, for I will explain to you the forces that work to keep us away from our children and drive us into exile.

Although *The Prodigal Father* includes the story of my personal experience as a father—a teen father and then an absentee father, a stepfather and then a reunited father—it is grounded in my work with many teens and parents as well.

I intend *The Prodigal Father* to be both a bellwether and a map toward wholeness for fathers, mothers, and children alike. It will work for you despite whatever differences in circumstance or specifics your story may entail.

Reunion is the goal. While it may seem distant, it is not an impossible journey. With each chapter your children will be nearer to you. With each chapter you will be nearer to your true self, the man who loves his children and shares with them that love.

1

THE HAUNTING

THE LOSS

In January of 1972, under a gray sky filled with falling snow, I
drove from Ohio State University in Columbus to Virginia to
visit my son, Scott, then twenty-two months old. I was an
eighteen-year-old college freshman, two years married and on
the brink of divorce. Scott was living with his mother, Betsy,
my soon-to-be ex-wife, and Betsy's parents in our old
hometown.

Driving all day in my little red Volkswagen through the
Ohio farmlands, along the Pennsylvania Turnpike to the
Appalachia Tunnel, and on through the night, I wondered
what I would say to Betsy. Did she sense, as I did, that our
attempts to hold our marriage together were failing? Did she
feel, as I did, a sense of hopelessness, despair, and failure?
Surely we had ruined each other's young lives. Was it as
painful for her to sense our broken dreams as it was for me?

Betsy, my first love, a tall, slim beauty with dark hair, had
become pregnant during our junior year of high school (just

as more than a million teenagers a year still do today). We were both from strict military homes, with religion at the center of our upbringing. When Betsy became pregnant, abortion was not an answer. It wasn't even a question.

"Do you love her?" my father asked me.

I answered truthfully, "Yes."

That left only one right choice: marriage.

Even though we were legally underage.

When Betsy and I fell in love, I was a geeky kid, president of our high school class, an honor student, a hard worker bound for the Ivy League. Dreaming of the stage, Betsy was the class princess, beautiful and bright. We planned a brilliant future for both of us. Our pregnancy would end all that.

Betsy and I married, at age sixteen, in a courtroom in Elizabeth City, North Carolina; we were too young to be married in Virginia. Betsy and I, our mothers, and my sister, Paula, had made the sixty-mile trip together. I remember pulling out of the driveway as my father watered the lawn and muttered epithets under his breath. (Betsy's father was a navy man away at sea, but he welcomed me into the family by way of a rumor that he threatened to kill me the minute he returned.)

I do not remember much of the long drive to and from North Carolina. Once there, I know I laughed nervously as the service began while all the women cried. I remember thinking I had broken the heart of every woman in that room.

The old magistrate jokingly charged me a hundred dollars for the wedding, said he'd take four dollars now and I could pay the rest to Betsy at a dollar a year for the next ninety-six years. A hundred years? I couldn't imagine myself much past thirty. By then, I reasoned, my son would be reaching his teens and I myself would be grown up. Clutching Betsy's hand, I silently promised that I would be a good father, although I couldn't see how, given the terror I was feeling.

That night, as sixteen-year-old newlyweds, Betsy and I sat down to watch TV with her family. We were stunned. We did not know what else to do. It was as if everything and nothing had happened. We were newlyweds with no home of our own. How were we supposed to act? We had no idea.

What we did, that night and for the next year and a half, while living in the basement of my family home, was to try to act like grown-ups. We didn't feel like grown-ups; we felt young and scared and overwhelmed. An all too grown-up world became our grim reality very quickly. The school called my parents and informed them that I could not attend high school as a married student and would have to attend night school. I got a day job as an orderly in a hospital. On weekends I worked as a grocery clerk. Betsy had to quit school, too; she prepared for motherhood. After a few months my entire family moved to Ohio to escape the stigma of our hometown shame.

I remember being embarrassed by not having enough money to rent a place of our own or even buy a car. I did not know how to comfort Betsy, or even myself. Late at night we would curl up to watch television. She would drift into the oblivion of sleep, and I would hold her in my arms, staring blankly at the screen and into our future. Scott was born just as Betsy and I turned seventeen.

Instead of making us feel grown up, his birth only emphasized our immaturity. Small humiliations seemed endless and personal. I remember saving enough money to take Betsy on a night out—dinner and a movie. She wanted to see *Midnight Cowboy,* which was rated Adults Only. Despite our babe in arms, we were carded at the door and refused admission. Looking young but with adult responsibilities, I felt my whole identity threatened and demanded to see the manager. He let us into the theater only after a public scene and my plea about our "adult" lives. The victory was short-lived. Scott began to cry midway through the movie and we had to leave.

Meanwhile, our new Ohio acquaintances were college students with nothing much to do beyond party and attend class.

I envied them greatly. I grew resentful about my situation but felt powerless to change it or to ease my guilt at getting us into this predicament.

By the time Scott was eighteen months old, Betsy and I, our old lives shattered and our new lives too difficult to continue, agreed to separate, hoping that by spending time apart, we could somehow recover our equilibrium as individuals. I remember the pain of this separation, as I prepared to move in with college friends, visiting Scott weekly.

I have a strong vision of Betsy standing by the door, the light spilling onto the snow, me in my coat and boots saying good night and turning to go. That hovering moment of heartbreak and loss. My cold breath floating upward. Turning to watch her close the door. Turning back to walk in the silent night. Full of an uncomfortable freedom, remorse, and self-hate. Empty of answers.

I can only imagine that it was as confusing and painful for Betsy to watch me walk away as it was for me walking home alone in the cold Ohio winter.

Soon after we agreed to separate, I moved Betsy and Scott home to her family in Virginia and went back to Ohio to continue college. I did well my first quarter, though my talks with Betsy became less and less frequent as guilt and befuddlement about my role as a husband and father became more and more intense.

By the time I made the long and snowy drive to Virginia in 1972, Betsy and I were barely speaking, and all my thoughts were of anger or self-recrimination. I felt worthless, and I was soon to act that out.

Driving through the storm, I thought about Scott. Where would I take him later that day? Would he remember me? Was it that important for me to see him? Would my visits be just hurting him? What about our father-son outing? Should we go to the zoo, perhaps, or the park? The zoo was a favorite with us, as was the beach. Usually we'd end our visit with a meal at Shoney's Big Boy, and then I would take him home and put him to bed. I never knew what was the best thing to do. I had no place of my own to be with him in a comfortable way.

I remember hearing a friend say that it was particularly important for the father to be with his child for the first three years of life, but I did not know why. And was I really what they meant by a "father"? Invariably, after a father-son visit, I would be overcome by sadness and would cry all the way home, overwhelmed by the terrible feeling of distance between me and my son. These tears made me feel unmanly so I told no one how I was feeling.

Shouldn't I know what to do with my son, what to say to him, and how to make our weekend together meaningful? I had no idea how to be a parent, how to care for him as a single dad, or even how to take good care of myself. My father was so angry at me that he could barely speak, though he tried to help in every way he knew. Still, he raged that I had "ruined my life."

The irony of my situation was that even with so much family around, I felt isolated and alone. I wish I'd had someone to talk to. I now know that counselors, members of the clergy, and grandparents can be of tremendous aid in such a crisis. They often have the long view, the compassionate view, the view that acknowledges the time and place and the history of the event. I was not that close to my grandparents, however, and it never occurred to me to seek professional help, even from a school guidance counselor. If I had, perhaps what happened next might not have happened.

When I arrived in Virginia, Betsy told me that I would not be allowed to see Scott this trip or ever again.

"What do you mean?"

"I mean I've made a new life and you are not part of it."

I remember our standing in her garage discussing her

decision. While we talked, John, her former boss, ten years our senior, and now her boyfriend, waited in the kitchen to lend her his support. Betsy was in love; she had moved on. We would never be a family again. I tried to take it all in.

More important, I was to be denied contact with our son. I wanted to argue the injustice of her decision, but John was an intimidating presence. Tall, soap-opera handsome, and successful in the world, he helped Betsy stand her ground. I was tongue-tied and intimidated.

As we entered the kitchen, John moved to her side, their arms immediately entwined, and I could see that they were a couple. They were a team. And they would raise Scott.

> I shall tell you a great secret, my friend. Do not wait for the last judgment. It takes place every day.
>
> —ALBERT CAMUS

Though I don't know if she actually said it, all I could hear that day was that I was a loser in Betsy's eyes. That I did not deserve this son any longer. That Scott was better off without me in his life. All of it seemed part of a bad dream. Too confused and scared to challenge Betsy morally, let alone legally, I got into the car and headed back to Ohio. I wept throughout most of the ten-hour trip. I felt isolated, cut off emotionally from myself and others.

Returning to school, I "accepted" Betsy's decision. Deeply depressed, I stopped attending class. I saw my grades slip from A's and B's to F's, a free fall that no one at school seemed to notice—not a teacher, not my boss at the hospital where I worked, not even my parents. This invisibility seemed to underscore my worthlessness.

For the next decade I continued to act out this sense of worthlessness. I drifted out of school, into depression, into alcohol and drug abuse, into a self-imposed exile, as I tried to hide from my failure.

Betsy was left to raise a child, while I was left without a child to raise.

THE HAUNTING

When a father is separated from his children, a piece of himself is ripped away, and he is haunted by that deep inner knowledge that somewhere, somehow, this missing piece must be regained. Until he is able to do that, no matter how he may try to deny it, a man is divided. The distance a man is from his children is often equal to the pain he still carries.

In many spiritual traditions this is called "soul loss": the abandonment of a central and integral part of oneself—namely, fatherhood. This loss of self never stops visiting a parent who is estranged from his children.

I call this marrow-deep memory The Haunting. It is a dramatic term, I know, but it accurately names the shadow of sadness that darkens even the brightest times with heartache. In my experience, a man does not merely remember his children; they inhabit him in his very soul.

What I call The Haunting, some clinicians call "parental emergency." The term for the feeling a parent has whenever he sees children playing. The sight triggers the sudden memory of his or her own child or children, wherever they may be, whatever they may be doing.

I remember passing a school yard, watching one of the boys and thinking, "Scott must be about that size." I remember going to visit an old friend and wincing when his young children came tumbling into the living room. They were Scott's memory come to life.

When a man loses a child to divorce, there are a million small losses—his daughter's first dance class, his son's nightmare, the braces, the bikes, the Band-Aids. His friends and family often act as if he brought the loss on himself. Many times they're right. This doubles the grief until the grief can be overwhelming.

Rather than get help, he tries to "be a man and tough it out." You cannot tough something out without deadening it as well. Grieving fathers often deny their feelings for their children. In doing so, they kill a part of themselves because their *children* are not dead; they're very much alive, just captive, behind the lines of failed communication, failed compassion, failed dreams. At bottom, men's feelings for their children are not dead, but deadened by the mechanism of denial—cultural and personal. This is how it works.

I once met a man named Jules who had convinced his friends and even himself that his seven-year-old son was dead because, he said, "It was the only way I could deal with the pain of not knowing him." His was a *literal* haunting. Men who have lost their children hide a horrible pain—one that they may go to great lengths to mask from themselves and others.

DENIAL OF THE HAUNTING

For almost a decade I used alcohol and other drugs to aid my denial, to medicate my soul loss. Although other men may do it through work, through a series of frantic new relationships, or by repeated moves—"geographic cures"—the central point is that men who lose their children often miss them keenly and go to almost any length to avoid facing this painful fact.

> *The beginning of health is to know the disease*
> —MIGUEL DE CERVANTES

Commonly, the pain of this loss is deadened by a set of denial mechanisms that we erect to keep our real emotions at bay. The denial sounds like this:

"They're better off without me."
"I don't care anymore."
"I'm sure they've forgotten me."
"Their mother has turned them against me anyway."
"Actually, I'm not sure he's my kid."
"I'll go back when I have enough money."
"They have a new dad now. Having me in their life will only confuse them."

"I'm tired of fighting with their mother. I can't deal with her
  anger."
"My new girlfriend treats me great, and she wants kids."
"I could not possibly afford to support two families."
"I will never make it as a husband and father."

Rationalizations and regrets isolate men from their fellows and from the best part of themselves. Without a family, men may lose their satisfaction in their accomplishments, because there is no one to share them with or to benefit from them. They may lose their ambition and drive; they may lose the ability to feel joy *and* sadness as their grief keeps them bottled up; they may lose their sense of identity as a father, a husband, and a man. Often, they carry so much personal pain and anger that their days seem unfulfilled.

And yet many men do abandon their children. They do—as I did—leave behind beloved sons and daughters. They renege on their promise to provide support, both monetary and personal. How can they do this? What makes this possible? It is easy to see how such abandonment can look like a lack of love. In some cases, it may well be. Not in most. Many people dismiss and blame men for having lost their children. Yet our culture sets the stage for this absence. The media, even many self-help books, portray men as emotionally absent, unavailable. We deny men a mythology that shows their presence to be important, and then we wonder how they can walk away so cavalierly.

> *O*ften we attack and make ourselves enemies, to conceal that we are vulnerable.
>
> —FRIEDRICH NIETZSCHE

The bad press that absent fathers receive reminds me of the bad press that Vietnam vets get. Vietnam vets are frequently depicted in our media as troubled people who can sometimes become dangerous psychopaths, even murderers. The sad truth is, as Robert Bly, a leader in the men's movement, has said, more Vietnam veterans have committed suicide since returning home than died in Southeast Asia—more than 55,000 men. We still do not understand their pain.

Absent fathers, the MIAs in the war between the sexes, are similarly acting out a cultural expectation. They are literalizing an emotional distance we expect.

> *In nature there are neither rewards nor punishments—there are consequences.*
>
> —ROBERT INGERSOLL

This does not excuse absent dads, but it does help to explain them. How can a man leave behind children he loves? By the same deadening process that enables a soldier to kill a man his own age who might in other circumstances have been his friend. In other words, in order to leave his children, a man must first leave himself. As a culture and in the courts, we unconsciously—and unconscionably—invite our men to do this.

Psychiatrists tell us it is the limbo loss that creates the lingering, festering wound. This is the loss without closure, without clarity, without the ceremony of grieving—in this limbo loss men lose their children.

Faced with losing his children in small increments, a man may unconsciously want to "get it over with." Already feeling distanced, he feels that a geographical separation won't really make any difference—and the new job in a distant city pays more. So he tells himself, "I can make more money and put them through college when they are old enough." The problem with this plan is that without their father they may never get to college.

Father unemployment and absence can result in desperate problems of poverty, depression, violence, and neglect for the mothers and children left behind. But even in more stable family circumstances an absent father may not know how important his presence is to his children's schooling, gender identity, emotional stability, security, and self-confidence.

Unable to tabulate even the subtle costs of his absence emotionally and intellectually, the father may try to tabulate it financially: "I'll have more money for child support, and I can make up the visits later." But paying child support is no substitute for a father's presence, and it's only part of the story. Men offer many kinds of support beyond money.

> *We make a living by what we get, but we make a life by what we give.*
>
> —Winston Churchill

THE PRICE OF DENIAL

As I would later learn, and as the experience of many others would confirm, an absent father's shame about his departure often deepens a negative self-image that can begin a vicious cycle of failure after failure in other areas of his life, sabotaging career and schooling. Even for those able to achieve some worldly success, the haunting can make their accomplishments feel hollow and undeserved. I have heard this scenario repeated too many times to dismiss it casually. Abandoning his children may become the beginning of a failure script a father will fight throughout his absence.

Steve is a former law enforcement officer. I know him now as a big sunny man, gifted as a musician and generous as a friend. I know him to be kind, honest, and gentle—not a man who would leave his children. And yet, like me, he did.

About six years ago Steve lost his job. The added pressure and shame of unemployment ended his already shaky marriage, as it often does. Research has confirmed that less money equals more divorce. When Steve lost his job, he also lost his wife and two children, ages six and eight. Steve says he also lost his mind.

"I moved from Colorado to Texas," he explains. "It was just too painful to stay in Los Angeles. I received a severance settlement, but I just blew it. I didn't work for two years and lived in a cabin in the mountains at 8,500 feet, chopping wood and carrying water."

During this time Steve had virtually no contact with his children. His ex-wife was hostile. He felt unwelcome, and he was. He also felt worthless and powerless—both common feelings experienced by divorced men.

Steve's pain, the result of his denial, rendered him effectively mute. For Steve it seemed that he did not have much to say—"To her or the kids. Or to anybody else really. You might say I lost it."

Working with the fathers of divorce, I have heard those words, "I lost it," over and over. Divorce has become so common that we seldom acknowledge its real emotional brutality for fathers as well as for mothers and children.

Steve gradually got himself back into the real world, into a new job, into a marriage with a new wife, a stepdaughter, and a new child of their own.

Despite Steve's hopes, the new family did not heal his pain over losing his first one. Many months ago he wrote a letter to his children in California and bought them gifts for Christmas, but has been unable to send the children either the letter or their gifts. When asked why, he says he does not know.

DENIAL CREATES EXILE

The absent father may distance himself further and further from the pain of missing his children by denying their existence. He may stop talking about them, no longer show pictures of them to his friends or display them in his home. Tangibly absent from his own life, he may reside in a fantasy, in an elaborate mental construct, about the kind of relationship he will have with the kids someday: "If I can just make a go of this new construction deal, I'll get a real showplace with a pool and invite the kid to join me for summers."

The more grandiose the fantasy, the more pain underlying

and blocking the return and the more difficult and finally rewarding the reunion work will be: "My daughter probably thinks I'm a real deadbeat. I'll bet her mother tells her I am. I'll wait until I can get her a pony and prove that I really love her."

Living in this fantasy world has the unintentional consequence of paralyzing a father, preventing him from ever going back into his child's life: "I don't know what to get him for this birthday. I ought to get him something really special. I ought to at least call. . . . What am I supposed to do, just call up without a gift or anything? Next year . . ."

> I'd like to get away from earth awhile And then come back to it and begin over.
>
> –Robert Frost

The fantasy, comforting as it is in the short term, makes any realistic attempt at reunion seem confusing, uncertain, even impossible: "Where would we even start? Hi, I'm your dad. I know I haven't talked to you in two years, but, you see, I was . . . I was what?"

When the "what" comes up, many men cannot imagine admitting even to themselves that they were afraid or hurt. That's somehow too human, too normal, too real, too weak. Don't their kids deserve a "real dad"? The kind who has the answers?

What their kids deserve is having their own dad back, just as he is, but most men can't see it that way when they are in the grip of The Haunting.

BREAKING THROUGH OUR DENIAL

The first step in healing The Haunting is to acknowledge that it exists. We need to come out of our denial about it and look as squarely as we can at the emotions we are feeling. Much of the pain of The Haunting is voiceless, not merely unvoiced.

I am at a dinner party. Talk turns to children. A dinner guest, Larry, whom I do not know well, falls silent. When asked, he mentions that he has four children, three of whom are grown, but then he falls silent again, not speaking further about them.

His good mood disappears. He finishes his dinner quietly. Later I learn that Larry has no contact whatever with his kids.

> Men may rise on stepping-stones of their dead selves to higher things.
>
> —ALFRED, LORD TENNYSON

Afterward, while we are doing dishes, I press him a little. "Larry, I noticed you got quiet when we talked about children. Would you want to talk about it?"

He says, "My kids are grown, so I feel it's too late to do anything for them." Again he falls silent.

I do not mention that he uses the verb "to do" when speaking of the role he might play in their lives; like many men, Larry doesn't think that "to be" in their lives might be enough.

"How old are they?" I ask.

"Twenty, nineteen, eighteen, and fifteen," he says.

I tell him that almost every young adult I have worked with fantasizes about finding his or her biological father. And many of them often seek their fathers very soon after getting out on their own. It seems to mean a lot to them.

> Oh, that one could learn to learn in time!
>
> —ENRIQUE SOLARI

Larry clears his throat. "Well, I guess I just thought if they needed me they would look me up." He turns back to the dishes.

His pain hangs over us like the memory of a lost love.

Not wanting to press him too far, I ask if he thinks of them a lot. "Oh, yes, all the time. I just don't know what to do about it. Imagine how they would feel? Me calling after all these years."

"I don't know," I tell him. "How would you feel?"

After a moment a big grin crosses his face.

In a small town in New Mexico where I used to live, I drove to the post office to pick up our mail. One sunny morning a few years back, just after Christmas, I slid my truck into a slot just as my friend Jack was leaving. A tall, handsome man with dark hair, blue eyes, and a movie-star smile, Jack didn't look at all like himself that day. Usually affable, he barely returned my hello. His long face was sallow, his jaw tight. I suddenly remembered that his daughter, Elizabeth, had just left after her holiday visit. She lived in Chicago.

"How's it going, Jack?" I asked.

"Oh, you know," he said. "This time of year . . ." Silence.

"Elizabeth?" I asked.

"Yeah. She went back."

Silence again.

DISGUISING OUR DENIAL

I have taught many workshops in which men like Larry and Jack are able to drop their denial and face their sadness once they feel they are in a safe environment. Until then many do not admit they are haunted by the loss of their children. Many seem unaware of it until they are questioned. I usually start by asking what they are doing with their lives.

"Oh, the job's really got me buried."

"I'm dating this new woman. She's pretty interested in me and says we could start a family ourselves one day."

"Maybe I'm drinking a little too much, but . . ."

More often than not, the denial has driven them into different forms of medication to hide from the pain of the absence of the children they left behind.

Listening to the stories of men, I understand their not being able to pick up the phone, acknowledge their loss, or mail their presents. I hear these stories all the time.

Another reason that denial is so prevalent is that absent or visiting fathers often imagine they will encounter rejection and continued loss if they make contact with their kids. Men like Steve do not acknowledge that their kids may be as haunted as they are.

"You mean they will accept me as I am?"

I've come to a theorem: the stronger the fantasy of a grandiose reunion, the more pain a man holds about the separation itself. The more anger he feels at the loss, the greater his pain over that loss and the greater the distance of drift away from contact and connection. Ironically, the more pain a man carries, the more pain he may inadvertently cause.

Father absence does not mean pain for the father alone, but pain and loss for the child and pain and loss for the mother, for the relatives and friends, for an entire network and fretwork of interconnected lives. This means, of course, that father absence brings pain and loss for society at large.

As a culture we place too heavy a burden on mothers. It's not only best, it's vital for kids to have access to and the nurturing support of two loving parents. We all know that, but our courts and our culture help promote something else.

Women are told that they should be the custodial parent after divorce. Men are told their financial support is all that matters. Women, trying to balance parenting and work, feel like failures as they struggle to make ends meet. Men find themselves reduced to a checkbook instead of part of a system of checks and balances needed for raising healthy, happy kids. Without a different kind of expectation and support, men and women do not have much incentive to view themselves any differently than society views them. What happens next? The daily shame, humiliation, confusion, and loss are simply too much. Families drift apart, and everyone suffers, particularly the children.

Many studies indicate that the most severe harm to children is from conflict, either in or out of a marriage. Other studies tell us the cost of paternal absenteeism to children is lowered self-esteem, lessened ability to form intimate relationships, a fear of disappointment in love relationships, increased compulsiveness and delinquency, increased likelihood of suicide, decreased gender affinity in female children, and overactive "masculinity"–meaning violence and misogyny–in male children.

Yet despite these proven statistics about the importance of a father–or, when that's not possible, at least positive male modeling–in the normal development of healthy, happy children, we have only recently begun to look at the tremendous, staggering impact of single parent child-rearing on the parents.

What I am talking about is the grief and anger felt by mothers who are struggling to do a two-person job and the terrible pain for fathers of losing their children. Exhausted and often embittered, the mothers lose their gaiety and miss out on the joy of motherhood. Displaced and often discounted, the fathers lose the dignity and satisfaction of being fathers. We all suffer the pain of losing our children's childhood.

> **A** *rock pile ceases to be a rock pile the moment a single man contemplates it, bearing within him the image of a cathedral.*
>
> –ANTOINE DE SAINT-EXUPÉRY

If even those parents who are doing the divorced-dad and single-mom routine in the best of circumstances must struggle to hang on, is it surprising that those less stable, or less healthy or less fortunate, give up?

If you have recognized or been moved toward emotions you have been "stuffing" for years, good. This is all the opening you need for changes to begin.

Nothing in my life means as much to me as my return to active fatherhood and my reunion with my son. You will find the same is true for you.

> **D** *ivorce and especially the abandonment by fathers may do particular violence to children's ability to trust others as adults.*
>
> –RICHARD WEISSBOURD

Once you can become aware of your feelings, express them, and unlearn the negative behavior patterns that may have contributed to your exile, and *relearn* your strengths, then you are already well on your way to reunion.

THE ROLLER COASTER OF RECOVERY AND RESISTANCE

The exercises and tasks at the end of each chapter are meant to guide you to a new acceptance of yourself. They are an emotional boot camp for men. Like the rigor of boot camp, answering these questions and doing the simple tasks asked of you may seem simplistic or absurd or unreasonable. You will want to complain to the drill sergeant. For that matter, you may hate the drill sergeant.

This means you may need to buck your own resistance and knuckle down, just as I ask you to with these tasks. If nothing else, think of them as "prep"—a sort of dry run for the challenges you will be facing in your real life.

One final proviso: if this book provokes you to anger, use that anger as fuel to get you over the obstacle course.

> *There is nothing as easy as denouncing. It don't take much to see that something is wrong, but it takes some eyesight to see what will put it right again.*
>
> —WILL ROGERS

This work will be hard at times. You will become frustrated. Some of you are probably feeling angry right now—like throwing this book across the room. Some of you may be so excited to learn that there is a solution and that you are not alone in your feelings—you're eager to start. These emotions will come and go. Such is the nature of the important task at hand—a mix of anger, fear, sadness, joy inevitably accompanies reunion. Try to remember: everything worthwhile comes with a price.

Make a resolution to complete this process without constantly voting on whether or not you will. There will be days when it is the greatest thing you have ever done, days when the payoff doesn't seem worth it. I assure you it is. Just accept that you will not do any of this work perfectly. There will be days when you may space out and fall asleep, when your body will ache, when you hate everyone you know. But at the end of this process you will suddenly realize that The Sergeant knew what he was doing all along and you're a better man for it. We've all seen those army movies where the gruff curmudgeon becomes the beloved mentor. Imagine that you're living that movie when you find your resistance at its peak.

I have presented throughout the book a wide variety of stories. Many of you will recognize yourselves in them. Good. This is the beginning of the awakening that happens when we suddenly have our old ideas changed for the better—even the ideas about who we are. As you learn their stories and begin to recognize their experiences embedded in your own, you may

> *We did not all come over on the same ship, but we are all in the same boat.*
>
> —BERNARD BARUCH

even come to love the men who went to this boot camp before you. Many of you may never have done "personal growth" work; no therapy, no pastoral counseling, no formal meetings with others for support. Others of you may have done so much "inner work" that you want to quit the job! So what's a guy like you doing with this book?

Don't call it coincidence. Call it grace.

Someone may have given you this book, maybe even your ex-wife. If she did, *great.* That means she is willing to listen to your side of the story and help you along even if you two aren't the best of friends. She is handing you an olive branch. Take it.

Some of you may be recently "clean" and "sober" and in support groups like AA, NA, or Alanon, searching for some guid-

> *Recovery is strongly related to mourning. Loss and the incapacity to mourn appropriately is one core aspect of most types of psychopatholgy.*
>
> —GIL NOAM

ance on this specific issue. Some of you, by honestly doing this work, may end up there. The tools of this book are meant to work within the twelve-step framework. Yet I need to add some words of caution:

No parents, mother or father, should be with their children if their behavior could be dangerous to the children. If you are still drinking, using drugs, physically or emotionally violent, or unable to hold a job, you must take steps to end your dangerous or counterproductive behavior before you try to participate in your child's life. If you are well enough and courageous enough to do this work, you are courageous enough to change your behavior.

Because it is grounded in the actual experiences of men and women, this work is not theory but practice. As such, it will help you and guide you to sources of community and professional assistance.

I approach this work as a teacher, not a therapist, but I highly recommend therapy as a support for anyone who can undertake it. If money is an issue, support groups are available at no charge, or you can complete this work with a group of supportive, positive friends or members of the clergy.

HOW THE PROCESS WORKS

The questions that follow each chapter will help you reframe your past and give you a chance to finally tell your side of the story. What you learn from this work may surprise you.

The exercises are arranged to walk you gently along a path of knowledge and action. Change, even positive change, however, can sometimes cause anxiety, sadness, anger, and much more. In my work with returning fathers, I have found that the early stages of reunion can be so exciting and joyful that emotional backlash can occur: fathers blaming or berating themselves for not having acted sooner. Avoid the self-blame trap.

> Don't find fault, find a remedy.
>
> –HENRY FORD

This work is not about blaming anyone, including yourself. It is about finding solutions. How do I recognize and fix what is wrong? How can I make my life and the lives of my children better? For me, it was my resistance to change that made life so difficult, not the change itself. Any negative feelings you experience in this work will always pass eventually–IF you keep doing the work. They will not go away if you keep trying to hide from them, bury them, run from them.

You are here to change something important in your life. It is never too late to change your life. Never.

THE DRILL

1. *Buy a notebook.* I ask you to keep a Reunion Notebook in which to record your feelings, thoughts, and progress. Fill one page a day. This book will become an important part of your memorabilia that you will want to keep, so I suggest that you buy a large school notebook or journal. You will be amazed at what you find when you look back on it a year or two from now.

2. *Choose a quiet place.* Start spending one hour a week in your own company. Find some solitude, a place to meditate, pray, or think, someplace you can be alone. It does not have to be a different place each week, but it can be. It does not have to be a sacred space such as a church, synagogue, or mosque, but it can be. An hour or two outdoors in nature can help. This process is at times unsettling, and it will be beneficial to have a place to go for a brief retreat and, most importantly, to give yourself time to hear your own inner wisdom.

> Faith is the bird that sings while it is still dark.
>
> –ANONYMOUS

3. *Choose a friend.* Think about your network of acquaintances and look for some friendly, positive, and sensible support. It is very possible that your current friends will NOT be much help with this work.

When I ended my negative behavior and set out on my path

to reunion, I did not have many friends that I really trusted, nor could I be trusted to know who had my best interests at heart. I had to look outside my own circle.

If this is your situation, call a member of the clergy, an older family friend, a therapist, or a hospital, or attend a support-group meeting. You can ask for guidance at a church, a mental health clinic, or a therapy center.

Our counselors and support teams hold our hands while we cry and rage and release long-suppressed anger, sadness, grief, frustration, loneliness, and abandonment. This important healing work allows us, finally, to live productively in the world community as well as in our own skin. This is sometimes called Grief Work. I call it Joy Work.

4. *Watch your health.* If you can, get a checkup. It is very important that you keep yourself healthy in mind, body, and spirit as you work toward reunion with your child. Get plenty of rest and exercise. Daily walks will help.

> I*t ain't over till it's over.*
>
> –YOGI BERRA

You will need to exercise at least three times a week to burn off the extra anxiety that this work may uncover. Any exercise is better than nothing, but strenuous exercise is best. Many men find that aerobic exercise is a powerful way to get in touch with what they are feeling.

When I started, I could run only a few blocks, but within weeks I was running regularly for longer and longer stretches, and eventually I ran two Chicago marathons. I believe running made my long-hidden feelings accessible for the first time. I remember running along the sandy shore of Lake Michigan, sobbing as long-buried feelings and events surfaced in my consciousness. At other times the running would provoke waves of enthusiasm at the recognition of the distance I had traveled, figuratively and literally.

5. *Pray.* Stop right now. Take three deep breaths. Close your eyes and say "thank you." You have just prayed. We tend to

overthink prayer, as if it's something complicated or connected to our childhood religion. We forget that God speaks all languages, especially the language of the heart.

Prayer is a tool. In fact, it is the one tool you will have always available to you. It costs no money. It takes very little time. And it works. So use it.

"Pray unceasingly"—or whenever you think of it. Pray in your own words. Pray in your own way. Pray in the quiet motion of your breath as it moves in and out of your body.

In: "help me."

Out: "thank you."

That's it. You don't need to believe in a God to do it. You can think of it as invoking your ancestors or simply some inner strength. You can, in fact, not think about it at all. Just do it.

Use the Serenity Prayer: "God, grant me the serenity to accept the things I cannot change, the courage to change the things I can, and the wisdom to know the difference." It will give you gratitude.

No need to discuss it with anyone.

THE TOOL KIT

The tools you use in this work will help you build a new emotional framework. They are meant to start things cooking in your unconscious. There are no right or wrong answers to the questions below. Just answer them as quickly as you can in your Reunion Notebook.

As you answer these questions, you will recover your memories of your children. This will give you a starting point on which to focus your reunion efforts. Remember that it is for those children, the ones you first knew and want now to know better, that you are doing this work. By remembering them anew, you will begin to remove

> *Vitality shows not only in our ability to persist but in our ability to start over.*
>
> —F. Scott Fitzgerald

the emotional blocks that prevent you from giving them the love they need and receiving the love they have to offer you.

THE EMOTIONAL MAP

1. What are the names and birthdays of your child or children? What are their nicknames?
2. Where were you when they were born? When they came home from the hospital?
3. Were you present at their birth? When did you see them for the first time? When did you see them last?
4. What is your earliest memory of them?
5. Where were you living when your children were born?
6. Who was around your children for their first year of life? Any special friends, relatives, pets?
7. Where were you when your children took their first steps? When they said their first words?
8. What were your earliest dreams for your children?
9. What activities did you share with your children when they were little? Making faces, making sounds, playing, watching special TV programs, reading at bedtime.
10. What was your child's favorite toy or game? What was your favorite toy or game as a child?
11. What is your favorite memory of your child?
12. What do you think is your child's favorite memory of you?
13. How do you feel when you think of being reunited with your children?
14. What circumstances caused you to lose touch?

> *I am larger, better than I thought. I did not know I held so much goodness.*
>
> —WALT WHITMAN

Let these answers gel in your mind. No need to do anything now; you are building a bridge and it will take some time. Avoid self-judgment.

POSITIVE INVENTORY

1. List five positive traits about yourself. Do not be surprised if this is difficult to do. Be specific and think small: I'm always on time for work; I pay my bills best I can, keep the car tuned, keep my apartment pretty clean. . . .
2. List five accomplishments you are proud of: I worked a paper route, anchored the wrestling team, served in the army, visited Mom every week when she was sick, got my union card, finished college. . . .
3. List five personal strengths. Again, this may be difficult. Ask a supportive friend for help, if necessary.
4. List five compliments that you remember and cherish about yourself.
5. List five actions you can take to care for yourself: keep healthy food in the refrigerator, cut back on junk food, call a friend instead of toughing it out when I'm lonely, go to a movie, renew my library card, clean out the trunk. . . .

MUSIC AND MOVIES

To help you release emotions, pick out several of your favorite CDs or audiotapes and several of your favorite videotapes—some upbeat, some tearjerkers. Make a list of music that will help you to cry—country music and ballads are good for this—and a list of music that will inspire you or lift you up—anything from the *Emperor* Concerto by Beethoven to Bruce Springsteen, Keith Jarrett, Greg Brown, or Garth Brooks. What you choose is up to you. This is a very personal list, and I ask you to keep using the music and movies like exercising, to get connected to your emotions. Feeling blue? Watch a sad movie and cry it out. Feeling great? Play something loud or exciting. Music and movies can assist you when you need a cry or a flight of the spirit. The music and movies will keep you in touch with the energy that runs through your body.

List a few sad movies, some funny, and some lift-me-up films to watch over the next few weeks. Humor is especially important; laughter is a healing medicine.

MOVING ONWARD

You have begun in earnest. Congratulate yourself. There is more to do—on another day. Get plenty of rest. You do not have to hurry.

2

THE SHARED TRAUMA OF SEPARATION

THE DARKNESS

When I returned to Ohio after my final visit with Betsy and John in 1972, I stopped being consistent at work, clocking in some days, spending some days in bed, unable to face the day. Too young to have been tempered by failure or to understand it, I began to hate myself and everyone else. I grew more and more ashamed of not being able to study or work; I was shocked at how lazy I had become, how apathetic.

As my money dried up, I fell behind on my child-support payments. I fell behind on everything. I was nineteen. I was losing myself—abandoning my education, my dreams of a career, my wife, and now my son.

This was my first taste of the emotional power of The Haunting, the power of shame to make me feel inadequate and unworthy. To make those feelings a reality.

I know now that I was experiencing a clinical depression, a medical condition that often includes listlessness, anxiety, anger or irritability, and thoughts of suicide. A depression should be medically treated with therapy and/or antidepressants, but I didn't know that. It was months before I began to function again.

My depression would return regularly throughout my twenties, often exacerbated by bouts with alcohol or other drugs, and a narcissism that grew into self-pity. Yet, despite being a smart kid, I never thought to see a psychiatrist or therapist. Therapy wasn't a part of my family background.

> *Self-pity is our worst enemy, and if we yield to it, we can never do anything wise in this world.*
>
> –HELEN KELLER

Now I understand that Betsy had plenty of her own pain to carry, but back then I was so overwhelmed and self-absorbed that I could not see past my own anger and frustration. Betsy was angry too; teen pregnancy, marriage, and divorce had hurt her deeply. Her losses were just as real as my loss of an Ivy League education. Teenage parenthood had curtailed Betsy's chance to attend college, limited her career options, isolated her from many of her friends, cast her into a role that she was also too young to fill, and changed forever her previously unencumbered future. Is it any wonder she saw John as a savior? Is it any mystery that she would wish to shut the door on me and the painful past?

However, I was Scott's father. He had a right to know me, and I had a right to know him—yet it seemed that no one else believed this. My parents and my friends seemed to believe that Scott was better off without me. I know now that this was not the case.

Focused on my own pain, on being shut out by Betsy and her new husband, daunted by the image of them as better parents for Scott, I gave ground, telling myself that my absence was the best thing for him. I missed my son, but I did not allow myself to imagine that he might also miss me. Bad enough that I was haunted. How much worse to feel that he was haunted too. Under the chill of my shame, Scott was slipping away from me, and I did not know where to turn.

Eventually when Scott was about seven, he was adopted by John. "He'll feel better at school," Betsy told me. Believing her, not knowing what was best, I acted without counsel and lost all legal rights to my son as he lost my name. "He'll be better off," I told myself.

SCOTT'S STORY

Scott is now a bright young man in his mid-twenties. I did not see him from the time he was a toddler until he was eighteen. I asked him to write about the years we were apart:

> *I remember as a child having thoughts of and wondering about my father. What was he like? What did he do? What did he look like? I didn't understand why he and my mom weren't together. I soon got a stepfather who was great to me, but I wanted to know about my biological father, also.*
>
> *I was curious about him, but my mother felt that I didn't need to know or was too young. So his presence was intangible to me. I stopped asking questions for a while, but in the back of my mind I was frustrated by not knowing anything about him.*
>
> *I couldn't help but think maybe I wasn't a good enough son for him. I wondered if he had found a better little boy or maybe a girl whose father he wanted to be. I thought about my father at every sporting event I ever took part in and at all the birthday parties I was ever given.*
>
> *I pictured my father coaching the son he wanted or throwing a big party for the daughter he wanted. I imagined hitting a big home run or scoring a touchdown to*

> Believe that life is worth living, and your belief will help create that fact.
>
> —WILLIAM JAMES

win a game, and my father would rush out of the stands and hoist me up on his shoulders like he was the proudest man in the world because of me. My "new dad" wanted to do sports things with me, so I wondered why my own father didn't want to.

I hoped to be a professional ballplayer so he would want to come around and meet me again. Something told me that if I became famous he would want to be my father.

THE BIGGER STORY: FATHER ABSENCE HURTS US ALL

What I hadn't realized was that neither Scott nor Betsy had forgotten me. This shortsightedness is, I have found, common among absent fathers. And yet we fathers need to know their pain if we are to confront the truth of those we left behind.

Their pain as well as your own will be soothed by your return. This is the reality you must look at now, as the first step toward reunion. Your children have not forgotten you and will often express their haunting in self-destructive ways. Their mother has not forgotten you, and your absence, although it may have been officially "welcome," may have left her overburdened and unfairly exhausted and without a partner to share in the major decisions of child rearing.

Carla is a college-educated single mom of thirty-two. Her son, Nicky, is two and a half years old and does not know his father. His father has chosen not to know him. Carla does not know how to soften this blow for her son, but she tries.

Carla says, "When I read stories about families I always change the word 'daddy.' I say 'mother' and 'man' instead, so that my son won't ask me what a daddy is.

"Last week Nicky and I were at the park playing on the slides. We had been playing for a while, and he had climbed to the top of the slide again. As I stood at the bottom to catch him, he looked over the edge of the slide and shouted something that I couldn't quite understand, so I yelled, 'What?' But he just kept saying something over his shoulder that I couldn't catch.

"Suddenly I realized he was saying, 'Daddy, watch! Daddy, watch!' to two men standing near their kids on the swings. I had never heard him use the word 'daddy,' and I had never used it in our house. But I felt so bad for him because he was really trying to get those two men to notice him.

"The men didn't hear him, so I walked over to them and said, 'I think my son is talking to you. He doesn't have a father.' The men understood and came over to watch him go down the slide. He kept saying 'Daddy, watch, Daddy, watch.' They were very nice guys and oohed and aahed over Nicky, but I went home and cried."

Evelyn, a forty-year-old single mother and artist, is raising her three-and-a-half-year-old son by herself. Although she generally feels good about her parenting, she says, "I often wonder about the future. Who's going to teach Adam how to be a man. I hear other single mothers say things like 'I'm just going to be this child's father *and* mother,' but how do you do that? I cannot be Adam's mother *and* father."

Janet, a teacher who raised her daughter alone, explains, "After our marriage broke up, I think my daughter lost both her parents, not just her dad. This meant that I was always trying to be tough enough to do the job. Trying to handle both roles, I think I lost a lot of my time for mothering. My daughter may have had bread on the table, but I didn't have time to make cake.

"I always felt like I wouldn't be strong enough to cut it in the world. So I stayed sort of armored. Carrie probably felt I was inaccessible to her. I was always busy, busy, busy. When I think of it now, I was a sort of an android, a kind of robot parent, always on the alert for harm. I used to have these recurrent nightmares about being left alone and hungry. The dream was just terrible. These dreams stopped when I finally remarried. We built a stable family life and my daughter had a father figure. I know it sounds sexist, but we both needed him. I needed a man and she needed a daddy. But Carrie still worried about her real father."

Celia, an erudite theologian and college professor, has also had a recurring nightmare since her divorce. Although the details vary, the dream is often the same.

"It is night, or near night," she explains, "and the air is growing chill. It will soon be cold and dark. I have my daughter by my side. She is small again, four or five years old, and she is tired, hungry, and a little frightened. I try to reassure her, but I am frightened myself. I have realized we have no home or that home is too dangerous to go to. I have no money, no resources, no friends. Somehow I must keep my daughter safe, and I don't know how I am going to do it."

Celia's and Janet's dreams, like the recurrent nightmares common to combat veterans, are a reaction to traumatic stress. Celia's fear for her own and her daughter's survival persists despite her substantial income and support from family and friends.

Dreams often reflect the nightmare pain of divorce. Though this book concerns fathers, the pain of women and children lies under every line.

IF YOU ARE COMTEMPLATING DIVORCE

If you are reading this book, the chances are that you are already divorced or separated from your spouse. But if you are still living in an intact family, I urge you to take the following to heart.

Divorce, contrary to popular opinion, has a profound and negative effect on children. I am not speaking of children living in violent and abusive homes but the millions of children whose lives are disrupted because their parents have decided that they can no longer live together. We have been led to believe that after a period of adjustment, the children are better off because the parents are happier. You should know that recent studies show that by almost any measure—self-esteem, competence, ability to make friends, ability to relate to men in young women, ability to form a loving bond with women for young men—a child of divorce is at a disadvantage. I am not advocating self-sacrifice or staying in the marriage at all costs, but I am pointing out the realities that you need to factor into your decision.

You may believe that your children will not be at a disadvantage, and perhaps they won't be. But statistics tell us that 88 percent of divorced mothers are given custody of the children, 26 percent of divorced fathers live in a different state from their children, and 50 percent of divorced fathers have not seen their children more than a few times in the past year. The fact is that maintaining a meaningful relationship with your children after divorce will require diligence and effort.

> *Because divorce is so deeply unfathomable to children, because it renders them so helpless, because they are so likely to feel rejected and disillusioned, it is critical that children have opportunities to talk to adults who are able to help make this experience comprehensible.*
>
> —RICHARD WEISSBOURD

For the sake of your children and your wife and yourself, I urge you to do the following before committing to divorce:

Get counseling and continue for at least twelve sessions.

Live through your problems for six months to a year and see if, over time, you have a different view of your situation. You would be amazed at how often intractable couples find that by detaching and tolerating their problems, readjustments take place between them, leading to a renewed, stronger bond.

If divorce is finally your decision, seek mediation rather than litigation. Mediation will enable you to make arrangements where your children are the first priority for you and your wife. Mediation will enable you to get through the process with the least damage between you and your wife, whom you will continue to deal with regarding visitation, and the least damage to you and your children. By putting your children first as a couple, you will avoid the armed-camp mentality that causes so much emotional havoc.

I also urge you to seek joint custody. Joint custody yields better results for all concerned, and fathers feel much more supported by sharing legal custody when (as is usually the case) they do not have physical custody. With joint custody, you will have equal input and decision-making power in the lives of your children. You will be a father actively involved in every aspect of your children's lives. Your consistent relationship with your child, your continued financial and emotional support, will enable you and your ex-wife to grow as parents. Joint custody will also enable your wife to have the time to develop a life of her own. But most important, it will enable you both to do the best possible job in bringing up children who are emotionally and psychologically strong.

THE COST TO MOTHERS—IN DOLLAR TERMS

"Downward social drift," a term originally used to describe the alienation from friends and the steady deterioration of living and working conditions experienced by the mentally ill, can today be applied to the plight of many single mothers and children.

Newly divorced women and single mothers suffer an economic catastrophe second to none in our culture. The average woman loses most of the man's contribution to the total family income, usually between 26 percent and 73 percent, following a divorce, while her workload increases. If a large industrial company lost the same amount of income so quickly, the government would immediately step in and arrange a loan or a bailout.

I know a young mother named Cathy. She is a single mother of a three-year-old boy. Her child's father does not visit or pay support. Cathy spends her mornings with her son and works three afternoons a week. She asks her employer to pay her cash, because the $250 a month she gets from welfare does not cover her rent and groceries. Do you know anybody who can live on $250 a month? Many welfare mothers work, even if only a few hours and even if they are paid under the table.

Studies show that 20 percent to 50 percent of single mothers and their children live below the poverty line. Remember, these are the minimum subsistence levels established by the U.S. government. Poverty affects more than 14 *million* children. Even families with far higher incomes experience severe financial strain.

Jean a divorced woman whose successful ex-husband is generous in providing for her and her son, says he sometimes went through dry spells and was unable to provide much. A former nursery school teacher, she was unable to find a teaching job, and took whatever odd jobs she could find. "It was so awful," she recalls. "I tried to keep up our middle-class lifestyle –the day camp, the piano lessons, the braces, the Nikes, by borrowing, getting loans, and typing envelopes for $4.00 an hour. I mended a lot of jeans, and we ate a lot of pasta. And still, I would often not have enough to pay the rent.

"One Saturday, when my son and his friends and I were dyeing Easter eggs in the kitchen, the cable TV guy came to the door and announced that our service was suspended. He marched right in, unhooked the box, and took off. I know it's no big thing, but it seemed like the last straw." Her voice falters. "I just put my head down on the table and cried right in front of the kids. . . . This was our home. How was I ever going to keep it going?"

> *F*all seven times, stand up eight.
>
> –JAPANESE PROVERB

Some version of this story is played out a million times a day across the country, and it touches all strata of society from Park Avenue to park benches.

THE COSTS TO FATHERS

What can a man do when he is unable to be with his children and unable to parent them? How does a father make sense of who he is, or the meaning of life, or the aging process without a future with his children? How can he replace that day-to-day love he lost? Without an outlet for their fathering instinct, lost fathers can become emotional amputees. They tell their stories with their silence.

The silence is ensured by the influence of shame-based media stereotypes of "deadbeat dads," "welfare mothers," and by misguided government programs that withhold financial support to the mother if the father is in the home. Our cultural vocabulary reinforces the distance between fathers and children with terms like "broken family" and "children of divorce."

Our instinct to father is discounted in our cultural heritage and ignored—in fact destroyed—by our mass-media images of the Lone Ranger, the solitary combat hero, and the often sad or silly fathers of the silver screen. Make no mistake, the cinematic cowboy, frontiersman, and war hero are the dominant masculine media stereotype. These images reinforce the devastating notion of men as loners and of family as something they leave behind.

> The deepest need of man is to overcome his separateness, to leave the prison of his aloneness.
>
> —ERICH FROMM

In many films and TV programs today—*Forrest Gump*, for example—the father is invisible. The single mother and the children act as if he never existed, the children never seem to miss him, and he is replaced by the mother's new boyfriend.

In real life, this is not men's or children's emotional truth.

No matter how far into exile they may stray, many men carry with them images of family, hearth, and home. Children wonder about their fathers and often blame themselves for their absence.

Our cultural denial of a man's real emotional bond with his children causes a terrible lie at the very heart of his life. The images of the isolated male mask a pathologically dysfunctional model of adult masculinity that is damaging to our self-esteem, our sense of responsibility, and our success. It is also historically inaccurate.

Men work at jobs–have always worked at jobs–that demand long hours away from their families. They are often asked to travel, to work late, to work weekends. They do this at great sacrifice to the time they would much rather spend in family bonding–only to be told that since they are absent so much, they have no bond! Every time a father walks out that door to provide for his wife and children, he is saying, "I LOVE YOU."

But instead of understanding, he gets blamed for not spending more time with his children.

THE COST TO THE FUTURE

For the man, the terrible pain of losing his children can affect every interaction he has with a female afterward, and it becomes part of the reason for the wave of second and third divorces or his downright refusal to marry again and have children again, or both. It is easier to leave a second marriage if a man has lost his children in his first one. The exit door is opened by his feeling that he will never hurt like that again.

> *People are lonely because they build walls instead of bridges.*
>
> –JOSEPH FORT NEWTON

This fear of commitment in men and fear of abandonment and economic disaster in women can make a marital union seem pretty tenuous. It is not something that will last long, so why bother? Looking at this dance of avoidance, is it any wonder we are becoming a country of multiple short-lived marriages? A country of men and women who have become frightened, angry, and lonely? Everyone seems to have lost their ability to be fully human.

NOT "DRAMA"—TRAUMA

The loss of a mate is traumatizing, though often the severity of the emotional wounds remains unrealized until well into the breakup. Divorce is a severe psychological event. In the bible of psychiatry, *The Diagnostic and Statistical Manual IV,* the only events listed as more severe are the death of a spouse, rape, serious physical illness, death of a child, suicide of a spouse, and a devastating natural disaster.

It is not uncommon for partners going through divorce to suffer depression, anger, sleeplessness, irritability, a loss of focus at work, accident proneness, and any of a host of other stress-related problems.

Claire, newly divorced, didn't answer her phone for months. Her husband had left her for another woman, taking his two children, her beloved stepchildren, with him. The blow sent Claire reeling. She had lost two roles, wife and mother. She had lost two identities and her entire family. Friends worried that she was drinking herself to death or going out every night with a different sex partner. The truth was that by seven o'clock every evening Claire was in bed asleep, in the throes of a clinical depression. The loss of her spouse and the children she had grown to love was simply too much to face. This is an unacknowledged agony many stepparents, and stepchildren as well, experience.

David, a graying, barrel-chested mountain man, was divorcing after twenty-five years of marriage, having raised two sons and a daughter who was still in high school. He began having sudden bouts of chest pain. His heart would suddenly speed up or slow down. He was fitted with heart monitors and forced to follow a strict dietary regimen. He had lost not only his wife but his identity as a father.

"I thought I was dying," David remembers. "I didn't know heartbreak could be so literal."

> *After two days in the hospital, I took a turn for the nurse.*
>
> –W. C. FIELDS

It was only when his daughter, Marisa, came home from boarding school to stay with him and he and his wife became friendly again that David's physical symptoms began to ease. After a year of intense physical and psychic pain, his irregular heartbeat went away as quickly as it had appeared.

Not only illness but also accidents threaten the newly separated. I had just finished telling my friend Larry, divorcing after three decades, to be watchful of accidents when he realized he had let the sink overflow—water poured all over the floor while we were talking. Another friend, Richard, says that within two weeks of his divorce his Toyota looked as if he had played bumper cars with it. He was constantly running into a tree, a mailbox, or a parking garage wall.

While divorce usually follows a period of discontent by one or both parties, it brings with it a period of fragility with a high potential for further damage to self-worth and physical well-being. Remember, it represents a loss of our most basic relationship with our closest friend, ally, and lover—our spouse. This loss is devastating.

John is a computer operator who was recently divorced. Normally articulate and discerning, he becomes tongue-tied when he tries to talk about his divorce.

"We had been married for fifteen years and for whatever

reasons a marriage fails—the stress of success perhaps, different paths in our careers, or the pressure of being work partners as well as husband and wife—our marriage began to fail.

"I'll tell you right now that our marriage was always a bit rocky. Though I consider myself an open-minded man with a lot of soul, we are both hardheaded career people, and we often clashed over creative ideas and issues of power.

"After a great deal of arguing, I moved out. Our divorce followed swiftly after that—too swiftly, I thought. I was not prepared for the emotional tidal wave that swept over me. It took me out to sea a long way from any kind of land I recognized. I did not realize how adrift I would feel without my home and my daughter.

"It was all I could do to keep showing up for work. Many days in the first couple of months, I couldn't accomplish anything. I was lucky my business year was winding down and I didn't have much to do. I could not have held a regular day job."

John shudders, remembering, "The week I moved out, I found myself on the streets of Boulder, walking for miles in the middle of the night just to work off my anxiety so I could sleep.

"The house my wife and daughter and I had shared, the land we had cultivated together, the horses we had walked with all night in the middle of a blizzard, the orphan dogs we had cleaned up and adopted—all of it was gone for me."

John says he thought of suicide occasionally. "I was in no real danger; I know that 'suicide is a permanent solution to a temporary problem.'"

> The only courage that matters is the kind that gets you from one moment to the next.
> —MIGNON MCLAUGHLIN

John lived the frequently male truth of a divorce: removed from the home he knew, alone in a sublet trying to make sense of what went wrong. He vacillated from being angry to being tearful; from being sure he was right to feeling sure he was wrong; from knowing he was the good guy to wondering if he was the bad guy. Nothing seemed real, yet John had to build a new life. Like many men in the initial throes of a divorce, John had a suitcase full of clothes and just enough money to set up a modest apartment. It was quite a blow.

One morning at three A.M., John woke up with an anxiety attack. He walked to the hospital with his heart pounding "as if it would burst." The doctor gave him a shot to calm him down and scheduled him for a cardiac stress test. His heart tested fine. They didn't have a machine to test his feelings.

While many depressions are a sort of generic divorce grief, others are grounded in remorse. Most marriages do not end without some very ugly arguments and scenes we would often rather forget. These memories add to the trauma of the divorce itself.

Although two million Americans undergo it every year, divorce is an assault on our spirits, our bodies, and our emotions. Many of us emerge so wounded that love of any kind seems a distant option and security looks like an impossibility. Is it any wonder we have problems being friends again?

THE PAIN OF THE CHILDREN

If men and women are traumatized by divorce, what about the children? The things that children say about their loss, especially little children, will break your heart.

"When is Daddy coming home?"

"I don't want you to go."

"Will I have to find a new dad?"

"I want to live with Dad and I want you to come, too."

Stephanie remembers the weekend she visited her film-maker husband on location with their three-year-old son. Her husband had been "distracted with the film" for the past three months, and on her visit she found out that he had become deeply involved with another woman; he announced that he wasn't coming home. For two days, they stormed and raged and wept while their son, Chris, was off with baby-sitters. Finally Stephanie realized she had to go back to the East Coast alone. "In the hour-long cab ride from the airport," Stephanie said, "Chris asked for his father and I told him he had to stay in California." Chris began to cry. No amount of consoling helped, and he just sobbed uncontrollably through the whole, dark, trip back to our house. He seemed to know something was unalterably changed–that Daddy was gone–that things would never be the same. When I entered him in nursery school a month later, the teacher told me he was very withdrawn and needed to see a therapist. It was several years before we were able to establish a routine where Chris visited his father regularly and was "normal" again.

Cornelia talks about the years when her daughter made weekend trips to see her father, who lived a three-hour train ride away. "Each Sunday night, I would tuck her in bed and she would say 'I miss Dad' or she would cry and say 'Why did Dad ever go and live with Ann? Why can't he live with us again?' People who are thinking about divorce should know these things. It's so heartbreaking to see a little child so unhappy and not be able to do anything about it."

John recalls the afternoon when he left his family and his home. "We had decided to divorce, and though my wife was still extremely angry about the unraveling of our marriage–I made some big mistakes–we tried to put the kids first in our divorce agreement. I found an apartment nearby, but it was the actual leaving that unhinged me. I was standing out by the car with my bags and Carrie, who was four, came out screaming, yelling 'Daddy, don't go, don't go'–crying hysterically and clinging to my legs. She gradually accepted the fact that I live some-

> *Suffering presents us with a challenge: to find goals and purpose in our lives that make even the worst situation worth living through.*
>
> —VIKTOR FRANKL

where else and see her regularly, but she still has a very hard time with any kind of departure, whether I drop her off at nursery school or say good-bye after a visit. There's that kind of wild-eyed 'Daddy, Daddy, don't leave yet.' It makes me feel very bummed out to see her so upset."

THE COST TO CHILDREN: INVISIBILITY

It is very hard to accurately see what is going on between yourself and someone you live with, whether it is a husband, a wife, or children. We can lose focus on what is really happening in *their* world, how they are experiencing life.

Fred, a twelve-year-old boy, says, "I never get asked about school anymore. My dad might mention it on a visit, but neither of them seems to know what I am doing, the guys I hang out with. I don't think I would even show them my report card except that I have to get it signed."

The single parent, overworked and overloaded, is often unable to set proper limits or boundaries for his or her child. This can be disastrous in adolescence. It is not healthy any other time, either.

Sara, a fifteen-year-old, is battling an eating disorder and depression. "I get good grades, and that is all they care about. I don't see my dad, though he talks to Mom about me every now and then. It's always about money."

Concerned parents tend to get too close, so that they're unable to focus on the child's experience. In other words, the parent becomes a friend and even sometimes makes the child into a surrogate spouse, losing sight of the important structure that makes a child feel safe. Or the parent is too far away, distanced by work and financial demands, to adequately supervise the children, counting on them to be, indeed, their own keepers.

This can happen in dysfunctional two-parent families as well, but it is particularly prevalent in single-parent homes. The boundaries a parent should be concerned with, according to a study from UCLA, are "school attendance and promptness, consistent homework, frequent and supportive parental contact, and limited, supervised dating."

The kid whose parents are too close, too close to focus, feels suffocated. The kid whose parents are too far away feels neglected. Being able to judge the correct emotional distance between the parent and the child is tricky, because it changes over time, throughout the various developmental stages in the child's life. It takes more than one person to properly adjust the depth of field and to place a child in perspective.

A kid who looms either too large or too small to his parents may lose either his constraints or a sense of safety. Then, like the kids so often reported on in the press, this child may pick pockets, set fires, or get into some other kind of trouble in an attempt to get attention.

This is what therapists mean when they talk about a cry for help. Drug use, school failure, bad companions, violence, theft, fire-setting, sexual promiscuity, isolation, and lack of motivation are all unconscious attempts by the child to be noticed, to become visible to the parent. Invisibility can become a way of life. They think, "Since no one notices what I do anyway, I can do what I want."

The solution—what this book is really aiming for—is a reunion that results in co-parenting, something more interactive and improvisational than mere court-dictated visitation. It's an almost constant adjustment, with one parent saying, "Give them some room," and the other saying, "We didn't spend enough time together this week." Between the two they gain a 20-20 perspective on their child.

Betty, the strong-willed, loving mother of Viki, realizes now that her daughter grew to adolescence as an isolated child. "I spent lots of time with her. She had pets, good toys, plenty of things to do, but she lacked playmates, and I didn't see that. We had a great time together—visits to the zoo, the Natural History

Museum, shopping trips. I realize now that she should have been sharing some of these experiences with her peers."

When Viki turned twelve, Betty met and married her second husband, Troy. He was able to help Betty see that they would have to teach Viki how to make friends. She had spent too much of her childhood in a world of caring adults, a lopsided world created by one parent who was too close, trying to do everything right. Troy helped focus Betty's view of her daughter.

Many parents underestimate the extent to which their children need a father—to physically see and touch them, to offer emotional support, and to provide financial contributions that keep them out of poverty. Few divorced mothers can bear to look squarely at their children's loss or their own, much less convey it to the father.

WHAT A FATHER GIVES

Working as a counselor, I not only hear of fathers like me, who have left their children. I see the cost daily to the children they have abandoned. I would like to share three brief examples.

Claude, a fourteen-year-old boy, was hospitalized because he could not handle his anger. I asked him to write down everything he knew about his father, the masculine role model he was missing. He wrote: "He was Italian, and his name was Tony. He screwed over my mother"—an assessment that hardly makes for a positive male self-image.

Eli is an eighteen-year-old boy, bright, honest, full of promise—and haunted. When I met him, Eli had just graduated from high school. He wanted to talk to me about his father. "I have not lived with my father since my parents were divorced. I was three. My father used to visit until I was ten or eleven, and then he stopped coming."

I asked Eli what that meant to him.

He said, "I've gotten what I needed from men like my grandfather, who really served as my father, and an uncle and a boyfriend of my mother's. I took from men what I needed and liked from each one."

I said those sounded like very good relationships that had worked well for him. Then I explained that during my years away from my son I had always had little fantasies about returning to him, and I often wondered if Scott had similar thoughts. Had he, Eli, ever had thoughts like this about his real dad?

The question pierced his denial.

Eli replied a little shakily. "No, but I often think I'm just going to drive to Georgia one of these days and show up at his door. I think to myself that he probably won't recognize me at first, but then I'm sure it'll dawn on him who I am. I also once saw someone at a football game at my prep school who my mom told me was my father's brother."

"Your uncle?" I ask.

"Yeah, some guy in a trench coat. I looked for him a lot after that."

"Your father?"

"No, my uncle."

"Oh. I see. Did you know where your father was?"

"Yeah, he's an architect in Atlanta. I just learned this year that my mother talks with him every six months or so."

"Ah."

Having gone this far, Eli finally allowed himself to touch his feelings.

"I used to think a lot about calling him. I would pick up the phone and think, The secretary will ask me who I am, and I won't tell her. I'll say, 'I want him to figure it out.' Then I would go through this big thing about how I would talk her into letting me speak to him without knowing who I was, and then she would say okay and put him on, and I would say, 'Hi, guess who this is' or something like that, and then I would wait to see if he recognized my voice."

"But I thought you said you didn't have any fantasies about your dad."

"I don't. I just used to have this thing in my head sometimes about it. Who knows? I might just drive down."

I told Eli, "It's Route 95 south to Savannah, then take a right."

We both laughed at the simplicity of this plan, its calculated casualness, despite the great emotional–distance it really was.

Janine is a nineteen-year-old from Pittsburgh. She is gifted artistically, but her promising professional trajectory is shadowed by her haunted past. When she was six years old, her father left the family and slipped into deepening alcoholism and estrangement.

"I always wanted to tell people ahead of time about my dad's alcoholism," she says, "so they couldn't catch me on a bad day, so they knew what the story was. I never missed him at Christmas, or anything like that." (I hadn't mentioned holidays.)

Janine says that she did not have any fantasies about being reunited with him. After all, he was homeless and on the street by the time she reached her teens.

"I was used to my life, and if I had a fantasy about my dad, it was that he had died. If he was sick and died, it would have been easier for me to understand. He is very intelligent, and to know he has a choice and chooses to stay drunk, refuses to quit drinking . . . better he dies."

And yet, although she claimed never to have thought about a reunion, Janine recently sought out her father, picking her way through welfare hotels and flophouses, alleys and shelters, until she found him.

"Meeting him was like looking at an empty shell. He was very sick, with nothing left in his eyes, as if the spirit had flown away. He said, 'I'm gonna get better, Janine,' but tears were streaming down my face because I knew he was gone."

"Why did you go see him, then?" I asked.

Janine continued, "I had to know where some of my art comes from; he used to be a good artist. I wanted him to listen to all the things I've done, to ask me about school and all my honors. I wanted to tell him all the wonderful things going on in my life. I wanted him to know.

"I remember I was his princess and very spoiled by him when I was a little girl, and I followed him around the garden while he did the yard work. When I saw him, I wanted to tell him what I thought of him and what I had done, but the whole time I talked I couldn't remember what I was saying. I just kept touching his hair. I was sitting next to him even while I was telling him to get it together, telling him how I felt about him never being there for me. I just kept touching his hair, because what I really wanted him to do was hold me and say he was sorry."

Often the cost of father absence shows itself in more subtle ways. It affects us all.

One fall day a few years ago, I was outside washing and waxing my car, something I rarely do. A boy I knew from the local high school, a sixteen-year-old named Aaron, drove by. Spotting me, he pulled his old red beater into the driveway, "just to say hi."

We visited for a while, and I continued the ritual of washing and waxing. Aaron grew very quiet, watching. He told me he had never waxed a car. I glanced up at him and remembered that his father lived out of state. I told him to "grab that Turtle Wax" and we'd finish my car and then do his. We did.

Two coats of wax later Aaron's old red beater shone inside and out like a new car. He was thrilled at his reflection in the once dirty hood. I smiled to myself, pleased at how the experience had affected him. I felt the same way. Looking at my own old Jeep shining under the trees.

That night I shared a chuckle with Aaron's mother when

she called to thank me. Aaron had bragged to her all evening about his hot little car, taking evident pride in his work. That week, two other young men, both friends of Aaron's, came by to ask when I would be waxing my car again and if they could learn how to do it. Neither had a dad living at home.

I am happy that I got the chance to teach Aaron how to wax a car. I am happy he got the chance to learn. The experience is a small treasure for me, and yet it evokes sadness when I realize all the treasures, small and large, I missed with Scott.

As a counselor I have learned to recognize the significance of the seemingly trivial. The children miss so many things with their dad: the short walk, an hour's work in the garden, a conversation over dishes, help with homework—these are the cornerstones of communication in a child's life. They provide mentoring for the children, and these seemingly insignificant moments are rites of passage for a parent.

THE EMOTIONAL MAP

The following exercises were designed to do two things: enhance your empathy for your former partner's situation, and bring into awareness your true feelings about your past with your children and your hopes for their future.

As before, record your responses in your Reunion Journal. Try not to overthink them. They are meant to come spontaneously. Do not be discouraged if your answers seem contradictory or even capricious. There are no right or wrong answers.

Be aware that some of these questions may annoy or pain you. Some may seem irrelevant. Others may not apply, while still others may feel intrusive. If you find yourself thinking, "This is glib" or "This is bull," label that reaction "resistance" and work with the question in point. For

> *Write injuries in sand, kindnesses in marble.*
>
> —FRENCH PROVERB

instance, why does that particular question bother you? Does it make you feel judged? Discounted? Ashamed?

1. Where are your children living now?
2. How do you think your absence has affected their mother?
3. How do you think it has affected you?
4. Have you talked to your children's mother about your absence? What was said?
5. Is there a stepfather in the house? How do you feel about that? Do the two of you have a relationship? Have you ever spoken to him about your children at any length?
6. What happened on your last visit to your kids?
7. Would your children recognize you? What, if anything, about you physically has changed since you last saw them?
8. How were your finances when you split up with the mother of your children? How are they now? What would you change if you could? Why? Do you owe any child support?
9. How would it feel to know your children?
10. Describe an ideal day with your child.
11. Describe your ideal relationship with your children.

ASSIGNMENTS

1. LOOK WITH YOUR HEART: Go to a mall or a park and look for a couple that reminds you of you and your child's mother when you were first together. Watch them for a while. Did any old memories come up? How did you feel? What did you learn?
2. LOOK WITH YOUR SOUL: Go to a school yard or playground with a friend to watch children who are the same ages as yours. (Make sure you take a friend so

that you do not frighten the kids. It is a sad but necessary commentary on this day and age that your solo presence might be misinterpreted as a threat to the children). How do you feel? What did you learn?

3. CHERISHING: Where do you keep the pictures of your children? When was the most recent one taken? If you don't have any pictures, try to get some. Frame one of the photographs and display it on a table or wall in your house. Pictures are an important way of keeping loved ones in mind and honoring their place in our lives. Be sure to display children equally. Two pictures of Mary? Then put up two pictures of John. It matters to them.

> *Seek ye first the kingdom of God, and all these things shall be added unto you.*
>
> —MATTHEW

MOVING ONWARD

1. Are you using your notebook? Try to fill a page a day, but even a page every couple of days is a big step forward.

2. Are you taking a weekly solitude break? This tool is about giving yourself a bit of peace and the dignity of respecting your own thoughts and perceptions.

3. Are you exercising? Sometimes our soul speaks when we are otherwise engaged. Are you letting yourself walk your way into a more heart-centered life?

4. Are you watching your health? Remember that this return is intended to be a CELEBRATION, not a shaming. You are learning a deep and valid lesson that you will teach your children. Stay healthy.

5. Are you remembering to pray? Prayer helps us avoid arrogance and increases our self-worth. It brings us to balance. Just a few moments several times a day will help—okay, call it a quiet time if you like.

3

GETTING READY: THE RETURN OF SELF-RESPECT

THE TURNING POINT

On March 10, 1983, my thirtieth birthday, my emotional defenses unraveled completely. For some time, my drugging and drinking had led to panic attacks that sent me to a local emergency room so often I knew the doctors by name. I had dizziness, stabbing chest pains, choking, and a bizarre swelling of my face. They checked me for tumors, allergies, and heart ailments and found nothing, but the attacks continued and were very real—soaking sweats, blurred vision, a sudden and catastrophic sense of impending doom. Each time, I was convinced I was dying.

In fact, I was. The life I was leading was killing me.

When I took my wedding vows that long-ago day in the magistrate's office in North Carolina, I had vowed to be a good father. I had promised myself and my unborn son that when he became a teenager, I would be solid and established—"by thirty."

As I stood holding Betsy's hand, both of us so young and

frightened, I promised silently that I would *be* somebody by the time my child was thirteen.

That day had come: Scott was thirteen, and I was thirty, and where was I? Still lost—without career or an education, without stability. I spent that birthday in a thirty-seventh-floor apartment furnished only with two lawn chairs. I was drinking and alone. I had spent many nights that way. This time, however, I suffered a nervous breakdown.

> **B**reaking wedding vows breaks hearts, no matter how many reasons we repeat to ourselves.
>
> –ELLEN SUE STERN

Facing the ugly truth of my life overwhelmed me, and I called the emergency room at Northwestern University Hospital, which I knew so well, and told the doctor on call, "I don't care what I have to do. I can't live this way anymore."

I meant it. I had hit bottom.

I could finally see through the wasted years. *I had become teachable.*

Once I surrendered to the idea that I needed help, I felt better immediately, but the panic attacks took some time to subside. The first time I sat in a therapist's office I felt nervous but also grateful, as if a huge weight had been lifted from my shoulders. Soon I understood what the word "resurrection" really meant. I was going to get a chance at a new life, though I learned quickly that it wasn't going to happen overnight.

For the first time since I was eighteen—since the pregnancy, the marriage, and the birth and loss of Scott—I spent an entire summer completely sober. I felt both saved and damned. The pain and guilt that I had medicated all those years by changing jobs or cities, by using alcohol and other drugs, hit me hard: I missed my son.

In the beginning, I felt just as broken as I had when I first left Scott and Betsy. This time, however, I had a therapist, and the difference was crucial. Now I was in a support group with people I could respect, people who knew how to make a sick man well. This time I had people around me who knew the way out. The return of hope for my life was a major turning point for me.

Once I was able to seek help, I stopped medicating my pain and partying irresponsibly. My cynicism also decreased, as did my distrust of other men, and my lying about my finances. My destructive lifestyle had to end before I could have the self-esteem necessary to reunite with my child.

It has been my experience that men and women who enter treatment for alcoholism or other addictions come very quickly to their feelings about their children, lost or otherwise. It was no different for me.

"I want Scott back," I began saying immediately. "I want my son."

"Just focus on yourself for now," I was wisely told.

"But–"

"Try to become the man you want him to meet."

I tried to do just that. Sober, I swam, jogged, got healthy, and reentered college. I began to build a life, one brick at a time. And through it all, it became obvious to me that Scott had been, and continued to be, the central fact of my life, even though I had not seen him since he was four.

The single most powerful experience I've ever had was a session that summer with my therapist, Sheila. I faced an empty chair and imagined Scott was there. I talked to him as if it was on the day he was born. I told him how I missed him, how sorry I was, how much I had lost by not knowing him. I told him how much I loved him.

> **Y**ou *must do the thing you think you cannot do.*
>
> –ELEANOR ROOSEVELT

The session lasted over two hours. I spent part of it doubled up on the floor, unable to do anything but sob and gasp for air. Afterward I was still so shaken that Sheila had to help me downstairs and into a cab. "You were releasing the pain," she said. "Take a bath and get some rest."

It took me several days to recover from that experience, but my steps felt lighter.

"Should I call him now?" I would ask.

"You'll know when it's time," Sheila would always reply.

TAKING TIME TO THINK

People who hear my story often ask me, "Why did you wait?" and of course, "How long did you wait before attempting contact?" What they are actually asking me is "How do you know when it is time?"

I want to say right here that I always recommend that a father initiate reunion as soon as he is able. By this I mean whenever he has gathered a support team around him, has taken a hard look at his own behavior, and is able to make a commitment to himself to stay in his child's life *as a healthy presence.*

In my case, John had adopted Scott, and I would have to honor his and Betsy's wishes regarding any contact. And because my case was complicated by my drinking history, I needed to prove that I could stay sober.

> Look *well into thyself; there is a source of strength which will always spring up if thou wilt look there.*
>
> —MARCUS AURELIUS

I continued the work to become psychologically free by attending meetings, getting therapy, staying in college, and asking for help. I call therapy, counseling, and support groups a "wisdom school." I learned to feel hopeful again, to recognize my emotions and what triggered them, to exercise and take care of myself, to have empathy for others, to take action instead of complain about the problems, to accept responsibility for my actions.

Most mothers know the child's pain regarding the absent

father; most want to heal it if they can. In fact, often the child—and the mother as well—could benefit greatly from some emotional and financial help from the father. For these reasons I believe that, when possible, reunion should be swift.

Significantly, the success of your reunion will depend on your being healthy enough and strong enough emotionally to help your children, to overcome your shame or hostility, and to protect yourself from any anger or bitterness on the part of your child's mother or her family. If you are clear about your feelings and prepared to face the feelings of others, your reunion will have a much greater chance of success.

Most fathers who have been absent from a child's life for more than a year will need help in assessing their situation. Getting help can also greatly aid those who are visiting their children but are feeling discouraged, disrespected, apathetic, angry, or bitter.

The place to begin getting healthy is with a look at yourself and your situation. Self-assessment is a part of all spiritual traditions and represents a coming of age, a coming to terms with yourself and with the world—an initiation, really—something that few men experience in modern-day life.

I joke with men I counsel, "It is easier to find yourself if you have several people to help you look."

Every time I got impulsive, I talked to my supportive friends, my personal support group—Charlie, Bill, Carl, and Michelle—and they always suggested I wait until I was really "emotionally sober." Until I proved that I could stay sober and hold a job, proved that I was no longer driven by resentment or blame, I was not ready to contact my son. Damn them, I thought. Then I thought again.

I had left my son—there was no denying that—but I could become worthy of being a father to him, and I could turn my *wish* to know my son into a *goal* by breaking it down into simple steps.

THE STEPS TO TAKE

1. Ask for human help. Actively search out the support and guidance that you need. Give up your isolation. Admit that you need support. The paradox you will discover is that your strength lies in your vulnerability.

2. Read the section on starting a study group at the end of this book.

3. Seek spiritual sustenance. In whatever form you can embrace, allow yourself an *open-minded* exploration of the possibility that there is a higher force that can guide you and sustain you in your path to reunion. *Ask its help.* Listen closely to the "still small voice." You may prefer to call it intuition or love or even your gut. Whatever you call it, if you seek its experience with an open heart, you will eventually know it as the reality of grace.

> T*hat deep emotional conviction of the presence of a superior reasoning power, which is revealed in the incomprehensible universe, forms my idea of God.*
>
> —ALBERT EINSTEIN

BUILD A SUPPORT TEAM

You may be keenly aware of how much you and your children need each other. This sense of urgency can sometimes cloud your judgment. In my case, the urgency with which I wanted to see Scott again after so many years caused me to be too emotional and impulsive. During this time my judgment was clouded; my supporters made the critical difference between blowing my chances and succeeding.

When did you last ask someone for help? What did they say? How qualified were they to give advice?

It is important for you to have a friend, mentor, or therapist on your side before you attempt reunion. You may encounter strong emotions from your children, their mother, or her family. Talking to mentors or friends in times of emotional turmoil or confusion will prevent you from overreacting and lashing out in anger or frustration. You will benefit greatly from having someone to listen to you as you move through all the emotions you may feel, including joy. Otherwise, a simple misunderstanding might harm your mission.

Even if your reunion with your child's mother goes smoothly, there are going to be emotions to work through. It may confuse you if the reunion goes well and yet you find yourself feeling sad. This is not uncommon. Every success brings a feeling of elation and loss, and a successful reunion can trigger the joy and the sadness you may have buried for a long time. Either one may be a powerful jolt of adrenaline to your system.

There are no gains without pains.

–ADLAI STEVENSON

Building a support team can be as easy as selecting several good friends who are willing to listen, or as formal as joining a therapy group. Many options are free, including Parents Without Partners, Alcoholics Anonymous, mental health clinic counselors, and church- or synagogue-sponsored groups.

Though close friends, current wives, or lovers can be great supporters and sounding boards, they can also be invested with their own agenda and feelings about your contact with your children. Therefore, you should look for a safe place where you can honestly unburden yourself. You need someone who can listen objectively to what you are experiencing and feeling, who will give you the reality check you need.

Babe Ruth struck out 1,330 times.

In a support or therapy group you will benefit from the feedback, experience, strength, and hope of the other members. Using the group will allow you to be more present with those with whom you are most intimate. The first step in this process is getting up the courage to go to that first meeting.

Don't be surprised if your inner critic, that voice in your head that is negative and cynical about everything, starts to voice an opinion about how the meeting will go, how stupid it will be, how little it will do for you.

This is the voice of fear, not truth. Do not listen to it. Do not let it influence you. Your heart and head will be one every time you take another step toward reunion, and even the negative voice will be secretly happier each time you ignore it and move closer to your goal.

SEPARATING THE MEN FROM THE BOYS

This work is what I call soul work. We are not intended to fix ourselves like a team of auto mechanics or surgeons. Rather, we are intended to heal communally with an eye toward our *shared* weaknesses and strengths. We are meant to develop into more mature adults. Nobody is perfect. Robert Bly and Michael Meade, authors and men's leaders, have done some wonderful work in exploring these ideals. With a bow in their direction, and some thoughts of my own, here is where we are headed:

> *The great thing in this world is not so much where we are but in what direction we are going.*
>
> —OLIVER WENDELL HOLMES

- When a man is in full possession of his manly powers, he will be able to set boundaries with himself and others. He will not yield to the weaknesses of youthful excess. He will no longer womanize or be overly dependent on a woman to give him his identity. He will not be grandiose or immature with money. He will be able to direct his life to higher purposes.
- A mature man will not let another's anger or disapproval deter him from his goals, if they are just and fair. A mature man can face wrath without running or becoming brutal. He will stick to the mission of knowing his children.

- A mature man will not use his sensuality as a way to escape his sensitivity. He will possess the discipline to discontinue those activities that harm him. He will see that he loses self-respect when drinking or drugging to excess. He will keep his self-respect and not fall victim to other subtle forms of addiction such as sports, food, gambling, or pornography, which could keep him from his children and dilute his strength of will and personal power.
- A mature man will not cheat or be cheated upon. He will have the strength to resist temptation and to leave those who do not respect him. Any cheating—whether on his wife, the IRS, or his child support—hurts his sense of honor and helps to drive away the people he loves.
- A mature man will not isolate himself from other men. He will be willing to ask for help and take guidance. He will try to show his true emotions, and will not wallow in self-pity or blame others for his failures.
- Finally, the mature man is not gullible. He will spot materialism for what it is, and he will recognize someone who wants to use him in some way. He might make mistakes—who doesn't?—but he will not idealize other people and he will be able to recognize ill will when he encounters it. He will be steadfast and work to increase his own power while avoiding unnecessary conflict. He will be able to earn and demand what is rightfully his.

POP QUIZ

1. How have you been tempted to violate your integrity?
2. List five ways you have been true to yourself.
3. How do you deal with disapproval from others?
4. How do you control your desire for ecstasy and stay within your personal version of integrity? Exercise? Spiritual practice? Creativity?
5. How do you express your feelings to others?

6. In what ways are you honest in your dealings with others?
7. Do you show up to help others as you would hope to be helped in time of need?
8. How do you show compassion for those less fortunate than you?
9. List five ways you could express your gratitude.

If the questions are a struggle, then there may be an even bigger payoff for you in working with this book than you have imagined. We all have to work toward perfection, living in what my friend Eli calls the paradox–that place in the present moment where you can be happy with who you are today, while working to be even better in the future.

These traits of personal strength can be greatly enhanced no matter how far away from the ideal you may be. Remember, you are honoring both sides of your nature here, the light and the shadow, and in doing so you are moving forward to reclaim whatever power you may have given away to others or hidden from yourself. As the poet wrote, "When the ego weeps for what it has lost, the soul rejoices for what it has found."

> *There is no substitute for hard work.*
> –THOMAS ALVA EDISON

The mature man with a true self will honor his commitments and enjoy giving of himself because he has a self to share. It is essential for your reunion that you be able to give of yourself. Being able to accept guidance and love from other men is crucial to developing this skill.

WORKING WITH A NARRATIVE TIME LINE

As part of your reunion work, you will gain a fresh perspective on your life. This means you must know your life–your version of it, not someone else's. All of us are raised to repeat certain stories about ourselves, but how many of them are really true? There is only one way to sort out the truth from the stories others tell about you, and that is to tell the story yourself, from the heart.

I am not talking about writing the great American novel. I am not even talking about autobiography. What I have in mind is more of a field report. If you stick to the facts, the emotions and interpretations will emerge of their own accord. I call this tool the Narrative Time Line. Julia Cameron and I have used this technique in The Artist's Way, The Vein of Gold, and Prodigal Father workshops for many years.

The Narrative Time Line is a life history in your own words. I prefer to write it by hand, as the hand often seems to lead me to a deeper truth than a typewriter or word processor. Whatever method you choose, simply write your story. Do not edit or rewrite. Just record the events of your life, starting at the beginning and moving right up to the present. Sometimes your memory will skip around—that's okay. Write down all of your recollections, in any order, and keep on moving until you have told your whole life story. I like to think of it as driving from coast to coast—don't dally too long in any one spot or you'll never get there!

Like driving from Los Angeles to Boston, the start will seem exciting. Then you may have some tears, then some rock-and-roll music and singing in the car. Then you may get angry because you got a speeding ticket in Iowa, then happy again while stopping to visit friends in Chicago, then excited as you resume the drive and plow through rain and fog all the way across Ohio and New York and home to Boston on a bright sunny morning. The trip could take five days or five months. Your time line will feel as if it goes on forever, and then suddenly, you're finished.

> You cannot teach a man anything. You can only help him to find it within himself.
>
> —GALILEO

The payoff for this writing assignment is immense.

One way to work through any lingering resentments and attitudes or hurts about your past is to write them out. Remember, this is not meant to be an in-depth personality study or a poetic rendition of your life story, though it might be. It is meant as a trigger for memory that can be seen as a fable upon which to reflect.

This does not have to be "WRITING" as in serious art. It is meant to bring up emotions and forge a new understanding of the events of your past.

Begin by writing down the significant events of your life, starting with your birth and proceeding in five-year increments. Tell who, what, where, and when. From your birth to age five, who were the important people in your life? What important events occurred? What places were important to you? What event was the most painful? What was the most fun? What was the most memorable? The most important? Fill this history in with as much detail as you can, remembering to list any grudges you still hold, anything you might be embarrassed to reveal, anything you are proud of.

Now do the next five years, from age five to ten. Answer the same questions. Then age fifteen to twenty. Then twenty to twenty-five, and on and on until you reach your present age. Include your relationship with your child's mother, and write about your children's births and anything significant you can remember about their lives.

> Do not veil the truth with falsehood, nor conceal the truth knowingly.
>
> —THE KORAN 2:42

Take the time to reflect: How would you figure in your children's time line? What years were you with them? What kind of contact have you had? What could you do now that might change their version of their life story? You may want to do your child's Narrative Time Line.

Be alert for places where your values and your actions

diverged. Lies take a toll on our self-esteem as well as on our ability to move forward in life. Writing them down privately will begin to clear away their damage. Write down whatever lies you can remember telling. And any lies told to you.

You may have been lying to yourself for a long time about some of this material, and I ask that you suspend self-judgment and just tell the truth. For, as Mark Twain said, "the best thing about the truth is that you never have to remember anything."

I repeat: do not edit your thoughts. Just write everything down, no matter how trivial; you can sort it out later.

REFRAMING THE PAST

This excursion into your history and therefore the history of your children is rich soil for growing a new perspective on your life. Remember that no matter how bad it may have been, or be, you survived it. The pain of the past is no longer an excuse for failure, and there is always room for hope.

These days, when I hear people describe their childhood as bleak and terrible, I know that they have not yet gotten to the other side of their work. They have not quite reframed their experience by working through their emotions and reaching forgiveness. John James, founder of the Grief Recovery Institute in Los Angeles, defines "forgiveness" as "giving up the hope of a better or different yesterday." (This may also be the definition of "sanity.")

Learning to be optimistic can make important changes in our lives. One benefit of the reunion work is gleaning a hopeful outlook from our experiences so that our vision is focused on the future instead of the past. This is what I call Emotional Ecology—valuing our personal resources, our strengths and natural gifts, and the advantages our heritage grants us. This is what best prepares the way for the next generation. Forgiveness, not blame. Honor, not shame.

Many of the men and women I have worked with have found in the midst of their writing about their childhood using the Narrative Time Line that while they had indeed lost or repressed many upsetting experiences and emotions from that time, they had also repressed many of the good things about it as well.

> *Confidence and hope do more good than medicine.*
>
> —GALEN

My father once talked to me about my early childhood, and he reminded me of many wonderful things that he and I had done together or that he had done for me. I had completely forgotten those experiences in the years of my exile: the model airplanes we built and flew, the propeller of a navy plane that hung in my room, the days he took me to work with him at shipyards and navy bases.

Many happy moments came streaming back into my memory after that conversation: playing basketball at the garage hoop, the nights playing football in the backyard with my friends and my dad, the only grown-up. I look back on that now and I can't believe that I didn't have ready access to those memories—they were such happy times—and I now know that memory is a tricky thing, never to be regarded as gospel. I also know that memory must give way to the present if we are to be truly healed.

Once the wounds and rifts of the past are cleansed and bandaged, once we recognize and grieve our personal short-comings and those of our parents, we can forgive "those who have trespassed against us," and we can have lasting peace.

Reexamining your history with a compassionate eye will allow you to bring some old hurts and pleasures into aware-ness and blend them into your new foundation for reunion. Each success remembered will help cancel out a failure; each painful moment reexamined will reveal a positive counterpart or payoff. This is the exercise of "reframing."

Let me give you an example of reframing.

Alan married when he was in college, trying to "do the right thing" by his pregnant girlfriend. After three years, his marriage failed, leaving Alan as a twenty-four-year-old divorced man, and in his immaturity he left his wife and their young daughter. For the ten years before he began the reunion work, Alan beat himself up over the fact that his marriage failed, that he was dumb enough to get married so young.

> *Anything in life that we don't accept will simply make trouble for us until we make peace with it.*
>
> —SHAKTI GAWAIN

Writing out his Narrative Time Line, Alan gained a new perspective: "I suddenly realized how brave I was to marry Ann. No one cornered me or held a shotgun on me. True, we were young and it didn't work, but I had the guts to try and I did love her, and that's what I focus on now. I could not stand up to her anger back then, but I can now."

By shifting the focus from his "cowardice" to his courage, Alan felt a shift in his inner worth. He now knew that even though he had been estranged from his former wife and the child they'd had together—like Betsy, Ann had remarried and formed another family, which excluded Alan—he would have the courage to move toward reunion.

For many men the new perspective offered by work with their Narrative Time Line dismantles shame.

"My memories are my memories now," Richard says. "Before I wrote about them, they were land mines."

With a loaded past and no way to mature out of it, a man may stay stuck. Once the maturation process is jump-started again, once the blocks begin to move, he may experience a genuine physical withdrawal—the growing pains of youth that were stifled by immature coping mechanisms like drinking, womanizing, and worka-

> *Suffering is a journey which has an end.*
>
> —MATTHEW FOX

holism. This withdrawal is a good thing, although it may feel mysterious and even frightening in its power.

"You mean I was holding that much pain in my body?"

"Yes."

"Is this going to kill me?"

"No. You're already dying. It's time to come back to life."

You may wake up sweating in the middle of the night, feel shaky at work, feel like crying over television commercials, or become angry at small aggravations. These feelings are good signs that you are beginning to take charge of the demons that have sabotaged your life, your happiness, and your relationship to your child. You are taking your life back, withdrawing your personal power from old behavior patterns and placing it into yourself.

THE GRATITUDE LIST

Go through your Narrative Time Line when you are finished with it and make note of all the successes you wrote about yourself in a separate "gratitude list." Try to find fifty things you are grateful for. (I know it seems like a lot, but keep going.)

Alan's list began like this:

1. I am grateful I had the courage to marry Ann.
2. I am grateful I hung in for three years.
3. I am grateful I didn't forget my child when I left—even if I wasn't healthy enough to keep up contact.
4. I'm grateful I am healthy enough now to renew contact.
5. I'm grateful I have help to do it.

Many men find that it takes them a long time to do their Narrative Time Line, sometimes several weeks. As a Buddhist teacher remarked to a friend of mine, "In the eye of eternity, that's just a wink."

It is better to concentrate on the fact that you are doing it than on the minor fact of how long it takes you. You will use this time line as a basis for writing about other reunion issues. It will surely evoke memories, some painful, some sad, some joyous. It is supposed to do this. These memories will produce insights into your personality and the forces that shaped it, and will, hopefully, HOPE FULL Y, instill a sense of grace into your life. Make your responses as honest as you can.

> **M**iracle doesn't lie only in the amazing living through and defeat of danger; miracles become miracles in the clear achievement that is earned.
>
> —RAINER MARIA RILKE

Some of you may additionally want a trained therapist's support. (There is empirical proof that good therapy does work.) Take a consumer's guide approach to finding your therapist. Neither gender, race, age, nor religion has been shown to have an effect on a therapist's effectiveness. What matters is that they are supervised, have grounded skills, and can establish a personal rapport with you.

SHARING WHAT YOU'VE FOUND

Think of your Narrative Time Line as a way of taking stock—a sort of life inventory. The object of this inventory is to bring into consciousness any behavior patterns, attitudes, or feelings that might be standing in the way of your reunion efforts. Sharing these discoveries may help you put them into perspective.

Select one of your mentors or a safe, interested, but neutral party. Tell that person your story. You will build on this story many times.

I suggest that you explain your mission simply: "I want to tell you my story. Can I have a couple hours of your time?" Select a quiet and private place—a beach, perhaps, or the corner booth at a diner—and set aside about two hours.

Explain: "You don't need to solve my problems or analyze me. Just listen."

Telling your own story will alert you to your own negative behavior and to attitudes or feelings that you may need to change in order to be mentally, spiritually, and emotionally ready to make contact. Listing your successes will help you gain a better sense of your strong points.

Bullying your way into your child's life because of some imagined sense of entitlement will not help anyone. This process is designed to help you become whole enough to be a good father ready to see his child.

You are seeking to be a man for whom his child is a treasure, a father whose child would want to know him and love him. Telling your story will help you find the traits you feel good enough about to share and help you see the areas where you'd like to do better. Confession is not only good for the soul; it will also teach you things.

> It takes more courage to reveal insecurities than to hide them, more strength to relate to people than to dominate them, more manhood to abide by thought-out principles rather than blind reflex. Toughness is in the soul and the spirit, not in the muscles and an immature mind.
>
> —ALEX KARRAS

Rick had been divorced from Bobby for five years. His visits with their children had been sporadic. Working with his Narrative Time Line, he realized that his visits became erratic whenever he began dating a new love interest. The pursuit of a new lover would take precedence over his children.

"I began to see that I was trying to use a new love to give me a sense of worth," he said. "Now I realize it's fine to want to get to know someone new, but it's a lot more important to see my kids on schedule and make the date wait. She respects me more for it, too."

Chasing women was not the sport that deflected Ted, but nearly all other sporting events were.

"I saw in writing out my time line that I used TV sports

like a drug," he explained. "I actually was addicted to big sporting events. I made excuses about why I couldn't see my children during the playoffs. Now they watch with me. The big games, anyway."

"I wish my problem were something like women or sports," says Michael. "Maybe I'm a dull guy. For me, my big excuse was work. Writing out my time line, I saw that I'd been too busy with work to make seeing my son a priority."

You and your support team will be able to see what works for you and what does not. This simple process can change your life for the better. You already know what you need to do.

THE PAYOFFS IN PERSPECTIVE

It is not only his relationship to his children and his past that a man's Narrative Time Line casts into clarity. Very often the rewards of writing and sharing his story will also cast light on many of the darker areas of his nature. Sometimes this darker self can give us strength. For this reason I often think of the Narrative Time Line as an exercise in mapping our own unknown territory. In writing a Narrative Time Line we become cartographers of the self.

> *All we are is a result of what we have thought; it is founded in our thoughts, it is made up of our thoughts. If a man speaks or acts with pure thought, happiness will follow him like a shadow that never leaves him.*
>
> —BUDDHA

In writing the narrative of his life, Reggie realized that he hated anyone or anything that made him feel "less than." He hated colleges because they could reject him, he hated his parents because they weren't rich, he hated his ex-wife because she fell in love with another man, he hated himself for getting married in the first place, and he hated working for "idiots." Reggie's list of resentments went on and on. In short, he hated his life.

By sharing his list of hates, Reggie saw that the real issue wasn't other people's attitudes but his own. He was always perceiving a disrespect that actually emanated from within himself. He needed to work not on changing others but on changing his own behavior so that he could build his own sense of self-worth.

"How come self-realization is always bad news?" Reggie jokes. "Funny, but a little shift in perspective can give you a whole new life."

Meaningful change was something Reggie could accomplish once he was willing to look at who he was angry with, what he was afraid of, and at what kind of smoldering grudges he held—all of which became apparent to him as he wrote his life story. Today, whenever Reggie is angry at something or someone, he asks, "What was my contribution to this problem? What did I do that helped cause this?" In other words, he has learned to check his responsibility before allowing himself to blame others or to be invalidated by someone else.

A WORD OF WARNING

Simple as it may be to describe, the Narrative Time Line is an extremely potent tool for self-transformation. Those who have worked with it over time swear by its effectiveness, but while they are doing it, they often just plain swear: the Narrative Time Line brings up emotions, memories, and often uncomfortable personal revelations.

> I*t takes a rare person to want to hear what he doesn't want to hear.*
>
> –DICK CAVETT

Brian began writing a Narrative Time Line. After the first week he told me it seemed as if his feelings were attached to his ignition key.

"What do you mean?" I asked.

"I mean . . ."

Brian explained that he always spent the hour before he left for work writing in his journal. Behavior patterns that surfaced had sabotaged his life—like being totally irresponsible with money. Then he would get in the car and turn the key.

The first commercial on the car radio always seemed to be a father and mother planning for their family's financial future, and this would make him cry.

"Then my glasses would fog up so badly, I'd have to pull over and wait for the sadness to pass."

"That's rough," I said.

"That's not half of it," Brian snarled.

It seemed to him that no sooner had he calmed down and proceeded down the road than another driver would fail to use his turn signal. This, Brian said, would result in an eighty-mile-an-hour chase through the streets of St. Louis, his head hanging out the window like a mad dog's, screaming at the other driver, foam and obscenities pouring out of his mouth.

> He *who conceals his disease cannot expect to be cured.*
>
> —ETHIOPIAN PROVERB

"You're exaggerating," I protested.

"Sure." Brian laughed. "I was there."

Then Brian would pull into the parking lot at work, wipe away the foam, comb his hair, and stroll in as though nothing had happened. The last thing he wanted anyone to see was that he was susceptible to feelings.

Eventually Brian realized that this out-of-control display of emotions was due to his trying to hide the truth of who he was and what he was going through. With a lot of support from his friends he began to give himself permission to articulate his feelings: "I am angry," "I am sad," "I feel great."

WHAT TO DO ABOUT EMOTIONS

- Take a walk.
- Take a shower.

- Watch one of your movies. Cry.
- Watch one of your movies. Laugh.
- Listen to soothing music.
- Listen to a friend's troubles instead of your own.
- Paint something for fun.
- Clean something like there's no tomorrow.
- Pray.

Happy or sad, these feelings are a source of energy—energy you will need to sustain the efforts you are making at reunion. Feelings are fuel and a map at the same time. For instance, a man who acknowledges that he is now ready to stop drinking or using drugs or to stop spending compulsively may find it sad that he has made such glaring mistakes in his life. This sadness is important. It is his soul telling him he needs to make a change; and sadness can turn to elation if he is listening.

> We are never as fortunate or unfortunate as we suppose.
>
> —FRANÇOIS DE LA ROCHEFOUCAULD

I used my anger at feeling like a failure to go back to college. Every time I felt worthless, stupid, or angry, I went to the library or to class. One class at a time, I graduated. I was thirty-three years old.

You can change who you are—if you *use* the feelings and not let them use you. Recognizing and naming your feelings and writing about them, working to remove stress from your body with physical exercise (even walking works), and changing the habits that make you feel guilty will become a way of life that is its own reward.

THE OKAY JOE

As you prepare for a reunion with your child, it is important for you to recognize the negative patterns that no longer work for you. Now you can begin to get rid of them.

For years I felt emotionally frozen as the sixteen-year-old boy I once was, and it took me some time to feel like a grown-up –but I do. I am not the same man who started this work, and you will not end up the same man who started it either.

Many fathers say, "I'm still in the house with my children," or "I'm visiting my children, and I don't have problems like alcohol or drugs. How will this work help me?"

There are many benefits to writing a Narrative Time Line for you fathers who are still visiting or living in (for mothers, for that matter). Most men report that doing the time line, inventory, and gratitude list alleviates much of their frustration, supports them for being fathers, and leads to a deeper understanding of their value to their children. It also helps them get more in tune with their kids in general.

THE EMOTIONAL MAP, ROUND THREE

Answer the questions below in as much detail as you can, writing down everything that comes to mind. Let your pen flow across the paper and don't edit your thoughts. This writing is private and is not to be shown to anyone while it is in progress. You can say anything you please.

Write about the memories that surface at each question and any feelings they evoke. It is not uncommon to feel hungry, get a headache, space out, or forget what you are doing.

Write down all the responses that come to mind, no matter how silly they sound. It will be just as important for you to see your good traits, though you may be acutely aware of your failures.

1. Are you able to make commitments and stick to them? List the many commitments you have and how you feel you have met each one. What strategies might you use to make yourself more consistent? Don't worry; no one is perfect.

Consistency is very important for children. Though you will have to start somewhere and take the relationship one day at a time, it is better if you have long-term intentions. It is critical to remember that you are making the trip home not just for yourself but for your children's best interests.

2. Are you able to work?

What sort of work do you do? Do you like it? Are you good at it? How could you do better? One of your important commitments to your children will be financial. Children do not need the moon, but the returning father will need to contribute financially if he is not doing so already, and there will be travel to arrange. The ability to work is essential for your self-esteem and will serve as a good example for your children. They will learn more about you and about life by watching what you do than by hearing what you say.

> A *shortcut is often the quickest way to some place you weren't going.*
>
> –CLASSIC CROSSWORD PUZZLE

The ability to work is a measure of your emotional and social health. If you are unable or unwilling to work, you need outside help to deal with this issue.

3. Are you able to accept responsibility for the part you played in your absence?

It's easy for all of us to point the finger and say we'd never have been absent if "she" or "they" had made it easier for us. Turn the focus toward yourself and take an honest look at the role you played in your exile.

4. Are you sober and reliable?

This question relates again to your being consistent, a crucial determinant for you to succeed with the reunion process. Many people are surprised at how silently chemicals, including alcohol, drugs, and food, became a part of their lives to cover their pain. If you cannot stop drinking or using drugs, particularly if you are violent, you may not yet be capable of moving forward in a loving, nonhostile way. If this is true for you, as it is for some, you will need to seek professional support in order to get sober.

Addictive substances can sabotage any attempt at reconciliation, so they must be dealt with first. Remember, recovery *is* possible, no matter how far down the scale you have gone, as AA says. Ask for help and you'll get it.

THE TEST FOR ADDICTION

If you're a teetotaler, you may skip this section. If not, you need to spot-check yourself for addictions. I have worked with millionaires and judges, politicians and doctors—this work may seem like an affront. Take pen in hand anyway. If this idea angers you, ask yourself why. Wouldn't you want to know your child's well-being was being placed in the hands of a sober, loving, and responsible person?

This test, designed by the Johns Hopkins University Hospital and subsequently published by Alcoholics Anonymous, can help you determine whether or not you have a drinking problem.

If you drink alcohol or take other drugs, recreational or not, please answer yes or no to the following questions. You may substitute the phrase "drinking or taking other drugs" for the term "drinking." Also try using the words "depression" or "anger" in place of "drinking." Any revelations?

1. Do you lose time from work due to drinking?
2. Is drinking making your home life unhappy?
3. Do you drink because you are shy with other people?
4. Is drinking affecting your reputation?
5. Have you ever felt remorse after drinking?
6. Have you ever gotten into financial difficulty as a result of drinking?

7. Do you turn to lower companions and an inferior environment when drinking?
8. Does your drinking make you careless of your family's welfare?
9. Has your ambition decreased since you started drinking?
10. Do you crave a drink at a definite time daily?
11. Do you want a drink the next morning?
12. Does drinking cause you to have trouble sleeping?
13. Has your efficiency decreased since you started drinking
14. Is drinking jeopardizing your job or business?
15. Do you drink to escape worries or troubles?
16. Do you drink alone?
17. Have you ever had a complete loss of memory as a result of drinking?
18. Has your physician ever treated you for drinking?
19. Do you drink to build up your self-confidence?
20. Have you ever been to a hospital or institution on account of drinking?

If you answered yes to any of the above questions, there is a possibility that you may be alcoholic; if you answered yes to two or more, you probably are an alcoholic; and if you answered yes to three or more, you definitely should seek help.

If you answered yes to three or more of the questions about your drinking, you now need to look at this issue more deeply.

- How has your addictive behavior, depression, or anger interfered with your relationship to your children?
- How have your addictions, depression, or anger affected your relationship with the mother of your children?
- How has your drinking or drug or food use affected your relationship with your own parents?
- How has your ex-wife's addictive behavior affected your relationship?

- Are you ready to take immediate action? If not, why? Will you call Alcoholics Anonymous or Narcotics Anonymous, a psychologist, hospital treatment unit, or member of the clergy?

MOVING ONWARD

Before you move onward from this chapter, take a look at the victory you have won here. Give yourself a token of your appreciation–a dinner out, a new shirt, a night at the theater, a drive in the country. Something for you.

In writing your Narrative Time Line, you have told your life story and won the right to reshape it as well. Keep the time line private; it will come in handy later. As Marcel Proust advised: "We are healed of our suffering only by experiencing it to the full."

4

MAKING AMENDS TO YOUR CHILD'S MOTHER

REACHING FOR REUNION

I remember the night I finally got up the courage to try to
locate Scott. Just as I'd been told, there was actually a moment
when I knew the time had come. But how was I to find him?

I knew he and his family had lived in Los Angeles—John
had worked as an actor—and in New York City. But I had heard
that they might have moved back to Virginia. I started there.

I picked up the phone, dialed Information, and asked for
John and Betsy's number. No way, I thought, and then the
operator said, "One moment, please, here's your number." I
sat back, stunned.

All those years. All that distance. And all I had to do was
call Information and ask. I never expected it could be that easy.
I picked up the phone again and redialed Information to
confirm—but this time Betsy answered! Even after all the years,
I recognized her voice immediately. I had meant to call Information but I had dialed Betsy instead, and there she was on
the line.

"Hello? Hello? Who is this?" she said.

Terrified, I hung up. The hour was late. What would she think? What would I say? What should I do?

I did what I'd learned to do—ask for some advice.

Over the next few days, I talked to my mentors, Bill, Bob, and Charlie; my therapist, Sheila; and my friends Marie, Dan, and Michelle: "I've found Scott—and Betsy!!"

I was flabbergasted. Thrilled. Jolted. I was so excited I jumped up and down. They listened to my elation and gave me some very important advice: "Mark, calm down."

Sheila said now was the time to write Betsy an "amends" letter, explaining what had happened to me in the years since our last contact. She urged me to be straightforward about my negative behavior and lost years and to explain that I was now sober, stable, and willing and eager to establish a meaningful contact with my son.

> Compassion is ... a spirituality and a way of walking through life. It is the way we treat all there is in life— ourselves, our bodies, our imaginations and dreams, our neighbors, our enemies. ... Compassion is treating all creation as holy and divine ... which is what it is.
>
> —MATTHEW FOX

"Be clear, honest, responsible, and humble," my mentors urged. "Explain what you want and apologize for any harm you have caused her by your actions or your absence."

"What about *her* mistakes?" I wanted to know.

"Sounds as if you need to work on your anger a little more," I was told.

This was sound advice. A successful reunion is not easy when unresolved hostility exists between the mother and the father—and it almost always does exist. It certainly existed between me and Betsy. I knew she must feel abandoned, just as I felt driven away. There was validity to both our perspectives, but I could see this only after repeated sessions with pencil and paper, writing through my wounded feelings until I could see not only the pain but the painful facts: I had surrendered my rights and my power to Betsy—and tried to blame her for my wrongs.

I was told to make amends, so I wrote to her.

In my letter to Betsy, I apologized for hurting her with my drinking and drug use, for my immaturity, and for my carelessness of our welfare while we were married. I humbly explained to her that I had changed—I no longer drank or used drugs, and I was working hard. I told her that I had loved her very much and was grateful for the time we spent together.

Sheila checked the letter for any hint of hidden anger or blame. She said, "Redo it, because you *still* sound as though you are blaming her instead of taking responsibility for your absence." Humbled and grumbling, I redid it. Sheila liked the next version. I mailed it. The real journey into Scott's life began then.

I had now been sober for over a year and had stabilized emotionally. I was attending school on a government grant, living in the attic of a friend's house, working full-time as a clerk. Financially I was still struggling, having returned to college at age thirty. What I had to offer—all I had to offer—was myself, the self I was building. I had no money in the bank or even a job that paid decently.

Betsy answered my letter. "You can't see him," she wrote. Not what I had wanted to hear. Not until "you pay us $10,000 for child support for the time you've been gone."

Regardless of my sentiments, then or now, it was money I did not have. Nor did I have any expectation that I would get my hands on that large a lump sum in the foreseeable future. I was heartbroken and furious.

> Be *swift to hear, slow to speak, slow to wrath, for the wrath of man worketh not the righteousness of God.*
>
> —James

"She shouldn't deny me visitation!" I raged.

"You could have sent *some* child support over the years. And remember, John adopted Scott," my mentors countered.

"It's blackmail," I sputtered.

"They raised your son," they replied. "What can you do to right things *now?*"

I should have sent small child-support payments and hoped their hearts softened. Instead, my grandiosity made me feel I would somehow, someday, be able to send the $10,000 in a lump sum. It took me a while to dismantle that thinking.

"I don't have it to send!" I raged.

Okay, then, Sheila and Charlie said, "Wait. Don't rock the boat. Write Betsy another letter and ask her what you should do."

I did that.

Finally, Betsy and John suggested a compromise. I could not see Scott, but I could write to him. They would not give him the letters, but they would save them until he graduated from high school. Scott was then fourteen; I would have to wait four years. I was not happy with the decision, but I no longer had a legal right to see my son, so I had to accept their terms.

The letters were hard to write because of my anger. I felt inadequate because I could not afford to "buy" my way back into his life. Nevertheless, I did send letters over the next several years. Carefully casual in tone, they described what I did, where I lived, who my friends were, where I was going to school. They were intended to get my son current on my life and circumstances, but, more important, they were intended to show him I missed him.

> Our prayers are answered not when we are given what we ask, but when we are challenged to be what we can be.
>
> —MORRIS ADLER

I carefully phrased each letter, making sure that I did not blame Betsy or John or say anything that would cause conflict for Scott. I kept the letters brief and tried to express what I really felt. I wanted him to know I loved him and wanted to meet him as soon as he thought it possible. I always showed the letters to Sheila, and after her approval, mailed them.

Disappointed at not being allowed to see him, I told myself to be patient, and I continued to work to get stronger, to become the man Scott would want to know when the time came. As I continued the routines that would advance my recovery, I was humbled by how much I didn't know about life, mine and others, but proud to be learning. I finished college and went to graduate school.

During this time I worked with young men and women who had chemical dependencies, behavior addictions, and money problems. I found I enjoyed counseling kids. Many needed help, just as I had needed it: I was glad I could be there for them. I wondered how different my life might have been had I gotten the counseling I needed.

Although I never cast it in these terms, I was learning the skills of fathering: consistency, patience, attention. My only heartache was not having my own son to use them on.

I continued to write to Scott, but sending letters into the void without receiving a reply was difficult. The wait was long and hard for me—and, I later learned, for Scott as well. We were both in exile from a part of ourselves.

REACHING OUT TO THE MOTHER

Many of you will meet with situations that will not fulfill your wishes or your fantasies about reunion, just as I did. The hard truth is this: reunion does not often come to us on our own terms. Our job is to see to it that it comes to us no matter what.

Reaching out to the mother of your child is the next stage in the reunion process. It will be much easier if you, as a returning father, find a way to establish, or at least attempt to establish, a more cooperative partnership with her. In order to cooperate with the mother of your children, you must now become able to see her and her point of view.

This reunion with the mother is the step with which you begin to move out of the shadowy world of The Haunting—the world of guilt and loss and fantasies—into the brighter, and often glaring, world of reality and solution. The contrast between these two worlds can be both startling and painful.

> *Love is an act of endless forgiveness, a tender look that becomes a habit.*
>
> —PETER USTINOV

The burden of striking up a new relationship with the mother is up to you. Whether this is fair or not is irrelevant. Life isn't fair. You will have to offer her the olive branch. Sometimes this meeting can go so smoothly and joyously that you forget why you lost touch in the first place.

I can already hear you chuckle—

"That's easy for Bryan to say—he doesn't know my ex-wife."

"There's no getting through to her; she has a heart of stone."

"My ex hates my guts," etc. etc.

Fair enough. No one said it would be easy, just better. I'm even willing to concede that maybe YOUR situation is different from the other hundred stories I can think of, but the majority of men I know have told me the same things—and a lot worse—about their children's mothers.

Emotion can block a man's view of his ex-wife, the mother of his children. Because he often views her as an antagonist, the barrier between him and his children, he may not see her as a valued and vulnerable human being anymore.

Recently I was driving through my neighborhood when I saw Bob and Sharon, a couple in the throes of a separation, coming toward me in their car. They were slowed by construction, and as they approached me, I saw Bob raise his hand, gesturing dramatically in exasperation. His anger was apparent from fifty yards away.

I sat in my car, alarmed for Sharon, his wife of many years. Although I know Bob is a good man who has never been violent, his anger scared me. Neither of them noticed me, and as they passed, I saw Sharon shrinking with fear in the passenger seat. It occurred to me that Bob could not see her and didn't realize she was afraid. She had become emotionally invisible to him.

> *There is nothing stronger in the world than gentleness.*
>
> –HAN SUYIN

INVISIBLE WOMEN

Women become invisible to men when men get so angry that they go into a rage, as Bob did. In the throes of divorce we are nearly always blinded by our rage and grief. Bob could not see how frightening his behavior was; he would probably be indignant later when Sharon told him that he'd frightened her.

I can hear Bob saying, "I would never hurt you, you know that." *He* knew he would never hurt her, but the fact is, she was scared. He would have to better understand her feelings; he would have to come to better understand his own.

TAKING THE X FACTOR OUT OF YOUR EX

The following exercises will help you gain a new perspective on your past relationship with your children's mother. Remember that your interactions with her will help or hinder your visitation with the children. Therefore, you need to answer these questions to reevaluate your former alliance and to help you come to a place of respect or at least acceptance of your child's mother.

TRIBUTE, NOT JUST TRIBULATION

These questions are meant to remind you that at one time there were things that you liked about your child's mother, whether you and she had a short-term relationship or a long one that ended badly.

There are no right or wrong answers to these questions. Stay alert to your emotions as you answer them. It is okay if you can't answer all of them.

1. When you first met your child's mother, what were you like when you were with her?
2. When you first met, what was she like when she was with you?
3. What are the things you liked about your child's mother?
4. What favorite memories did the two of you share?
5. What did she do that made you happy?
6. What did you admire about her?
7. What do you think she admired about you?
8. What attracted her to you in the first place?
9. What do you remember that made you most angry?
10. What made her most angry?
11. What did your parents think of you and her together? What did hers think?
12. What do they think now?
13. What do you wish you had said to her before you two broke up?
14. What do you wish you could say now?
15. What do you wish she had said to you before you left?
16. What do you wish she would tell you now?
17. What three things do you wish she had done differently?
18. What three things do you wish you had done differently?
19. What is the most romantic thing she ever did for you?
20. What was the most romantic thing you ever did for her? With her?

> *Gratitude is the heart's memory.*
>
> —FRENCH PROVERB

CLEANING YOUR SIDE OF THE STREET

Remember this: you can focus on the problem and it will get bigger, or you can focus on the solution and the problem will get smaller.

"Love is action," my mentors told me, and they were right. My actions during the years away from my son were unloving, no matter what I had in my heart. There was nothing I could do about the past, but I could do something about the future. I did what I now ask you to do: take an inventory.

THE PERSONAL INVENTORY

You have already written a Narrative Time Line and gotten a clearer perspective on your life. You may have also made a habit of recording your insights and discoveries in your reunion notebook. Now, in the same notebook, take a Personal Inventory.

What precisely do I mean? I mean take an accurate look at the attitudes, not merely the actions and events, that have made up your life. List all of the fears, grudges, angers, and resentments that you harbor. Also list any guilt and all of your secrets, particularly those relating to your ex-wife and your divorce.

Listing your mistakes and mishaps is an essential step toward reunion. Any business that does not take a regular inventory usually goes broke. This personal inventory will keep you from getting broken.

> Truth is a demure lady, much too ladylike to knock you on the head and drag you to her cave. She is there, but the people must want her and seek her out.
>
> —WILLIAM F. BUCKLEY, JR.

If you are working in a twelve-step fellowship, you can use your fourth step from AA, NA, or other program and go over it with your sponsor. Either way, while doing your inventory, remember to count both your mistakes *and your successes.*

You will be identifying your negative behavior attitudes, and your positive ones as well.

If you are working with a men's group, simply work these exercises into the fabric of your other rituals and activities. Writing and then reflecting on what you have written will lessen your anger; it will also make you more understanding of your value and more compassionate about your former partner's situation. Keep your ears and eyes open to coincidences that have meaning for you—something said by passersby, perhaps, or a book whose title strikes you as interesting, or the odd bit of humor that may pertain to your situation. Be open to clues.

Listing your resentments, fears, joys, and accomplishments may also enable you to appreciate the efforts your child's mother has made, changing old grudges into appreciation and distance into cooperation.

> *All truth is an achievement. If you would have truth at its full value, go win it.*
>
> —MUNGER

Discover the role you played in causing your absence by writing down all the fears and resentments you have about your relationship with her and about your reunion with your children. Old angers and attitudes that helped drive you away should surface as resentments at people or institutions, and writing them down to be studied, thought about, and reframed will help you accept them as part of your truth. Do not lie or deny. Just list them and let the answers cook for a while.

PEN IN HAND

1. Be specific. List every time you hurt someone else and every time someone else hurt you. Write down each incident and what you could do to set things right.
2. Look at your list of those who hurt you. Are you prepared to forgive them?

3. Can you think of what they may have been thinking or feeling to cause them to make the choices they made?
4. What actions of yours do you hope will be forgiven? What amends are you willing to make? What changes?
5. What underlying emotion was your anger trying to mask? Most often, underneath anger or a grudge, you will find fear and feelings of sadness or inadequacy.
6. How is your job going?
7. How do you handle anger?
8. When are you most fun to be with?
9. What are your living arrangements?
10. In what ways have you been fearful, selfish, or self-centered about your children?
11. What are your fears and resentments about your reunion?
12. What did you do wrong during your marriage? During your divorce?
14. How can you change your behavior in the future?
15. What can you do now to improve your relationship with your child's mother?

> I *have learned silence from the talkative, tolerance from the intolerant, and kindness from the unkind. I shall not be ungrateful to those teachers.*
>
> —KAHLIL GIBRAN

Doing this inventory will help you heal these old wounds for good by reframing the past and taking responsibility for your part, seeing how others contributed to it, and forgiving their trespasses against you. This sets your final course for reunion.

SHARING THE INVENTORY

After writing your Personal Inventory, ask someone you trust to listen to it. Be certain you choose someone you can rely on to keep a confidence. Again, the listener's job is not to fix you, merely to listen with his heart. He need not say anything.

This simple gesture of sharing begins to break the bonds of

silence that chained you to your past mistakes. Talking it out with others will help you overcome any sense of self-pity, that righteous feeling of "She done me wrong," or "I'm a loser," or "After what I've done I don't deserve it," or "I can't do it."

You can do it. You already are.

REFLECTIONS, NOT RETALIATION

Sometimes a look in the rearview mirror can be as painful as watching a car crash. It was for me.

Never forget that you can change the way people react to you by changing the way you react to them. You can now begin to prepare for your amends.

> A man who studieth revenge keeps his own wounds green.
>
> —FRANCIS BACON

Remember your quiet place? Go to it now and spend an hour reviewing your findings. Look at your answers and make a commitment to change any behavior that has worked against you—overwork or laziness, alcohol and drug use, womanizing, carelessness about your home environment—whatever. Don't forget to celebrate your successes. Sit for some time and try to breathe them in.

You have probably started daydreaming about the reunion by now. This may affect your sleep patterns and dreams as well. You may think often about what the reunion will be like, what you will say, how the kids will look, what they will say to you. Such reveries are not uncommon, and as your self-esteem deepens, the idea of reunion will grow more plausible.

THE AMENDS LETTER

The inventory questions you answered are the building blocks for the amends letter you will write to your child's mother. You have listed your mistakes and the actions that hurt her or the children. It is these mistakes you must now confront head-on.

Present yourself to her as a sane and rational man seeking legitimate contact with his children for their benefit and hers as well as your own.

You should be prepared to tell the truth about your current living arrangements, your financial situation, and your interest in your child. Be prepared to thank her for all she has done for the kids.

It is important for you to express your gratitude to her for all she has done and to tell her you're sorry. The amends letter is a matter of standing tall and accepting responsibility for your actions that have caused harm to others—in this instance, your ex-wife.

It is more important to share the nature of your wrongs than to list every specific incident: "I'm sorry I was such a pessimist," "Sorry I was not more attentive," "Sorry that I have not paid child support, that I have been gone, that I was violent, that I was so jealous, that I didn't call on the holidays, that I didn't trust you, that I drank too much . . ."

This letter must promise—and deliver—a change in behavior.

You are promising that you will no longer do the negative things you did before and that you will work diligently to change any behaviors that have kept you from being a proper father. One word of caution here: do not include information that will harm you or someone else. For instance, do not list affairs that your ex-wife to this day doesn't know you had. You do not have to say you were across town with Mary in order to say you are sorry you were unfaithful. Just make a promise to yourself to live as an honest human being and put your children first.

If she knows you were seeing someone before your divorce, you can apologize for it, but it is not okay to name the other party. You are promising to be a better man in order to be

> "Honesty" without compassion and understanding is not honesty, but subtle hostility.
>
> —ROSE FRANZBLAU

more present for your child. If it was your ex-wife who left you or had the affair, you will have to forgive her for her past actions, too. But our focus is on you.

Some of the information in your letter will probably be specific: "I'm sorry for the time I drove like a madman when we were arguing." The rest will be more general: "I'm sorry for all the times you tried to tell me what was bothering you and I didn't listen."

This letter is not a platform from which to blame the mother of your children for anything that went wrong–"I hated it when you flirted with every guy on the block," or "How did you expect me to eat what you put on the table" is not exactly what I have in mind.

You should in this letter promise to provide regular child-support payments, whether you were ordered to or not, whether the amounts are sufficient or not. Send whatever amount you can handle. I regret that I remained stuck in my idea that I had to have a lot of money before I could contribute any to Scott. Even small amounts are helpful. This act will bolster your self-esteem as well as help your ex. Most fathers pay child support if they are involved with their children, are a part of their lives, see them on a regular basis, and help make significant decisions about their lives.

> *Character consists of what you do on the third and fourth try.*
>
> –JAMES A. MICHENER

Some men are so close to the poverty line themselves that to provide the court-ordered amount of child support would plunge them into poverty while the mother and child would rise above the poverty line. I understand this is tough. Regardless of our financial status, we have to deal with the truth: we owe the money, we want to see our children, we pay what we can.

Whatever your situation, in your letter you need to tell her you will make some kind of monetary contribution, even if minimal. You should, of course, apologize to her for being in arrears and indicate when and how you think you'll be able to pay what you owe.

One night in group, Charlie said he had written his amends letter and met with Maggie, his ex-wife, the night before. He told us that he had made reservations in a chic little café, but about halfway through dinner Maggie stomped out. He knew then that improving the relationship with his ex was going to be harder than he had hoped.

I asked him if he had read his amends to her as his mentor had suggested. He told us that he was reading her the last line–"If there were ever two people on the face of this earth that deserved each other, it was you and me"–when she walked out.

The rest of us burst into laughter.

I asked him how his mentor had let him write an amends letter that included such a line. He said he had added the line as an afterthought.

I sent him back to his mentor. He rewrote his letter and mailed it to her with an apology and a request to meet again. It was several weeks later when she responded.

Once she had some time to sit with her feelings and read a more proper letter that was free of blame and rationalizations, Maggie's heart softened. Reading this list of "I accept responsibility . . ." coming from the man who had been her verbal sparring partner in round after round for eight years, led her to try another meeting with him.

As you can guess, this meeting went much better than the first. There were still some sparks and fire. Each jockeyed for top dog, a pattern left over from their marriage, but as they parted she agreed to meet again and go over his plan for starting visitation with their children.

I have yet to meet a man who couldn't find something to apologize for or something that he could change about himself that would make her—and him—happier. And I have never met a man who did either one who didn't feel much better about himself afterward.

A BUSINESS RELATIONSHIP

As you work to reestablish a child-rearing partnership—or at least a cease-fire—with your children's mother, you may need to be patient and consistent to slowly undo the damage of the past and rebuild a basis of trust.

This is potentially the most volatile part of the recovery process. The meeting with the mother can stir up feelings of sadness, powerlessness, or anger that must be cleared away to make room for the new business relationship between you, one that puts the children, and the children's need for both parents, first.

> Because a thing seems difficult for you, do not think it impossible for anyone to accomplish. But whatever is possible for another, believe that you, too, are capable of it.
>
> —MARCUS AURELIUS

Even if your children are well into their teens, it is important that you reach out to their mother (and stepfather, if there is one) as a matter of respect. Any attempt to contact the child before discussing the visit with her will be interpreted as a sign of aggression and will most likely cause her to respond defensively.

The first goal is to honor the mother in your heart and in deed, so that the potential for conflict between the two of you is minimized. The writing you did in the first two chapters, about your early relationship with her, should clarify many of her good qualities and highlight volatile areas you will have addressed in the amends letter.

Remember: she is the gatekeeper of your child's life, and it is important to acknowledge her role and to appreciate the good she has done. Disrespecting her hurts your child.

If your child is eighteen or older, contact with the mother is not mandatory, but making amends to her shows her a courtesy, and will lift spirits.

In some instances, of course, despite a father's best efforts to elicit the mother's support, or at least her cooperation, she may still refuse his request. In this case, because you are now a better man than you might have been when you left, you are entitled to seek a legal remedy. But not yet. There is still more to be done. And some of you will have to watch for hidden expectations you may still have.

SPOT-CHECK INVENTORY: WHAT ARE YOUR MOTIVES?

While all of us want our reunion to be warm and loving, the reality is that it may feel more like a summit conference between wary and guarded nations than a love fest of peace and forgiveness. You are not there to be your ex-wife's lover again, nor should you expect her to treat you as if you were. You both are in the business of raising your children to be the best they can be, and the children will need all the help you can give.

Accepting your new role as business partner to your ex-wife or former lover may be a blow to your ego and your sense of entitlement, but these feelings are left over from the old myth that a woman somehow belongs to her man. A woman is her own person and has a right to her own life. You will have to let go of your expectation for fondness. Though you might receive it someday after your friendship warrants it, any expectation or demand for affection or approval from her is a ticket to disappointment.

> Let all bitterness and wrath and anger and clamor and evil speaking be put away from you.
>
> —EPHESIANS

Your child's mother may be bitter or cold. It is important that you be able to see this as her leftover emotions from the past. Stay honest with her about your finances and child care capabilities, and no matter how angry she is, do not make promises you can't keep and don't be scared off your mission.

THE MOST COMMON PROBLEMS

Men face some common problems in reestablishing contact with the mother. They may not have let go of their anger or, equally dangerous, their romantic attachment to her. Either emotion is an attempt at connection, and both are dangerous. Do not let them confuse the issue.

Kevin refused to join a reunion group when it was first suggested. He was certain he would be able to handle any difficulties or complications. Then he had his first meeting with Susan, his ex-wife, to discuss visiting their children.

Susan sounded friendly on the phone. "It felt like old times," Kevin told me. (My ears perked up when I heard that line, but I let it go.) Kevin was confident. He felt sure he could deal with Susan. It was time to see the kids; he had some money.

The night they were to meet, Susan sent the kids to her sister's and had Kevin over for dinner so they could talk "first." Kevin brought a bottle of wine . . . and I probably don't have to tell you the rest. One bottle of wine later they were in bed trying to "communicate."

In the morning the light dawned and the pain of their separation invaded the bedroom, ripping open the old wounds. Kevin and Susan had to separate again after a night of intimacy. By the time he was walking out the door, they both were angry and sad. And he still hadn't seen his kids.

BE ALERT FOR SELF-SABOTAGE

Without support, you too may attempt reunion before you have let go of your romantic attachment. There may be other land mines besides that are just as dangerous—for example, unresolved anger.

This was the case with Dirk. He still felt betrayed by the divorce settlement and usually saw red whenever she asked for money. He went to see the kids for the first time in a year, and that was the first thing she did.

"What about last month? You were $50 short."

"I didn't come to hear that!"

"What *did* you come for?"

"I don't know!" Dirk yelled, instead of saying, "I came to see my kids."

"You never did know what you wanted!"

"Well, I sure don't want you!"

"Then I suppose you don't want the children, either!"

By then the kids were cowering in the face of their parents' rage and the reunion became, for Dirk, another reason to stay away. He withdrew from his children again. He had gone in too early and without enough support.

Now in therapy, he is working out his feelings, learning to take time out when angry, and he has established a line of communication within the family at a safer distance. In Dirk's case, a formal group process was the best solution because it helped him to see that his ex-wife's request for money was not meant to shame him. The money was important to his ex not only because she needed it to feed and clothe the kids, but because it showed her he still cared about and honored her and the children. She did not realize he would take her demands as an attack on his competency as a man, and his ability to be responsible. Realizing she didn't mean it this way helped Dirk lighten up.

> *Communication leads to community—that is, to understanding, intimacy, and mutual valuing.*
>
> —ROLLO MAY

Another pitfall, one that is often difficult for a man to spot alone, is "too much togetherness" with his girlfriend or his new wife.

Jay, married at twenty-two, became a father six months later, and divorced at twenty-four. He loves his son, Austin, and would take him every other weekend and, some months, every weekend. He and his ex-wife, June, had a commitment to each other as Austin's parents.

Three years after his divorce, Jay remarried. His beautiful new wife, Laurie, loved Jay but was not interested in being a stepmother. To Jay's friends she seemed to want more attention than any man could give.

As the weekend approached during which Jay was to have custody of his child, Laurie would begin making plans. When Jay would say, "I'll have Austin," Laurie would pout and tell him that his son was more important than she was, that he was always canceling plans with her, and that it was breaking her heart. In love with his wife, Jay did not see this as manipulation.

When pouting didn't work, Laurie would up the ante. First she would get angry and attack. Then she'd say he didn't love her and that the marriage wasn't what she expected.

Jay's visits with Austin became more and more rare until they eventually ceased entirely.

I have talked to Jay about doing the reunion work, but he is always "too busy." Guess who keeps making plans for him? And guess who keeps giving in?

Is Jay simply a weak man? Maybe. My opinion is that he is a confused man, a man who wants to keep his commitments and is torn by having two commitments to honor.

> It is not the mountain we conquer but ourselves.
>
> —Sir Edmund Hillary

Remember your motive: reunion with your children and respect for yourself and their mother. If it helps, make "R and R"—reunion and respect—a sort of mantra. If you find yourself leaning into any behavior that feels uncomfortable, back off and repeat to yourself, "R and R—reunion and respect."

Having a mantra to guide you may seem far-fetched, but remember that men have always fought crusades under a banner they believed in. This is your personal crusade. Keep its standards high.

After you have sent your amends letter and are waiting for her to respond, spend some time thinking about the reunion and your new relationship with your child.

Sit down and describe your ideal future as a parent. Be specific. You may want to play some music to inspire you.

- How do you intend to handle visitations? How will you deal with picking the child up and dropping him off?
- What would you like your interactions with the other parent (parents) to be? Are there ways you can shape your plan to help their mother with her life?
- How do you envision your interactions with your kids?
- Think about holidays and vacations and lazy Sundays as well as shepherding the kids to the library and the Saturday Little League soccer game.
- List twenty things you like to do. Which ones would be fun to do with your children?
- Do you have a new family? How will you handle introducing your children?

Allow yourself to play with some ideas about what your visit might be like. Remember, this fantasy version will be shaped into a more realistic plan later. Enjoy the reverie.

IMAGINE YOU ARE FRIENDS WITH YOUR EX

Envision an idealized version of your meeting with your child's mother, a best-case scenario. Put an older and wiser mother and father at the center of the story. Think of it as if it were a story about unconditional love, a story of longtime friends who are separated for years by life's changes and who were caught in a storm and survived. How does this feel?

THE MEETING WITH YOUR EX

I have found that the more acrimonious the separation, the more formal and gradual the return should be. If she is still angry or if the relationship is volatile, you may have to write several letters before she responds at all, and it will take patience on your part not to get angry and try to force her hand or throw in the towel in frustration.

> Lord, make me an instrument of your peace. Where there is hatred, let me sow love; where there is injury, pardon; where there is doubt, faith; where there is despair, hope; where there is darkness, light; and where there is sadness, joy.
>
> —SAINT FRANCIS OF ASSISI

If you are still feeling hostile even after all the work so far, and this is not uncommon, you may want to write a few letters—which you *will not send*—to vent your anger or sadness or to say the unsayable so that you can get the rage out of your system. ANGER letters are never to be mailed.

After the first letter you mail, you may want to wait three to four weeks for a response before you send another letter. If within a month you have not heard anything, I suggest you send another letter. Then wait another month and send a third.

While you are waiting, continue working with these tools, and keep meeting with your team. If your ex has not responded to three letters, you might send a registered letter, call her to discuss her hesitation, or issue an appeal through a mutual friend or relative. Or you may want to send her this book. Do not get forceful, and do not threaten or demand.

Remember, she will have her own emotions to work through, and giving her ninety days to answer is not unreasonable. Sending three letters communicates to her that you will be persistent, that this is not a whim, and that you will remain respectful. She may test you, perhaps unconsciously, to see if you really mean this.

RESIST any temptation to show anger if she does not respond immediately. She needs time. Give it to her. Keep the tone of all letters warm and friendly. Remember she is the mother of your children, and the two of you have a sacred trust. This respect will help her to feel safe.

> It is only with the heart that one can see rightly, what is essential is invisible to the eye.
>
> —ANTOINE DE SAINT-EXUPÉRY

Once she has responded to your letter, the next contact may be by phone, but you will want to follow it up with a face-to-face meeting. This meeting should be held on neutral ground; a public place, such as a quiet restaurant, is perfect. The two of you could meet privately if it feels comfortable, but the civility of a public space is often a wiser choice.

Either way, pleasantly make your case for seeing your children, and then listen to what she has to say. Do not defend yourself, and listen to what she is feeling, not just to what she says. If the meeting becomes unpleasant, whatever the reason, you may want to meet a second time with a therapist or clergy member.

It is possible, of course, that she will not meet with you at all. In this case your feelings—and your mentors'—should guide you toward what to do next, whether it be continued dialogue or work with an attorney or other intermediary. Most communities now have skilled family mediators who will serve just such purposes. Mediation is always the best first approach, as it allows you to avoid a legal battle that could easily solidify you both into enemy camps. Another avenue for many men has been the intervention of a family member who is sympathetic to their cause.

> You grow up the day you have your first real laugh at yourself.
>
> —ETHEL BARRYMORE

A heartfelt appeal will usually open the conversation. Just remember: you must *earn* your right to be in your child's life again; you must not demand it. In order to know your children and help them in their lives, you must appeal to their mother's higher nature, and yours, and make an honest attempt at reconciliation for the children's sake.

Because emotions may be high, with everyone nervous, it is important, before you actually make contact, for you to decide exactly what you intend to say to her. This will lessen the chances of your saying something you will regret.

PREPARE WHAT YOU WILL SAY

Rather than speak from highly charged emotions, write out in your Reunion Notebook what you would ideally like to say. Next, practice saying what you really feel and imagine letting her tell you what she really feels. This may seem foolish or artificial, but you should rehearse this meeting as carefully as you would an important presentation at work.

It may aid you to rehearse with a friend or mentor. Sometimes, it is only in the speaking that you can know what it is you really want to say. Additionally, this will give you practice in listening to someone else. Your meeting may be as much–or more–about listening as it will be about talking.

And another word about what you say: take care to stick to the present. Anger expressed toward others damages many relationships, and it is important not to fight about old issues. You are here to be a supportive new partner in parenting the children, not to rehash any old arguments.

Going over with your mentor all of the correspondence and communication you will have with your child's mother *before you have it* will greatly enhance your chances of saying what you really mean.

WHAT IF IT GETS VOLATILE?

Regardless of what she says or does, you must remember to address her respectfully and speak to her calmly and civilly at all times, *no matter what.* Do not lose your temper or let an outburst of rage cover your nervousness or your understandably roiled emotions. If your anger should rise–and she may want it to–if you are able, take time out. Just say, "I'll be right back." Go to the rest room and compose yourself. If you cannot calm down, say, "I will talk to you tomorrow, and walk out the door *immediately.* Do not to raise your voice. It is better for you to leave her at the table with the check than to allow your meeting to escalate into an ugly scene.

> **F***air play is primarily not blaming others for anything that is wrong with us.*
>
> –ERIC HOFFER

Rehearsals and tested scenarios will help prevent you from sabotaging your efforts. The tendency to argue will be particularly prevalent at the times of meeting or leaving. I call this tendency separation syndrome–the sudden outburst of hostility that many couples experience when one of them is about to travel to a distant place or is returning from somewhere far away.

In order to keep this potential problem to a minimum, make your first interactions brief and to the point. It is easy to get too comfortable or overstay your welcome when talking with, writing to, or visiting your former spouse, particularly at first.

You may be greeted with open arms, with outright hostility, or anywhere in between, and I want you to be alert to the fact that all of these emotions are transitory. Even if you were once married or had a good relationship, remember that the longer you spend on the phone or at her house, the more chance there is for disagreement. Also, just because your relationship was volatile in the past does not necessarily mean that it will be that way now. You are both older and wiser.

> **A***nd if not now, when?*
>
> –THE TALMUD

You are not asking her to make you feel better about yourself. Your support group and your friends are doing that. Your contact with her is for the purpose of discussing your interest in your child and planning the reunion or visitation with your children. Period. It is imperative for you to realize how much emotion both of you will be carrying and to allow her to have her feelings without overreacting.

There is no perfect reunion. Expect moments of joy, of tears, of anger, of clumsiness, and plenty of mistakes. You will learn as you go. Congratulate yourself and each other on your progress.

Gary had not seen his daughter, Megan, since her mother, Constance, moved out of state six years earlier to make a new life for herself after the divorce. Megan was now thirteen. Last year he sent his ex-wife, Constance, several letters that Gary described as "the best letters I ever wrote."

Unfortunately, Constance was unmoved. Like many mothers, she responded that contact with him might hurt and confuse Megan. I explained to Gary that although such a fear is legitimate in cases of drunkenness or violence, Constance was just as likely to be having one of two more common reactions. She could be expressing her own fear of being exposed for her part in the separation, or she might fear that contact with Gary would reopen old wounds for her as well as for their daughter.

Gary sent her another letter, but Constance stood firm. He could not see their daughter. No way.

Gary's confusion about what to do caused him to give up for a while. Then, several months later, he decided to try another approach. He would just pick up the phone and call Constance. There was a catch, however: Gary did not know exactly where she was. Upon leaving the state, and fearful, perhaps, that Gary would try to legally force her to return so that he could be near their child, Constance had asked that child-support checks be delivered to a post office box. Gary had complied. And now that he wanted to reach his daughter, he thought bitterly, there was no way to do it.

Then he remembered his wife had called him collect to deny his request to see Megan. Resolute, Gary looked up his

October phone bill and, sure enough, there was the number. There had been never been any violence or abuse between him and Constance or between him and Megan. He had a right to see his daughter. Nervous but determined, he called at dinnertime, expecting Constance to answer.

Instead, Megan picked up the phone.

"Hello?"

"Hello . . . Megan?"

"Yes."

"Megan, this is your daddy."

Pause.

"Hi, Dad."

"Megan, I have been wanting to talk to you for a long time. I think of you a lot."

"Um-um."

"I would like to come visit you. Would that be okay with you?"

"Yes."

"Well, I'm calling to talk to your mother about it."

"She's not home."

"Okay, I'll call back. How's school?"

"Okay. I got good grades this semester."

Their conversation went on for several minutes, with Gary excited and his daughter fluttery and near speechless. Gary says hanging up the phone that day was the hardest thing he had done in a long time. He finally rang off by telling Megan that he would call again soon and asking to have her mother call him when she got home.

Megan said, "Okay, 'bye."

Five minutes later Gary received a call from his ex-wife. He was sure he was going to get blasted. He hadn't planned to talk to Megan; it just happened that way.

Instead, Constance was cordial, even friendly, and volunteered that Megan was "blown away" by the call. Then she added that Megan was in a phase where she hated men.

"Ah."

"Don't let that stop you from visiting her, though."

Gary was stunned. "What are you saying? Is it okay for me to come and see her?"

"Yes," she said, "but why don't you talk with Megan on the phone a few more times first and send some pictures—let the relationship develop, so to speak."

Gary was amazed. The response had shifted from "No, you can't see her" to a discussion about when.

Gary was impatient, but I told him that starting slowly with phone calls and pictures sounded like an excellent idea. "Start slow, but start—and then maintain contact no matter what as regularly and as consistently as you can."

What had happened to make Constance change her mind? It may have been partly her fear that the lack of a father was damaging Megan. But my experience working with reconciling families suggests that she was also waiting for Gary to make a kind of overwhelming argument for his good intentions. Her behavior, in fact, is common for many women in her situation.

> *Walking is man's best medicine.*
>
> —HIPPOCRATES

Understandably protective of their children, women feel certain of one thing and one thing only—that the prodigal father had better be willing to go the distance. If they have learned anything as single mothers, it is the value of sincerity and a promise kept. Often, when a woman sees that her former mate is really committed to connecting with their child, she finds the heart to help him.

ASSIGNMENT

Take a gratitude walk. Choose a time and a place where you can be alone with your thoughts. You are seeking on this walk to open your thinking to any guidance that may come to you through quieting your emotions. What you are doing is a walking meditation. It often moves us to a place of insight far more effectively than any other meditation form.

If your reunion got off to a good start with a positive meeting with your ex, that's wonderful. Reflect on that with genuine thankfulness in your heart.

Even if it did not, the fact that you have begun at all is worth counting. No matter which scenario you are experiencing—good, bad, or something in the middle—walk in solitude to reflect on your situation.

As you walk, move your thoughts deliberately to the sunny side of the street. Try to keep an overview of the progress you've made and celebrate instead of hoping for perfection. Remember that compassion is required for yourself and for those with whom you are seeking to renew contact. You can often gain access to your compassion by consciously saying thank you for the smallest gains.

> I*f the only prayer you say in your whole life is "thank you," that would suffice.*
>
> —MEISTER ECKHART

MOVING ONWARD

How are you doing at your self-care maintenance? You have embarked on a new lifestyle that will yield a lifetime of benefits.

1. Are you using your Reunion Notebook? Remember to aim for a page a day. If you make daily entries, you will do better at keeping current with your often turbulent emotions.
2. Are you taking a weekly solitude break in your quiet space? Have you given yourself the dignity of respecting your own thoughts and perceptions?
3. Are you exercising? Remember that "exercise" and "exorcise" sound a lot alike. Sometimes we need to chase our demons out physically!

4. Are you watching your health? Men often catch a mysterious flu when their emotions aren't being processed. Try to avoid the flu by letting yourself feel the emotions you are carrying. Remember that we also speak of exercising our options. You are opting for a new life. You need plenty of water, rest, healthy food, and vitamins. In other words, keep up your deposits in the physical bank.

5. Are you remembering to pray? By now you might have experienced the rewards of prayer as a practice. You may have noticed that whether you officially believe in prayer or not, something beneficial does seem to happen when you pray. Call it meditation or reflection; the name doesn't matter. You're calmer, steadier, more decisive—more, period. And it should feel good.

5

THE REUNIONS

When Scott was eighteen, just after he graduated from high school in June 1988, Betsy and John gave him the manila envelope containing the letters I had written him over the years. Within a week or so he called me at my home in Chicago. I was exhilarated.

Our first phone conversation was short and a bit strained. We both brought years of expectation and fantasy with us to the call. I found it hard to talk, and we spoke mostly of the weather, his school, and a recent business trip I had made. I asked him if I could come and see him, and he said he would like that. We made plans to meet for a brief three-day visit the following month in Virginia.

A month! That wasn't enough time for me to become rich, famous, or any of the things I'd fantasized I'd be when I came back into Scott's life. He would be getting the man I'd actually become by that point—sober but not yet truly solvent, recovering but not yet fully recovered. It would have to be enough.

Scott and I decided to meet at a restaurant. I drove into

town in a rented car, so nervous and tense I was a road hazard. I knew the restaurant from my early years. It was located in an old Victorian building on the main drag that catered to older, well-to-do locals.

I entered, chose a table, and waited for Scott to walk in—but I hadn't seen him since he was a child, and he had told me that he was now six feet two inches tall. Focused on the door, I sat in the restaurant and waited for him for about thirty minutes before I realized he was already there. He was that tall, thin, handsome young man sitting at the table to my right with a woman who looked vaguely familiar. Unbeknownst to me, Scott had decided to bring his aunt. I went over to their table.

"I'm Mark," I said.

"Oh, my. You've been here the whole time," Scott's aunt said.

"And you too."

"Right."

We were all slightly embarrassed by the mistake. I gave my son an awkward hug, with more hellos all around. How could I not have recognized him? He was a taller, skinnier version of me in my old yearbook photos—that eighteen-year-old, not-quite-a-man-yet-not-still-a-boy look that I remember as feeling excruciating.

I wanted the tone of this visit to be light and as natural as the situation would allow, but I was willing to accept whatever came. We ate dinner and joked anxiously. I don't remember much about it except that nobody cried, for which I was grateful. A part of me expected Scott to use this opportunity to curse me out or show hostility toward me in some way, but he didn't. Like me, he was shy and perhaps a little too choked by emotion to make more than small talk.

Once satisfied that we were not combustible, Scott's aunt left us on our own. For a minute or two, all we could do was stare at each other. "So this is him," we both were thinking.

"I've looked forward to this for a long time," I said.

"So have I."

The distance hung between us. I remember trying to be present in the moment, but I wanted somehow to heal the years of separation immediately.

Scott and I stayed at the restaurant a long time. Then we went to his aunt and uncle's house where I was staying.

Over coffee at the kitchen table we talked and talked far into the night. I talked too much. I told him how sorry I was that I had left him and that I had missed him all those years. He said he had missed me, too.

At about two in the morning we parted. He drove to his new apartment, and I went upstairs to my room. I closed the door and quietly lay awake for a few more hours, overwhelmed with images from Scott's early life.

That second evening Scott and I met again for dinner and then took a drive around his neighborhood, the same one I had lived in when I was his age. Many of the people I had known still lived there. The place looked unchanged, though amidst memories of my paper routes, high school, and first job, the houses looked smaller. It seemed surreal, as though little time had passed between then and now. Afterward we went to a movie and visited some more at a coffeehouse until late. We made plans to meet in Chicago.

Our last day together was a Sunday. We met for a workout at a health club and then took a long walk on the beach. The Atlantic was cool and blustery. I listened as he talked about his life and his plans for the future. He listened as I talked about mine.

"You know, I always wanted to be a millionaire or at least someone important when I came back into your life," I confessed to him.

"Why?"

"So you'd want me back. So all would be forgiven. I fantasized about it a lot."

"You're kidding!" Scott laughed. He had his own confession. "I dreamed of playing pro baseball so you'd have to come to my games. I wanted to become so famous that you'd have to want me back too!" Both of us smiled thinly, our smiles nearly as similar as our matching fantasies of somehow becoming "enough."

We were more comfortable with each other now.

As the afternoon ended, I dropped him off at his apartment and we hugged and said good-bye. I drove back to Washington and caught the Amtrak to Chicago.

SCOTT'S STORY

"I'm not sure where I got it from, but when I was a small child, five to seven years old, I started to make up wild stories about my father. When people asked me about my real father, I would say he died—usually something cool, like a motorcycle accident or a car chase. 'He died coming to see me,' I'd say. I'm not sure if I ever really believed this or not, but something made me think it and say it.

"Sometimes I thought maybe I was crazy and didn't have a missing father after all. Since I wasn't getting any information or confirmation from my mother, I thought maybe it was my imagination. But at the same time, I knew, I could remember going to see him as a very small boy.

"I could also vividly remember going to the adoption judge and all the visits to family court in New York City while my stepfather was trying to adopt me. I wasn't really sure what exactly was going on. I was six or seven. It was sort of a game to me.

"I was told that having the same name as my mom and dad would make it easier for me in school. It did, until I was a little older and met kids who did have different last names. While I felt guilty that I had not kept my birth name, I also felt that somehow my heritage had betrayed me as well.

"I was scared to ask my mother anything about my father, because it would make her very angry. Then she would either put it on me or ignore me totally, sending me to my room. That was her way of dealing with things that were hard to talk about: 'Go to your room.' As I got older, I became more openly curious again, but my mother always dismissed my questions. This would infuriate me and make me even more curious."

"When I was twelve or thirteen, I came across some of my mom's yearbooks from high school. I was snooping in the hall closet, although I didn't know what I was looking for. I remember opening one, and on the inside cover I saw 'Mark and Betsy Bryan.' This surprised me. I never thought she was in high school when she was married and became a parent, although I was aware of our seventeen-year age difference. Then I flipped to the picture pages, and there he was. It was like looking in a mirror. I was going through the beginnings of puberty at the time, and my father didn't look much older. I couldn't then, and I still can't, imagine what being a father at that age would be like.

"I stared at the picture for hours on end. It piqued my curiosity more. I showed all my closest friends. They were equally shocked. None of them looked so much like their fathers. I put the book back in the closet right where I'd found it for fear of being discovered. I pulled that book out every day just to stare and dream about what life was like for them back then. I would read all the comments from friends about what a great couple they were and what a beautiful baby they had made.

"The autographs in the yearbook made me wonder what had happened. If everything had started out so good, what made it go bad? Me? Did I make things so hard on them that I drove the perfect couple apart? I didn't understand and couldn't get answers from my mother, and was too scared to ask my dad. I wanted to know so badly, but I didn't want to hurt anyone's feelings in the process.

"When I graduated from high school, just after my eighteenth birthday, my mother and my dad handed me a stack of letters that my biological father had written me over a number of years. There weren't many, a dozen or so letters with minimum content, but they showed me that he did care. I was hit with an array of feelings: I was very angry that the letters had been kept from me, I was crushed that my parents hadn't shared them with me, but I was elated that my father cared.

"I agreed to meet with my father for maybe some of the wrong reasons. I wanted to hurt my mom because I was still furious with her about withholding his letters, but I also wanted to satisfy my lifelong curiosity. The summer I turned eighteen, my father and I met for the first time, though he had been waiting and writing for five years.

"I didn't tell my mother prior to the first meeting with my father. I was afraid of appearing disloyal, and I remembered her reaction to my inquisitions. She found out anyway, though–my family loves gossip–and she conveniently went out of town. It was never really discussed after that.

"I shouldn't have been ashamed–he was my biological father–and I should have been strong enough to tell my mother with no guilt. Of course, life doesn't seem to want to hear about should'ves, and so my uncle set up that first meeting.

"I was eighteen and was working for Domino's Pizza and going to school part-time at a community college. The three of us were to meet at a restaurant for lunch. I asked my aunt, my mother's sister, to go along as well. Sort of someone in my corner, just in case. In case of what, I don't know, but I didn't know anything about Mark, the man, and frankly I was nervous. What if he didn't live up to my expectations, though I really had none, or, worse, what if I didn't live up to his?

"As the time to meet got closer, I desperately wanted to cancel, but my excitement finally prevailed. We went to the restaurant and sat at a table near the door, and every time it opened, I wanted to vomit.

"Finally, after we had been sitting for fifteen minutes, I got really nervous. Did my father stand me up? Abandon me again? These were my first thoughts. And then I noticed a man sitting alone across the room.

"There he was in the flesh. My father. He hugged me, and I remember it felt very weird. Men in my family rarely hugged. I couldn't eat, and I just stared at him, at my aunt and uncle, and out the window. After a long time talking, my uncle, my father, and I went to my uncle's house. I rode with my father and wasn't sure what to say.

"As we visited with my uncle and his wife, there were a lot of 'Gosh, you guys look alike' exclamations and reminiscing between my father and my uncle. I was interested, but I didn't really remember most of the people they were discussing. After dinner my uncle and aunt went to bed, which terrified me. What were my father and I going to talk about? My mind was racing like I was seven again.

"Here was my chance to get all the answers to my lifelong questions, but as my father began to spew them out, I was too embarrassed to hear them. Like I said, I felt seven years old and here was this man, my father, laying all this incredibly heavy adult stuff on me. Even though I was eighteen, I still was confused.

"We managed to talk almost all night long. The next day we went to see a movie. I forget which one, but I remember thinking, 'Thank God, no talking for two hours.'"

RECONNECTION

I had been warned about my expectations for the relationship with Scott. My mentors said he might not be able to get over his anger at my abandoning him. I was also told that he might not be able to sustain a relationship with me due to pressure from his mother and John. But our visit had been so friendly and loving that I lost all fear of losing Scott again.

A week later, when I received a letter from Scott, I was ecstatic.

> *Dear Dad, (Mark),*
>
> *I'm sorry I haven't been home when you've called, but I worked during the day and went to school at night. Well, thank you for everything last week, I had a great time! I'd been waiting for that for a long time and I know you had been also. Of course, I was nervous, excited, anxious, and scared all rolled into one and you probably know that feeling!*
>
> *You are a great guy and I'm glad to say that you were everything I had hoped for. (This letter might ramble on and skip but I'm not exactly thinking as an English teacher right now, sorry.) I know you are upset about the past and everything there but don't even think about it. Think of only the good, not the bad. And if it helps any, I hold nothing at all against you! I just blow off the bad and say well, hey, it happened. Maybe it was the best thing for all involved. I'm not sure that came out right but I think you get the picture. . . . Well, I'll be writing again soon. And I hope to see you again in the near future.*
>
> *Love, Scott*

I was deeply touched that he'd addressed me as "Dear Dad." The word seemed to define everything right and everything wrong about our meeting after more than ten years. It promised so much more than I had ever delivered. It held the promise, too, of everything I still hoped I could become.

Sometimes children must grow to adolescence or adulthood before they themselves can take the actions necessary to bring about the reunion they long for.

Ann is a thirty-five-year-old college professor. She grew up without her father and with a negative view of her paternal heritage. Ann tells her story this way.

"I have never known my biological father. He left in 1958 while my mother was pregnant with me. According to my mom, Dad was from a 'hillbilly family' from Oklahoma. Mom was from an upper-middle-class family in Indianapolis. They had been married four years, and Dad had been working for Mom's father as a salesman in Grandpa's business.

> *Children begin by loving their parents; as they grow older they judge them; sometimes they forgive them.*
>
> —OSCAR WILDE

"Mom wasn't critical of Dad. She just said he never fit into her clan because he was a dreamer and a wanderer and was overwhelmed by our huge family and their high expectations.

"When I was four, Mom married an attorney, Patrick, who adopted my brothers and me. My name was changed.

"Because I was adopted I never identified myself by my birth name until one day, when I was about nine years old, I found a children's book with my birth name in it. It was printed in my own childish scrawl: Ann Schneider. It was a revelation to me. Now I thought all I had to do to find my father was search through the phone book for all the Schneiders.

"But it wasn't until I was thirty and struggling with depression and alcohol that I began to search in earnest. I asked my mom for help, but she was noncommittal. I started going to the library and looking up phone numbers for Schneiders around the country. After two years I gave up. I turned my search for Schneider over to God. All I had to show for my own efforts was a stack of phone bills. I changed my name legally back to Ann Schneider.

"A year later Mom finally sent me the phone number of one of my father's sisters, who gave me his address in New York.

"I prayed for the right words, and the next day I wrote him. The letter was simple, and I tried to word it carefully so that he wouldn't feel cornered. I asked him point blank: Are you an alcoholic and do you have a history of depression? I was sure the answers to these questions held the answers about my own life.

"I mailed my letter with a picture and waited."

One week later Ann received a reply:

> Dear Ann:
>
> I've been praying a lot lately to the Higher Power, not for justice, not forgiveness, not for the knowledge of His Will . . . not even for mercy but rather for strength to act and give life my best shots.
>
> I sincerely hope that you can believe that my decisions made during the late fifties, although clouded by booze, were motivated by love. My state of mind at the time could have only directed me on a path of total destruction had I remained in Minneapolis. I feel that it would be pointless to delve further or elaborate.
>
> You have my address. Our telephone number is . . . My wife, Pamela, totally endorses our communication.
>
> You and the children are beautiful. Here is my picture.
>
> Love, Harry

Ann says, "Never, not even when my baby was born, have I cried such tears of joy. I looked at the photo of my father, and sure enough, I had his feet, wide ones. I had his high forehead. I had his big upper arms.

> The feeling remains that God is on the journey too.
>
> —Saint Teresa of Avila

"I felt, though I had never spoken to him, that I was finally, complete. Here was my father. I knew then, too, that I was Daddy's girl. That sounds a little stupid, since I'm thirty-five years old. But I held that letter in my hands and read and reread and reread the words 'Love, Harry' over and over again. I read them with every emphasis that I could: *Love*, Harry. Love, *Harry*. Love . . . *Harry*.

"Later that day I was walking–well, more like floating–along the street, and I grabbed a total stranger and told him: 'I have a father. And he loves me.' The stranger just smiled at me and said, 'That's nice.'"

"I talked to my father often after that. He had never stopped thinking of me and my brothers, he said. "'I missed you every day of my life. Every hour.'"

Your child may be waiting too, hoping to hear from you. Like Ann, your children may even be actively searching. No matter how difficult it is, wouldn't you rather be the first to make the move?

Gabriel left his wife and two-year-old daughter, Angie, under the worst possible circumstances: he ran off with another woman. He did not go back, but he often looked back. In the rearview mirror of his memory, he saw his beautiful little girl growing up without him.

Like many such affairs, Gabriel and his new love lasted only six months. He had moved from the East to the West Coast to be with her. When she dumped him for another man, richer and older than he was, Gabriel kept right on running–first to Europe, then to Asia. He stayed out of the country for nearly two years.

"I think I was actually out of my mind with guilt over what I had done," he says.

Gabriel finally returned to America, determined to face the wreckage of his past and reconnect with his daughter. Through intermediaries he contacted his wife.

"Will you allow him to see Angie?" his friends asked.

She answered, very defensively, "Under limited circumstances, for a short time."

His wife did not want to see him. What she wanted was a quiet divorce, child support, and good riddance.

"What would you consider an appropriate visit?" they pressed.

"Her uncle Simon can pick Angie up and take her to him. She can spend an afternoon with her father."

Gabriel agreed to his wife's terms. Uncle Simon brought the child to meet her father.

"I was in this hotel room. It was Halloween," Gabriel recalls. "I hadn't seen my daughter in nearly two years. I didn't know if she would know me. Her uncle brought her in. I said, 'Angie, it's Daddy.'

"She looked at me with her huge brown eyes, paused a moment, and then ran to me like I had only been gone overnight. I couldn't believe I was holding her in my arms again. We went out and bought pumpkins and candles and carved faces in them. Then we put the candles inside, let them turn out the lights, and just sat in the dark staring at them. We made a complete mess of that hotel room, but it was a fantastic time. Simon took pictures of us and the pumpkins. I still have them. It took me a long time to work things out with her mother, but my daughter is eleven now and has been in my life ever since."

It was quite a long time before Gabriel and the woman he ran out on were able to be friends, but they did it, slowly but surely, by putting the needs of their daughter first.

Estrangement, of course, is not always the man's fault.

Terry lost his child under very different circumstances. He did not run away; his wife did. While Terry was out of town on a business trip, his wife took their son and left.

"I came home, and my entire house was emptied of all their things. I had no idea where my wife had gone or why. Over the next few years I searched for them but couldn't find them. Her family offered no information, and her friends were closemouthed. It took four years, but I found her, living in another state with another man.

"I went to a lawyer, prepared desertion papers, and petitioned for visitation rights to our son, but even though she had left me, the judge leaned over the bench and said, 'Son, here in Virginia we believe a child should be with its mother.' It took me another year to win the right to visit, and she made it plenty expensive for me.

"I was in medical school when I found them, and my ex wanted me to give my son up for adoption. I refused, then she refused to send him for a visit until I could fly out and pick him up–a very expensive proposition. I would fly out, pick him up, fly him back with me for a visit, and then fly back to drop him off. It was worth every cent, though, because he and I got to know each other.

"By that first visit, he was already in the third grade, so I went to his school with him. I saw so much of myself in him. He told me he'd been sent to the principal's office for getting mad at the art teacher when she didn't like his work and ruined it. The exact same thing had happened to me in the third grade: I got in trouble with my art teacher when she destroyed a pot I'd labored over and I got angry. How about that?"

Terry grins at this memory, proud to claim the smallest detail that connects him with his son. Today they are a regular part of each other's lives, and eventually Terry's ex-wife softened her position about flying, so his visits increased.

Martin was the angriest man I ever worked with. He was forty-five years old and the father of four teenage boys when he left his wife in a rage after she confronted him about his drinking. It took three years of sobriety for his anger to subside. During that time Martin had cut off all contact with his wife and kids, claiming that he was going to stay away from his children as long as they were in communication with their mother. This kind of power struggle is always a losing battle.

Martin's anger caused him much trouble despite his new sobriety. It cost him his job and a place to stay, and he ended up sleeping in the back of his camper truck, working at odd jobs.

Martin's anger, like that of many divorced fathers, had

made him unable to return home as a "visiting" father, even when he was sober as a judge. He was just too mad.

Finding himself in this position, even though he was a college graduate and a talented teacher, finally drove Martin into counseling, and he attended several sessions of a fathers group.

> **W**hoever is out of patience is out of possession of his soul. Men must not turn into bees who kill themselves in stinging others.
>
> –JONATHAN SWIFT

It didn't take long for Martin to soften once I pointed out to him that he was punishing himself and his children with his absence.

We often have to swallow our pride to walk back into our child's life, and this is not easy to do. It can be very hard to be treated like a second-class citizen concerning your own kids. I understand Martin's reluctance to ask for help or let go of his anger. However, doing just a few months' work with a group opened the door for his return to fathering the children he had loved for well over a decade. His anger died hard—a measure of his grief.

Martin was invited to his eldest son's wedding.

"I'm not going," he raged.

Nervous? Defensive? Hurt? Yes, but I could not get through to him.

Then, in group, Martin heard someone explain how sad it had made him when his father did not come to either his wedding or his college graduation. This helped Martin see the situation from his son's point of view. It cooled his anger just enough.

"What would I wear?" he thought. "I have no money right now."

Nervous, yes. Defensive, yes. But willing to listen.

Then a voice in his head answered, "It doesn't matter what you wear. Just wear something clean."

That voice was Martin's turning point. He drove all night on borrowed gas money and arrived in time to purchase a clean shirt and tie at a roadside Wal-Mart store and shower and shave. He entered the church just as the wedding march began and took a seat in the front row.

Later, when I asked Martin how it had gone, he said, "I cried my eyes out. I was even able to tell my ex what a good job she had done with the boys. Then she asked me to dinner!"

Martin and I both grinned about that.

He didn't go to dinner, but he did go back a couple of months later for his niece's wedding. And then again for another son's basketball game. Eventually Martin moved closer to his hometown so he could watch his boys play ball.

I always recommend that a father make every attempt to be present for important life events such as graduations and weddings. The child will remember your presence or absence his whole life. So will you.

Martin's anger lifted more slowly than most, a measure of his unresolved hurt. Rage is dangerous even when it's justified—and it's always justified in someone's mind. Whether hers or yours, anger is an enemy of good sense.

> *All of my life I been like a doubled up fist . . . poundin', smashin', drivin'. Now I'm going to loosen these doubled up hands and touch things easy with them.*
>
> –TENNESSEE WILLIAMS

Matthew is a successful thirty-eight-year-old sales manager at a large department store. Five years ago his wife left him because of his drinking and took their two children, ages seven and four, with her. Matthew was furious. In the middle of their divorce a year later, he felt something tugging at his conscience and began to see that maybe his wife had been right. Maybe he did indeed need to quit drinking.

Two weeks later, Matthew found himself in a therapist's office talking about sobriety. A week after that he attended his first AA meeting. Within a month he had stopped drinking completely, and he has not had a drink or used any other drug since. However, though he continued to go to AA meetings, he had not seen his children since that day five years before when his wife took the kids and refused him visitation.

Matthew says that the courtroom battle was touch and go for a while as to whether he was ever going to be able to see his kids again. When he was two years sober, Matt's ex-wife remarried and moved to the East Coast, the other side of the continent. She remained hostile and uncommunicative despite his best efforts to make amends and to prove to her he was a changed man. Their long and bitter custody battle continued.

Matthew says that one of the hardest things about not being allowed to see his children those last years was not allowing himself to return, volley for volley, the depth and volume of his ex's animosity toward him. His self-control was tested when court papers led him to suspect that she was poisoning his children's attitude toward him. Still, he persisted in his efforts to wedge himself back into his children's life, his anger rising with each new provocation. He eagerly awaited his day in court, ready to retaliate.

> With the help of my god I shall leap over the wall.
>
> —BOOK OF COMMON PRAYER

Finally that long-awaited day in court arrived for Matthew and the mother of his children. The children, then twelve and nine, sat in court with their mother and her attorneys. Matt entered the courtroom, having been well rehearsed by his lawyer as to what to say when called upon to testify. They took their seats and began to get ready. Matthew excused himself and went to the bathroom.

Once inside the rest room, Matthew recalls, "I knelt on the marble floor in my expensive new suit and prayed to God to forgive me and make whatever was best for my children happen. I rose from my knees, happy that nobody had caught me praying, and took my seat in the courtroom."

Matt was called to testify but doesn't remember a thing he said: "A sense of unreality came over me, and all the things my attorney and I had planned I say just went out the window. My attorney asked me one question, and I started talking about my love for my children and my mistakes and about how I had loved my wife. My attorney never asked another question. I just talked for twenty minutes, and when I was finished, I looked up and the judge had tears in his eyes.

"I had gone into that courtroom carrying a sword, but to my complete surprise, all my feelings of anger and hatred for my ex-wife were lifted. I just wanted to be fair to her and to do what was best for my kids. I told the judge I wanted to know them and have them know me as I am now, a sober and God-loving man."

What happened next was even more extraordinary. The opposing attorney offered to help Matthew's attorney come to an equitable agreement. They all met in the judge's chambers. The judge ordered Matt's ex-wife to attend and help pay for post-divorce counseling for Matthew and herself, and for the children, in order to reverse the pain caused by those years of separation. Matthew's visitation rights started immediately.

MOVING ONWARD

Now is the time to watch a couple of your favorite movies. I love *Orphans* with Albert Finney, *Field of Dreams, An Officer and a Gentlemen, Terms of Endearment, Rocky,* and even *It's a Wonderful Life.* Also watch a few funny movies. The Marx Brothers, *Beetlejuice* or Cary Grant does it for me; my friend Gene likes *Cold Comfort Farm.* Watch them over the next several days. See if you can get in touch with some sadness and some laughter.

Write in your Reunion Notebook any feelings you experienced while reading the reunion stories. Did you have any unusual dreams? Write them down.

Take a walk for reflection. If you do it daily, it will change your life. Spend just twenty minutes or so walking by yourself, to think, to ponder, to celebrate quietly. You are ready to meet your child—now. How does that feel?

6

FIRST CONTACT WITH YOUR CHILD

As many hardworking single parents know, no amount of work can compensate a child for a missing parent. Sometimes, the older a child gets, the more mature and assertive the fantasy of the other parent becomes.

Remember this: you have been missed. You may be walking into a whole gamut of emotions. They may avoid you at first. They may welcome you with open arms. They may be wary and watchful.

Melinda, a divorced physical therapist, has a fifteen-year-old son, Stephen, whose father has not been in his life since Stephen was three. She says Stephen always wanted his father desperately.

"At around six years old, when Stephen started spending time with a lot of other kids, he became more aware of the fact that he didn't have a father.

"He would ask me about his dad. He would talk about wanting a brother or sister, and I would say, 'Well, you know, there has to be a man around, there has to be a father,' and he'd say, 'How come I don't have a father? . . . How do you get babies? . . . Why don't we ask Dan [his father] to come back?'"

Kathy is the young mother of a four-year-old daughter, Peggy, who has not seen her father for several years. Recently, Kathy and Peggy were in an auto accident—a drunk swerved in front of them on a street in their small town. Though no one was badly injured in the collision, Peggy was very frightened. As they were waiting for a ride, Peggy started screaming, "Daddy! Daddy!" Kathy's distress over the accident was doubled by her distress over Peggy's pain.

If you listen enough to the pain of estranged children and their mothers, you will learn that many mothers, at their deepest level, want a father in their children's lives. Many mothers know their children *need* a father, but they are baffled about how to help.

YOUR REUNION WITH YOUR CHILD

You've made your amends.

You've met with your ex-wife.

Now it is time to plan your actual reunion.

"Okay, but what if my kids don't like me?"

I have found it helpful, in counseling other prodigal fathers, to remind them to relax. They are often nervous about the reception they are likely to receive from their children. But even an angry child will usually agree to meet you because of natural curiosity about her father. This curiosity will probably overcome any hesitancy about the first meeting, so that you will at least have this opportunity to communicate with her. If you have done the work of the previous chapters, you will present yourself well enough that your child will want to know you better.

How do you make this contact?

Where should you meet your child?

What do you do?

The best guideline you can follow is to think in terms of comfort: what sort of meeting would feel safest, friendliest, least threatening? Often it is a good idea to meet over a meal. At the very least, the food will give you something to do.

It is not a good idea to plan something intimidating or impressive. Do not, for example, take your child to a restaurant you can't really afford. Do not plan an elaborate outing to an amusement park where the tickets alone are a week's child support. Instead, keep the meeting simple and keep it heartfelt.

> *The secret of life is not to get rid of the butterflies in your stomach but to get them to fly in formation.*
>
> —ANONYMOUS

I urge you again to discuss your plan with your support team and to rehearse, either by yourself or with your team, what you intend to do and say. You may want to call your child's mother and work out the details with her help.

Here are some things to consider:

1. What do you want to say during your first meeting? I myself made the mistake of trying to say too much at once. On an emotional level, your child has enough to absorb simply seeing you. Remember, it is your job to understand your child's feelings, not vice versa.

   I suggest you do more listening than talking, though many children may be struck mute by emotion. Just keep the conversation simple. Ask your child about her life and about what she likes. If it seems appropriate, tell her how it felt to be without her and how it feels to be with her now. You do not need to make this dramatic. Your

> *Why, then the world's mine oyster, which I with sword will open.*
>
> —WILLIAM SHAKESPEARE

message can be very straightforward: "I missed you, and I thought about you often. It feels good to be here now."

2. What should you say about your absence? Avoid trying to justify your absence, and avoid blaming the child's mother or other family members, even if they were unfair to you. This will just cause more problems. Within a few visits there may come a time when you might say, "I'm sorry for being gone. One day perhaps I can explain to you what happened." You will know when that time is right. No need to rush.

3. How do you reassure your child that you will not leave again? Simple: *don't* leave again. Reassure him by setting up a second visit and then taking it one visit at a time.

    At the end of every visit, set the date for your next visit. This will help alleviate your child's fear of future disconnection. But beware of your natural tendency to be overexcited and promise more than you can deliver.

4. Be prepared for a potential backlash from your ex-wife's family—and for an emotional backlash of your own. Once contact is made, resistance from the family may actually increase. Men to whom this happens—and I was one of them—have a difficult row to hoe as they practice a combination of determination and acceptance in the face of fear from the mother or her family. This fear is natural and to be expected. Just treat it like the wind: let it blow.

Bill, a Native American from Arizona who has long black hair and tattoos, looks like anything but the devout Christian and Native American spiritual leader that he is. He looks as if he just got off the Harley-Davidson motorcycle that he sold years ago. (Too risky, he says.)

Bill has been a counselor and writer for more than twenty years. Four years ago he was married and, for whatever million reasons a marriage doesn't last, his didn't either. It broke Bill's heart when his ex and his daughter moved to California.

His wife and her family made it hard for Bill to visit his child. They were hostile and kept changing their schedule, leaving town when he was due to visit.

Bill prayed, asked for guidance, and remained patient, waiting until he could catch them in town.

They glared when he came to pick up his kid. He smiled and struggled to stay spiritually centered.

Then they hired an attorney.

He prayed and asked for guidance and was told to get an attorney too. He did. All without blowing up or making a scene.

Bill has been in his daughter's life since she was born. Even though she lives in California and he lives in Arizona, he makes the trip regularly and has managed to present himself to his child as a positive and consistent role model. She adores him and he has taught her the traditions of his native spirituality, the four directions, the language of his tribe. Though still wary, his ex-wife no longer begrudges him his visits. Bill made it through the fire of her wrath.

Human beings attempt to avoid pain. That's one of the most basic traits of human nature. We do not welcome situations that make us feel worthless or unworthy, that open us to deep personal attachments and then rip us apart. It's also human nature that much of what we do to avoid pain isn't conscious and isn't logical. It's often self-defeating, destructive to us and to those we care about, which only makes the pain worse. This is also true for the child's other caregivers.

What greater pain can there be than being separated from your child? Add to that pain the humiliation and awkwardness of having this most important relationship in your life reduced to formal visits dictated by the court and, in effect, enforced by an ex-spouse. The trauma of divorce is a deep wound that gets reopened every time you have to say good-bye to your son or daughter. Every time you watch your former spouse walk out the door and see the heartbreak on your child's face.

Bill had therapeutic and spiritual tools with which to understand and work through his emotions. Still, he says, it takes him a week to recover from his visits with his child. He says, "Leaving is hard. But not hard enough to keep me away."

THE UNCONSCIOUS UNDERTOW

As you prepare to meet your child, remember that you are on a sensitive political mission. Many uncomfortable feelings will lie just below the surface. Opinions about fathers and children are all around us, in the media and in the expectations of men and women.

In his statement about propaganda, a Russian poet notes that in war the enemies are always caricatured as less than human so that they can be annihilated with a clearer conscience. He calls this process "warnography." In our culture, the war between the sexes is so caricatured that it allows men and women to discount the reality of the other.

> *Within every man there is the reflection of a woman, within every woman the reflection of a man. Within every man and woman there is also the reflection of an old man and an old woman, a little boy and a little girl.*
>
> —CHEYENNE TEACHING, HYEMEYOHSTS STORM

In married households, we play *Father Knows Best*. In divorced households, we play *Mother Knows Best*. What we do not play is fair: we do not support shared responsibilities. We do not acknowledge that the real meaning of child support goes far beyond financial aid.

Women are often not aware of the underlying emotions that they feel for the father of their children. Perhaps it is a shield for the heartbreak of divorce, or maybe it's unresolved anger at past mistakes of the father. Whatever the reason, many women do not realize how they may undermine their child's father in voice and in deed.

On their part, men are often hypersensitive about being undermined and may look for insults where none are intended. In short, both sexes may overreact in dealing with each other, and both sexes occasionally act out of their lower rather than higher nature. This is only human. I call this tendency the Unconscious Undertow.

Jim is a construction worker married to a waitress named Tammy. When they decided to divorce, they both went to couples therapy, sought individual counseling, and were able to negotiate their divorce amicably. They were tender and touching in their grief for their former union and recovered faster than most.

Yet Jim recently called Tammy to tell her he was coming for their daughter's birthday. Tammy paused a moment and said, "I don't think so. She's very tired this weekend because we've been traveling. Why don't you see her next week?"

Jim held his temper. He felt she was being high-handed, treating him like a stranger. To his credit, Jim was able to do what most men don't in that moment of frustration: he was able to contain his flare-up of anger and state his case gently. He said to Tammy: "I bought her a present months ago and have been waiting to give it to her. If you have plans for dinner, I will come for lunch."

Tammy said casually, "Oh, okay, let me ask her." She came back to the phone and said, "She says she's anxious to see you. Come on, take her to lunch."

Jim is certain that Tammy is not aware of how he experienced the transaction between them. He knows if it had been reversed she would have felt the same way. He also admits that he, too, carries an unconscious undertow of unprocessed feelings that rear up every so often.

"Between the two of us, this stuff seems to show up as

control. One or the other of us will suddenly get very rigid about a pickup time, bedtime, diet, TV, almost anything. It's a little warning flag that we still have pain there underneath."

THE CHILD'S UNSPOKEN FEARS

Regardless of how well you have settled your working relationship with the child's mother—and with the stepfather, if there is one—you will now need to deal with the child's feelings of loss over the original separation and her unspoken fear that it will happen again. These feelings and fears will surface once you are actually in the process of reunion.

Thomas, a reunited father, told me, "Sometimes my daughter, Alice, seems to be deliberately obnoxious when we first see each other. It's like she's pushing me. Once I lay down the law a little, then she's fine, but she does like to test me."

Just as you want to put your best foot forward in reunion, so does your child. You both try to be extra nice, extra understanding, or, in the case of the child, extra good. Then, in phase two, your child, like Alice, may turn just a little bit "extra bad."

Sometimes this is best thought of as a sort of melting, a dissolving of reserve and defenses that will begin only when you get to know each other. That's when reality sets in. You unthinkingly swear in front of your kid. Your kid does something really annoying, acting extra bad instead of extra good. You both look at each other like "I'm going to be dealing with you?"

Yes.

> We love persons . . . by reason of their defects as well as of their qualities.
>
> —JACQUES MARITAIN

Jungians would call this letting your shadow side show. You might want to call it getting real. It's a dance of "Will you love me even if you know I am imperfect?"

Alex remembers, "My son asked me to play softball with

him and his friends. Suddenly I got really nervous. What if I couldn't catch anymore? What if I couldn't hit? Would he be embarrassed? I did all right, though, and that meant a lot to me. I'm sure he had his own concerns about what I thought of him, so I made sure to tell him that he was a good player and that I was proud of him."

This will-you-love-me-if dance, on one level or another, will continue throughout your relationship. No matter how much time goes by, the child will still fear the loss of the connection and will occasionally test it.

A word of warning: your child's extra-bad behavior can underscore your own fear that you aren't so wonderful and maybe don't have enough to offer, but don't let your child's fear that you will leave again become a self-fulfilling prophecy. This can happen if you are not aware of the possibility. Therefore, repeat to yourself these words (even post a sign on your shaving mirror): "I do not have to do this reunion perfectly, but do it I will."

KEEP IT SIMPLE AND GIVE IT TIME

At the first contact or soon after it, you may find yourself wanting to justify your disappearance or pose as a more financially successful man than you are. This is usually an attempt to overcome your shame at having left, and it's a natural human tendency. But remember, the simple truth is a much better foundation for a relationship. Tell the truth about yourself all the time. But do it in small doses.

Beware of talking tough about any grand adventures you may have had or how much trouble you got into. Don't act wealthier than you really are or try to blame anyone or anything for your disappearance. Practice restraint of tongue and wallet—no showboating and no breast-beating. Just show up. This is not easy.

Many children, perhaps unconsciously fearing they will be

asked to choose between their parents, make deliberately inflammatory statements. Do not take the bait.

"Mom says you weren't even the nicest boyfriend she ever had."

"Mom told me you never were good at sticking to things."

"Mom told me you probably just wanted to start dating other women."

"Mom told me you didn't love me."

"Mom told me . . ."

No matter what "Mom told" them, remain respectful and reticent in what you say about your children's mother. She may not have said any of it. Do not blame her, as this will raise loyalty issues for the children. Children need to know only that they are missed, that you are sorry for your absence, and that you will be in their lives as a positive force.

Children want to know that you care for them and are willing to be there for them from now on. The focus of your conversations, once the basics are covered, should be the present, not the past. Always remember your children's emotional maturity when talking with them. Always consider the effects of any disclosures on them. Why do they need to know this? How will it help them? How do you best tell them where you stand given their age?

THE MYTHS

A good thing to remember: your child may have a lot of misinformation about you. Children often invent elaborate fantasies, positive or negative, about their father. Often, they have blamed themselves for your disappearance. Sometimes they have been indoctrinated with negative opinions by their mother and her family. Some ex-wives paint the father as an ogre she unwisely married. Some men, to their surprise, find that they have been whitewashed by an ex-wife who has bent over backward to keep their image shining. In still other cases, the child's relationship with a stepfather may be a complicating factor if the child experiences a divided loyalty.

Do not compete.

Do not denigrate.

Do not disappear.

Your child needs both your presence and your presence of mind.

PROCESS YOUR FEELINGS ELSEWHERE

During the period after you have met your child, it is critical for you to continue with your support team. You will need a place to explore and sometimes to neutralize some very potent emotions.

Many women work to keep a link between their children and the absent father. Often, by card or call, they keep the father apprised of the milestones in the child's life. Along with the report cards, drawings, or photos goes the unspoken message: Please stay in contact. Your child needs you.

> It is not because things are difficult that we do not dare, it is because we do not dare that they are difficult.
>
> —SENECA

Now you are heeding that message, but it's not easy.

Hearing the mythology of your life from your child may amuse you, anger you, sadden you, or fill you with gratitude, depending on how you receive the information. You may need help to receive it properly. After the reunion celebration, many men fall back into isolation and an "I can do this now by myself" attitude. This can be catastrophic. Your support team can be even more important now than it was before.

Remember the reuniting father whose kid tested him? Well, she tested him so hard one summer that he flunked: he withdrew from his child for six long months because he was hurt by her mouthy behavior. He thought it meant he was unwelcome in his daughter's life. It was only when he compared notes—finally—with another father of an adolescent that he realized all teenagers could be difficult and that she didn't really hate him. Realizing that, he resumed his visits.

Continued regular contact with your support team will provide the important feedback with which to process the many feelings that learning your children's mythology about you can cause. Expect to feel a few reverberations as you learn the facts.

Remember Scott telling his friends that I had died in a motorcycle accident while going to visit him? Hearing that my young son had felt he had to make up such a lie to explain my disappearance made me sad and reminded me of the cost of my absence.

Adam, a construction worker, learned that he had been routinely characterized to his son as "your father the hippie who never held a real job."

> Behind an able man there is always other able men.
>
> —CHINESE PROVERB

Hearing this, Adam wanted to get right in the car and show his ex-wife his résumé. Instead he was told, "Tell your son about the jobs you've held, but do it casually over a few visits. That way he will get the idea that you have in fact always been a worker without it having to be some big drama."

Try to keep drama out of your dealings with your children. Don't get into a power struggle with your ex or her family about what's true. You will overcome the mythology by staying around and letting your children get to know for themselves who you really are.

It may hurt, but it should no longer really matter that your child's mother holds a grudge or that her new husband doesn't like you. Their feelings are their feelings. You may not be able to change them for a long time, if at all. You can take comfort, though, in the fact that you have cleaned up your side of the street. You must allow others to have whatever feelings they choose to have and not let their attitude prevent you from knowing your child. This is not a popularity contest.

EASY DOES IT—BUT DO IT

Avoid the temptation to rush things. Allow your relationship to mature on its own. However, set a regular schedule of visits and let your good sense and the children's evident comfort dictate how fast to allow intimacy to develop. Expect a few emotional hurdles, and when they come up, try to go around them instead of high-jumping them.

> *Slow motion gets you there faster.*
> —HOAGY CARMICHAEL

It is not uncommon for the returning father to want to take up where he left off with his children—in other words, to expect to share full decision-making and all the details of his children's lives. Rationally, you know there will be an adjustment period, and your head may accept that, but your heart might have a harder time with it.

"I don't really want to talk about it, Dad" can feel like a door slammed in your face. So can a kid who jumps out of your car without a good-bye hug or kiss and runs into the arms of his mother at the door. Be warm, but don't push your children to display affection.

Your children will grow to love you again in their own time and in their own way. It may take a while for them to know you well enough to like you. Do not expect to be treated like a returning hero. Let them tell you about themselves. Show interest in what they do, whether it be their favorite TV shows, pets, music, hobbies, friends, whatever. LISTEN to them. You will come to cherish this role. Let them tell you what they will, and let them decide how much to tell you and when to tell it to you.

Vicki, a young girl who was reunited with her birth father after a decade apart, told me that while she was thrilled to know *him*, she wasn't quite ready to let him know *her*. "I don't want him to think I'm dumb or anything, so there are some things I don't tell him—like about that math test I messed up."

> B*e not afraid of growing slowly, be afraid only of standing still.*
>
> —CHINESE PROVERB

When Scott and I first met, I tried in my excitement and nervousness to tell him everything about me and ask him everything about myself. I would do it differently now. I would let the discussions come about more naturally as he and I relaxed and did things together.

LIGHTEN UP

It's a hard line to walk between showing too much interest and appearing aloof as you wait for your children to make revelations of their own accord. You may be disappointed that your renewed relationship doesn't feel deep enough. Again, give it time.

Try to lighten up and keep a sense of humor. Remember, you are coming back into your children's lives for their benefit and yours. Make it fun. If you can stay good-natured enough to remain grateful, and wise enough to look for the humorous side of things, the reunion process will be easier for everyone. One way to do this is to take your child to activities that the child will enjoy. Then, while involved with something fun, allow your conversation to meander naturally. Avoid confessions, interrogations, and melancholy discussions of the past.

Donald was a newly reuniting father who was doing so well that he invited his ex-wife and daughter to stay at his house for a three-day weekend. Everything went wonderfully, with much warm feelings and laughter–until Sunday. That day brought flared tempers and strain as a result of too much togetherness too soon. Spending the night under the same roof with your ex is almost never a good idea, and it's particularly dangerous in the beginning. Be aware of it–and lighten up.

Regardless of how diligently you have prepared for reunion, you should expect to make some mistakes. There will be moments of joy, of tears, of anger, of clumsiness, and of everything in between.

You are not required to make everything right overnight.

BE CAREFUL WHAT YOU PROMISE

Once you reconnect with your child, it is important to remain consistent and do what you say you will do. Remember that you are trying to rebuild trust and that trust comes from the experience of safety and consistency. Remember also that the urge to be grandiose is just a cover for your guilt and pain. Children only want to know you love them.

When Tony and his daughter, Bethel, were reunited, Tony promised all sorts of things in his excitement at meeting her again. Even though he was remarried and had extensive financial commitments, Tony said he would pay Bethel's college tuition. He also said he would take her river-rafting on an elaborate shared vacation. He said he would visit regularly, even though they lived on opposite sides of the country.

> The measure of a man's life is the well spending of it, not the length.
>
> –PLUTARCH

He meant everything he said, but . . .

Then Tony's new marriage fell apart, and his financial situation became even more precarious. Unable to keep his promises, Tony let his focus shift from his reunion time with Bethel to his problems finding a new job. Stressed out and financially strapped, he spiraled into shame and isolation, all but cutting off the newly opened line of communication with his child. He didn't call her, and he didn't keep his promises. In his mind those promises were not broken, merely delayed, but his daughter had no way of knowing this.

"Dad's gone again," Bethel told herself sadly.

Bethel did not know that Tony was working hard to come through for her, thinking it would just be a little longer until he could. All he really needed to do to alleviate Bethel's feeling of rejection was to tell her the truth, but his false pride kept him from doing so.

"I almost lost her a second time," Tony says.

Fortunately for Tony—and for many of us—kids can be remarkably forgiving if they sense that we are basically sincere and committed to reconnecting.

Donald was separated from his father when he was just a toddler. His parents went through a very nasty divorce, and his mother's family closed ranks to practically drive his father out of town on a rail. Donald grew to his thirties without ever reuniting with his dad. When his mother died, Donald continued to live in his childhood home. In fact, he never left his hometown. He set up an auto repair store and worked a few blocks from home.

One day an older man came into Donald's shop. He was new in town and asked Donald a few questions about car repair and the town in general. They established an easy give-and-take, and the man dropped by to chat every week or so. Donald grew to enjoy their visits and to take an interest in how the old man was doing.

Several months later, Donald says, he "suddenly knew." Yes, the old man was his long-lost father, returned home to make reunion, but obviously too shy or ashamed to tell his lost son who he really was.

"Maybe it's better this way," Donald says. "I was so mad at my father for abandoning me that I might not have given him a chance, otherwise. As it is, we're friends. But I sort of hope the old man will come out with the truth one of these days."

While some children may reject efforts at reunion, at least initially, the overwhelming majority, when approached in good faith, are eager to know their prodigal fathers.

REUNION REPLAY

Cue up a piece of music that makes you feel safe and centered. Allot about forty minutes—long enough to play an entire CD or album. Some people like to play the same song over. Whatever works.

Write the story of your reunion in your Reunion Notebook. How did it go? How was it different than you expected it would be? What did you do that you are proud of? What did your child do that you are proud of? What do you wish had gone differently? How will you make your next visit better? How do you feel?

Write as much detail as you can about the time you spent together. The journal and the music are a valuable tool for the future and a good way to stay in touch with your emotions now.

> *Just be what you are and speak from your guts and heart—it's all a man has.*
>
> —HUBERT HUMPHREY

Write your children a note and tell them you love them. Mention specifically what you recall from the reunion that gave you special joy. Be sure to ask a few follow-up questions about the topics you covered in conversation. This note does not need to be great art. Remember that communication is the heart and soul of a successful reunion.

Mail your note.

MOVING ONWARD

1. Are you making regular journal entries? You may find that writing is actually harder after the reunion, when

there are many emotions to be processed and the writing could do the most good.

2. Are you taking care of yourself? Just as your journal-keeping may have a temporary lapse in the wake of reunion emotions, so may your self-care. Are you eating well? Are you sleeping? Are you using any "behavioral drugs" like junk TV or junk food to block your feelings?

3. Now is the time to exercise—and to exorcise whatever self-worth demons your reunion may have stirred up. Take a daily twenty-minute walk, get on your old bike and ride for a half an hour, or take yourself to the gym or the tennis court. Remember that we "embody" our feelings and that you probably will not be able to move your feelings through you until you move, period.

4. Schedule a spiritual rest. It doesn't matter how you define it or what you choose to call it, but at this point you need to step up your spiritual practice. Reunion work is soul work, and your soul needs food and fuel to make the journey successfully. Give yourself some spiritual sustenance, both as a reward for work well done and as a source of supply for the work that must now continue. Remember that reunion revolves around self-worth. Choose to nurture yours on a spiritual level. Here are a few of the ways some men have done so:

   - Ted joined a book club.
   - Doug went to a lecture series at his church.
   - Tony committed to a month's bike riding.
   - Daryl set up a workshop in his garage.

   As diverse as these approaches are, they give you the idea. Reunion can actually inspire you with renewed energy for other activities. Remember that this is a celebration.

5. Read the next chapter on the different development stages of children and requirements of each. It may help explain the behavior you encounter as you build your renewed relationship. It may also remind you of your value.

7

DIFFERENT AGES,
DIFFERENT NEEDS

One of the odd things that reuniting fathers often say to me is "It's nice to know how tall they are again."

This can be true psychologically as well as physically. Children need different things at different ages, and all kids are different. Young children need more time to play; older children need more time to talk. Younger children may seem to need you more and older children or teens may seem not to notice you at all. Do not be fooled.

"I don't want to intrude on her time with her friends," Richard remarked to me about his erratic visits with his thirteen-year-old daughter, Donna.

"Don't be fooled if she seems casual. She actually wants you to insist on seeing her."

"You were right!" Richard told me a week later. "When I insisted on visiting, she said, 'Aw, Dad!' but she sounded *pleased.*"

No matter how cavalier your children may occasionally

seem about reunion, remember that for them, as for you, an ongoing relationship is dead center, top of the list of the things that matter.

Learning to be a good parent again may require that you ask for guidance or read some books. You may want to take a class on parenting through your local high school or health department.

- How late should they be staying up?
- What if they won't eat?
- How much TV is okay?
- What's a normal homework load?
- Can you leave them alone in the house at night at age twelve?
- Do most kids have huge phone bills?
- What if your kid's got a sugar and soda habit?
- Is mall crawling really something that all kids do?

Though the potential problems and their solutions are too numerous to mention here, talking with experienced fathers and mothers will guide you. There are resourceful parent groups in most communities. In them you will pick up specific hints that can feel almost tailored to your needs. Here, however, are a few general guidelines:

- The younger the children, the less they need to know why you went away.
- The older the children, the more false information about you they may have invented or heard from others.
- No matter what their age, it is a psychological fact of life that your children may blame themselves for your absence. You will need to address this gently but directly.
- Communication is the heart of any reunion. Keep your visits regular. Keep them simple.
- Remember that scheduling an activity during a visit is

often a good idea. However, avoid making every visit a special occasion.

It is important that you not be defensive when your child asks direct questions. Remember that although you do not have to defend against the truth, you must consider your children's age and emotional maturity when asked about your absence.

DEVELOPMENTAL DATA THAT MAY SERVE YOU

Though all children go through predictable developmental stages, each child is unique in specific ways. Each stage presents challenges that move the child on toward maturity. And the stages are colored by each child's inborn characteristics and life experiences.

A discussion of child development is beyond the scope of this book. However, I would like briefly to illustrate how children of different ages may react to your return and how you might best plan your return for their benefit. It will help if you think of your child as an ever-evolving person whose challenges change as they grow older. I am using Erik Erikson's theory of psychosocial development as a point of departure.

Each major issue presented below continues as a variable throughout a child's entire life.

INFANCY

If your child is an infant, less than a year old, the mother will need all the support she can muster, for she will be expending an immense amount of physical and emotional energy.

In this critical early stage a baby learns either to trust or to mistrust the world in general. Anything you can do to lend the mother support will directly benefit your child. Any direct contact with your child will have long-lasting benefit to that child's well-being.

Fathering is important in and of itself. A father provides the child with something different from generic caring. A child develops a different set of responses to recognize the father from the ones it uses to recognize the mother, and a father's play style is different. Male presence, including fathers, uncles, brothers, friends—in other words, a culture of fathering—is a vital nutrient children need. There is no more important time to be involved than when a child is young. Remember that when divorce happens with young children, the child's world is effectively split in half.

Although babies may seem to be only dimly aware of their fathers, they will recognize the father's voice within a few days of birth. By regular gentle and loving contact, a father can help his child to know that the world is a safe place from the beginning.

T. Berry Brazelton, a beloved pediatrician, says that a child may actually develop different neural pathways in the brain that come into play when responding to the mother and the father. Although you will be helping immensely by just showing up, you can be most helpful in this first stage of life by providing a feeling of safety for the mother and child. The father's contribution here is to add to the secure base from which the child will learn to explore. The job of the father—returning or otherwise—is to support the child and mother emotionally, physically, and financially. This means making regular visits.

> We are not primarily put on this earth to see through one another but to see one another through.
>
> —PETER DE VRIES

Since the child's pattern of attachment to the mother and father will be based on experiences with each of them, and the individual ways in which each parent behaves, it is important for fathers to establish and continue attachment from the very first, if possible.

Arthur and Gail had known each other about six weeks when one night they let passion rule and left common sense about contraception in the closet. Gail got pregnant. After much discussion, they decided to have the baby. Because Gail was comfortable in her apartment, Arthur gave his up and moved in.

The combination of pregnancy and two people who probably wouldn't normally have continued dating was too much. Arthur soon moved out.

At first Gail's anger made it impossible for Arthur to help out. He called regularly, offering to run errands, go to birthing classes–whatever. Gail refused. She had one of her girlfriends take the birthing classes with her.

Eventually Gail got past her anger and realized that a third human being was about to put in an appearance. She called Arthur. He was present at the birth of their son, and when Gail came home they got a breast pump so Arthur could take the boy overnight and feed him from a bottle. These visits gave Gail some much-needed rest and Arthur a chance to bond with his son.

Your case may be far less extreme than Arthur's, yet needed interaction with your child remains the same.

TODDLER

The next developmental phase, the toddler years, from age one to age three, is a time when children discover their own will and begin to develop autonomy. This phase includes the "terrible twos," when children test the patience of everyone around them. During this period it is especially important for you to remember that your child's temper tantrums and occasional orneriness is not about you. His moodiness is not a sign of your being rejected but part of his attempt to become a separate human being.

At this point your child will test his limits and will need to be allowed to cling to you and then push you away without your getting angry. He is also likely to be extremely energetic and unruly at times. This stage is about asserting himself and gaining control of his world. Give him room, but keep him safe, and don't take it personally.

Do not let this difficult and moody stage of development frustrate you to the point of leaving, and if you are returning at this stage, give yourself time to learn the rhythm of the "come here, go away" behavior that is typical of a toddler's growth.

As a father, you can help the mother and child during this period by providing an intimate and familiar space for visits with your child. This will not only allow the child some time with you, it will give the mother some rest. A place of your own to be with your child can help the child become independent as you draw him out of the mother's magnetic pull.

Sometimes mothers have difficulty letting a child become independent; they feel abandoned by the baby who has been completely dependent on them. This is where the father can be an enormous help by giving the mother the time and space to care for her own needs. If a mother knows she will regularly have a free afternoon or evening, she can then take that pottery class or go to that movie with a friend.

> He who wishes to secure the good of others has already secured his own.
>
> —CONFUCIUS

Psychologists know that if a woman's need for emotional nourishment is unfulfilled, she may inadvertently stifle her offspring's struggle for independence with her "we're in this together, just the two of us" mind-set.

This enmeshment is not good for children. It can breed fearfulness, the inability to separate, and ultimately an impeded sense of self and identity. Fathers help lessen this struggle by gently drawing young children away from an overdependence on their mothers and into interaction with the world at large. This helps the child establish a sense of individuation and mastery that they will rely on throughout their lives.

If you go to pick up your toddler and your reception is less than warm, it may have nothing to do with you but be related to the child's need for independence. Or the child may be moody, almost as if you've been punished for going away. This happens after short separations as well as long ones. Your job–which is spelled like the name Job and may take nearly as much patience–is to be understanding about these dynamics.

EARLY CHILDHOOD

Age three to six is a time for developing a sense of purpose, the need to initiate, and the awareness of guilt. During this period I often observe children of absent fathers begin to blatantly ask other men, usually friends of their mothers, to be their father.

"Mom, I've found a daddy," Jessica remembers her daughter announcing as she dragged a blushing man by the hand to meet her at a neighborhood spaghetti dinner.

> Love received and love given comprise the best form of therapy.
>
> –GORDON ALLPORT

If you are reuniting with a child of this age your presence will help ensure that the child does not carry blame for your absence, or the shame of being somehow responsible for your being gone. The presence of a loving father NOW will increase the child's confidence and improve friendships later in school.

When Carl started visits with his five-year-old son, Ian, whom he hadn't seen since the boy was three, he wanted to give his ex-wife an award. Ian was the best child he had ever seen. He was quiet, obedient, helpful, a joy to be around. But then Carl was remarried and had two stepchildren, ages seven and four. Those kids wanted to kill Ian because he was making them look bad.

When Carl told his ex how wonderful Ian was, she thought he was talking about someone else's child. Ian was never such a Goody Two-shoes at home. What was going on here?

Carl and his mentors figured out that the boy was feeling responsible for Carl's absence and was afraid that if his behavior was anything short of perfect Carl would leave again.

Carl began to have brief talks with his son. He explained that Ian had no part in Carl's having to live in a different place, that Carl would always love him and would continue to see him, and that nothing Ian could do would drive Carl away.

Nowadays the boy's behavior is far short of perfect, but for his age it's terrific. He also gets along much better with his stepbrother and stepsister. He now feels safe enough to be a normal KID with his father.

CHILDHOOD

Between the ages of seven and eleven, a child develops competence. Support from the father can greatly enhance a child's ability to stick to a task and enjoy his strengths and talents.

It is important that you guide, praise, and help your children in this age range to learn new skills in a step-by-step fashion that will allow them to develop a sense of mastery. Your presence will ease any sense of isolation and help them to take creative risks. This expanded sense of proficiency will serve them well as they enter the turbulent teen years. Practice saying yes to requests like these:

- "Dad, can you come to Parent Night?"
- "Dad, Mom says I need training wheels, but I told her you'd teach me without them."
- "Dad, will you show me how to set up a computer game?"

Although Reggie's daughter, Candace, is now nineteen and in college, he still talks about the period when she was eight, nine, and ten. Reggie had allowed a furious, long, bitter divorce to drive him out of contact when Candace was two. When he finally reconnected with his daughter, she was eight. He didn't want her to fail, so in an effort to protect her, every time she started something, he would help her avoid doing it wrong.

If she wanted to go horseback riding, he would say, "No, I don't think so, you might get hurt." If she wanted to play outside, he'd say, "Don't hurt yourself." He'd even remark about how she stacked her Leggos. "Careful. That's too high. They're going to fall over. Let me show you . . ."—and he would take over her project. Candace would then become irritable and withdrawn.

Reggie couldn't understand why his best efforts were making Candace angry. He took it to his men's group, and they told him to back off a little, to let the child learn by herself. Slowly Reggie was able to break his habit of saying "Let me show you" and "Be careful" and let her do things on her own, including make mistakes. Eventually he could see the wisdom in this approach. Candace learned to experiment without making success the focus.

By reconnecting with your children at this age you can make their transition into adolescence easier for them and for you. As a teen counselor, I learned that a loving father's presence becomes more and more important as adolescence draws close. In the teen years, an abandonment wound can manifest itself as a lack of confidence, lack of direction, and particularly lowered school performance. In more extreme cases, father absence can lead to withdrawal, delinquency, or violence. Making connection now can help your children prepare for the hormonal firestorm that some teens experience.

> There is a time to keep silence and a time to speak.
>
> —ECCLESIASTES

THE TEEN YEARS

In their teens, ages thirteen to nineteen, children learn about loyalty and identity—hence the struggle with peer pressure. Your presence will help solidify their sense of identity.

Remember that this drive to forge an identity often motivates teenagers to seek their biological parents. I have heard of teens who got in the car to go meet their fathers as soon as they got their driver's licenses. Your presence will help ground the teen in her genetic realities. Who am I? Where do I come from? Your presence will help answer these questions for them.

The teen years are often marked by rebellion and self-absorption, but they are also a time for developing tenderness and a social conscience. Try to be patient when your teenager thinks that everything in the world revolves around him. It may be hard to get a word in edgewise, so listening may be the best gift you can give.

"Carly would get together with me and do a monologue," Charles remembers of his visits with his daughter. "I'd pick her up, and she would start talking and keep it up nonstop. I heard about every boy in her grade. It was exhausting, but I figured it was better she was talking to me about all of them than fooling around with all of them!"

Charles is right. With daughters in particular, your presence during the teen years will be an enormous help to her in establishing good boundaries and avoiding the sexual behavior that is often a symptom of a young girl's desire for male attention. As Blankenhorn writes: "A father's love and involvement builds a daugher's confidence in her own femininity and contributes to her sense that she is worth loving.... [W]omen who have had good relationships with their fathers are less likely to engage in an anxious quest for male approval or to seek male affection through promiscuous sexual behavior."

> *The first duty of love is to listen.*
>
> —PAUL TILLICH

Blankenhorn also writes eloquently on the crucial part a father plays in his son's development as a man. "The father is irreplaceable. He enables the son to separate from the mother.

When this process of male identity does not succeed–when the boy cannot separate from the mother, cannot become the son of his father–one main result, in clinical terms, is rage. Rage against the mother, against women, against society."

Once a relationship is established you can help your teen by reinforcing her mother's attempts to maintain structure. It is wise to discuss some rules with the child's mother that you will both work to enforce.

You can help your teen by enforcing the strict boundaries, supervising and helping with homework, and providing guidance about curfews, dating, and job responsibility that the mother and other caregivers are trying to impose.

Once you have established a relationship, one of the most important things you can do for your teen (or for your child at any age) is to encourage and support them in their schoolwork. Have weekly check-ins about homework and assignments, or a study night where you participate. These can forge a new bond and provide a focus for your role. And it can make the difference in your child's success or failure.

We began to hear girls at the edge of adolescence describe impossible situations— psychological dilemmas in which they felt that if they said what they were feeling and thinking no one would want to be with them, and if they didn't say what they were thinking and feeling they would be all alone, no one would know what was happening to them.

–Carol Gilligan

- "How'd you do on that biology test you were so worried about?"
- "I know Jeannie gets to stay out later than you do, but your mother and I both think that's not such a good idea."
- "This guy Chris sounds like a real jerk. Some of the other boys you've talked about sound like a lot more fun."
- "Your mother's right. No way you're going to that party unless there are parents in the house."

One of the biggest mistakes parents make with their teenagers is treating them like adults. It is the nature of adolescence to test limits. You must provide them.

A close relationship with your teenagers will help avoid the disasters—pregnancy, alcoholism, drug abuse, violence, crime, school failure, suicide. Reuniting with your teens, listening to them in a nonjudgmental way, treating them to respectful reminders about safe activities, and giving them loving supervision will help them far more than just letting them "work it out for themselves."

Too often parents respond to a problem like teen drinking or pot smoking by saying, "It's just a phase." It's more than a phase. It's a flag waved to gain your fatherly attention.

When his son's grades dipped from B's to D's, Carlos called his ex-wife. "What's going on?"

"It's just a phase," she answered—a little defensively.

"Are you sure something isn't upsetting him?" Carlos pressed. "Has anything changed?"

"Maybe he's worried about girls," his ex replied.

"I'm not sure that's it," Carlos said. "Why don't you ask him to call me."

Carlos set up an extra visit with his son just to do a little parental exploration. He found that his son was spending a lot of time with one of his male teachers outside of school. When Carlos asked about this, his son said, "Yeah. It's kind of confusing. It's like he wants to be my friend or something."

> The beginning of love is to let those we love be perfectly themselves, and not to twist them to fit our own image. Otherwise we love only the reflection of ourselves we find in them.
>
> —THOMAS MERTON

Carlos asked a few more questions. Were alcohol and drugs involved? Was this teacher also singling out other boys? The disturbing answers were yes and yes.

As you may have guessed, this teacher had a history of seducing his star students. Gently steering his son clear of the man, Carlos also doubled up on the time and attention he gave his son.

"His mother was really blind to this," Carlos recalls. "She was flattered that a teacher was paying special attention to our boy, which I can understand. I was cynical enough to ask some hard questions, and I'm very glad I did."

Older children and adolescents do what they see, and they will be very unforgiving if you do not "walk your talk." During this period loving support can make all the difference in their future, so strive to provide a good example of a well-lived life.

> A *father is a thousand schoolmasters.*
>
> –Louis Nizer

"I realized I was asking my son not to smoke dope and ruin his life, but I was getting blasted on beer when we watched football together."

"I wanted my eighteen-year-old daughter to respect herself as a woman, but I was dating a girl not much older than she was. When the three of us went out to dinner, I could have been out with two daughters–that's the way it looked."

"I asked her not to use swearwords, but every time we were caught in traffic, I'd be yelling a stream of obsenities."

Realizations like these can catch a man up short. Actions speak louder than words, and these actions were what these men's children were really learning.

Another common problem is particularly troublesome with teens. Children are adroit at playing one parent off against the other, manipulating both in order to get their own way. This manipulation can be very difficult to spot unless you are in clear and frequent communication with your ex.

When Gerald's wife, Annie, dragged him back into mediation to alter the visitation agreement, he was very, very offended. In his eyes, he had been a good dad to his teenage son and daughter. He loved them and supported them financially; he listened to their problems and helped them with solutions.

What came out in mediation was that Gerald was a highly permissive parent. When the children constantly violated their curfew, Gerald let them convince him it was all right. That choice, of course, put his teens at risk. It was also hell on their mother, who was trying to set and enforce reasonable limits. The kids would make huge scenes at her house until they were allowed to go to Dad's.

After the mediation hearing when he was chastised for being too permissive, Gerald sought help. A pastor helped him see that he was unable to set limits for his children because he was afraid of being rejected by them, afraid they wouldn't want to see him anymore. He was very invested in being their friend, as often happens with single parents. He learned he would have to risk angering his children in order to support their mother's efforts at control. "To children," his pastor said, "limits are love."

> Example is not the main thing in influencing others. It is the only thing.
>
> —ALBERT SCHWEITZER

Gerald was able to sit down with their mother and draw up a list of what was acceptable behavior and what was not. Enforcing the rules was tough at first. Both children rebelled and tested Gerald's resolve. They even did what he had feared they would do: they left in the middle of visits. He let them go. And their mother, standing firm, sent them right back to Gerald. The teamwork approach to parenting worked well.

Eventually the teens settled down. Gerald says now he can see the love in his children's eyes. He was astounded to realize that the love came as a result of doing what was good for the children, NOT what would keep the peace.

EARLY ADULTHOOD

Early adulthood is supposed to be a time of learning to love and to work.

Ideally, by this time, your children are developing their own interests, establishing their careers, and settling into serious romantic involvements. They may even have a spouse and children of their own.

However, many young adults I know are adrift in the world, without education, purpose, or plan. Though many work hard, they tend to react to their circumstances and environment rather than actively pursue a chosen path. If I saw this as experimentation I would be more encouraged, but too many young adults seem dissociated from themselves.

This can make it especially confusing for parents who want to help and don't know how.

If you are reuniting with grown children, it will be important that you honor their autonomy and their choices in life and become a friend first instead of a father. Use this friendship and your example to support them in their search for fulfillment, i.e., education, career, marriage. Include your child's spouse in your plans and in your gift-giving. Prove to them that you will be there as an ally for all of their family and friends.

> M*y father didn't tell me how to live, he lived, and let me watch him do it.*
>
> —CLARENCE BUDINGTON KELLAND

One warning here: it is too late to try to impose your value system on children of this age. They are grown up and will make their own decisions. The key here is acceptance. You will have to teach them love by example, not by imposition. Do not let differences in politics or ideology separate you. Do not try to play "father knows best."

Kevin was eager to be reunited with his son, Kenny, after a ten-year absence, but he says, "I was insensitive to the fact that Kenny was himself newly married and that his marriage needed to be his top priority. I did not pay enough attention to the bond between Kenny and his wife. I was not sensitive enough to her feelings. Instead of setting up solo meetings with my son, I should have visited with them more as a couple."

When David reunited with his grown daughter, Jessica, he treated her as though she were still his little girl. "The truth is I had missed her teen years and couldn't quite admit it to myself," he says. "Instead of treating her like the young adult she was, I came on pretty heavy-handed as the all-knowing dad. No wonder she resented it!"

Fortunately for many of us, children can be very forgiving. If we are essentially sincere in our desire to know and love them, they will give us the time and latitude to make necessary course corrections in how we deal with them. We will do the same for them.

IT IS NEVER TOO LATE

The end of The Haunting and the intimacy of friendship can be rewards for both you and your children at any stage of your child's development, no matter how old either of you are.

> The bitterest tears shed over graves are for words left unsaid and deeds left undone.
>
> —THOMAS CARLYLE

Even people in their sixties and seventies who were abandoned as children often tell me how much it means to them to think that their father, whom they did not know, may have missed them. The abandonment wound can still be healed even in late adulthood. If you are an older father, you might consider giving your children and yourself the grace of a reunion in order to set the stage properly for the next phase of their life and yours.

Your old age will be a time of deciding whether you lived a life of integrity or one that left you ashamed and filled with despair. In old age a forgotten parent may feel the full brunt of the loss of his children.

If you are in this stage of life and feeling despair and regret over the broken bonds with your children, you can still make a difference for yourself and them.

All a reunion between an elderly father and his child requires is that each of them tell the other how he feels, how much he loved or missed the other, or even how angry the absence made him.

I have talked to many people who were abandoned by their fathers, and they often say the same thing: "If only the old bastard would say he was sorry and tell me that he loved me. I could forgive him anything."

There is an old saying that the way a man dies defines how he lived. Reunion shouldn't have to happen on a deathbed.

MOVING ONWARD

1. Have you planned your next visit?
2. Are you taking care of yourself?
3. Take a rest from this work for a week or two. You deserve it.

8

FORGING
NEW BONDS

THE BACKLASH

After my initial meeting with Scott, he suddenly cut off all
contact. When I received my "Dear Dad" letter from him that
meant so much to me I did not know that I was not to see him
again for nearly four more years.

I had written back but never received a return letter. I
called several times and never got a return call. Eventually I
called Scott at work, and he said he didn't want to talk to me
just then. He was elusive about why, and he canceled our
planned meeting in Chicago.

A few days later, John called me and shouted, "Leave my
family alone!"

I was heartsick, angry, and confused.

What had happened? Something had gone terribly wrong.

First I blamed myself. Then I looked for a scapegoat: was
this John's doing? I had no real evidence that it was, and in
any case I owed him a debt of gratitude for raising Scott. Was

John afraid that my presence in Scott's life meant that Scott would abandon him? I had no evidence for that scenario, either. So if John wasn't the villain, who or what was?

The mystery tormented me. I got a good look at exactly how powerful—and negative—my imagination could be.

Was Scott afraid I would abandon him again? Was he feeling unappreciated? Or was Scott himself abandoning me? Was he playing out the last act of teenage revenge fantasy? Had I failed to live up to his expectations? Was he rejecting me permanently?

All I knew was that my fledgling relationship with my son was somehow being dismantled, and I could not figure out why. One more time I went back to my mentors. I was told to return to writing him. I did just that. I wrote a letter every few months. And, though sad, I went about my life.

I met and fell in love with Julia, a writer who had a young daughter, Domenica, not yet ten. I had rarely thought of remarrying. The pain of my estrangement from Betsy and Scott—The Haunting again—was too real for that. Despite my misgivings, our relationship grew stronger.

I found myself considering Domenica often, thinking about her life, her schooling, her friends. I wondered what would make her happy. As my romance with Julia deepened, so did my rapport with Domenica. "What is your son like?" she would sometimes ask me. She seemed to understand how my thoughts of Scott haunted my life. Absent but always there, Scott hovered out of sight but was never truly gone. And I realized I was watching—helping—Domenica grow through some of the rites of childhood I had missed with Scott.

Julia, Domenica, and I began to function as a part-time family, living separately but sharing meals, evenings, and occasional weekends. Then we began sharing chores like laundry and grocery shopping and dropoff and pickup at school. I watched Domenica grow. Finally, Julia and I were married and our little family moved in together and went full-time.

I still wrote to Scott, and though I often lost faith that he would ever contact me, my mentors did not. They said Scott was a grown man now and I would have to let him call the shots. I would hear from him when he was ready. In the meantime, my life went on.

My parenting skills matured as I began to intuit Domenica's moods, dreams, and disappointments. I could often tell very quickly when she was unhappy, depressed, overwhelmed. I learned when to set limits: "No, that dress is not okay for you at your age. No, you cannot stay out past ten."

I also learned when to loosen up a little: "All right, this is a special occasion and you can stay up."

Julia and Domenica became the loving focus of my life, and we moved as a family to New Mexico. During this time without contact from Scott, I threw myself into my work. Julia and I taught and wrote together for several years, developing a best-selling book, *The Artist's Way*, which helps people recognize and realize their dreams. I taught in many places, including Russia, but although this was rewarding, all of it felt somehow hollow. I told myself to count my blessings, and I did. But I still missed my son.

I started working as a counselor with troubled adolescents at a private residential psychiatric hospital. I had already been a volunteer in the field for many years. Additionally, I threw myself into the study of child psychology. Increasingly absorbed, I began to talk with experts. I didn't realize it, but I was preparing myself for the work I do now, teaching troubled families: prodigal fathers, overwhelmed mothers, and troubled kids.

Ever since my conversation with Professor Velez, on that train taking me to Scott, I had been convinced that there was a need for a book that would help men break their silence about their heartache over their estrangement from their children.

With this in mind, I began to talk with men on a more formal basis about their feelings, about their losses, about their lives. What the media called deadbeat dads I saw with ever-increasing clarity as brokenhearted dads. I discovered that not only did the courts, social agencies, and ex-wives not know what the absent fathers were feeling or why, but the fathers themselves didn't know, either. Our collective pain on this issue was so deep that it had struck us mute. As a nation, we suffered not only from father absence but also from father silence. I resolved to be at least one voice that would speak out.

I began to write, but found I was completely blocked. It seemed I could write about anything except my situation. How could I write a book about fathers when my own son would not even speak to me? The pain of this fact was too difficult to feel, much less to commit to paper.

"Write about the pain, then," Julia urged me. Finally I decided that if what I had to say to men was that I missed my son and was heartbroken that he would not see me, then so be it. That was what I would write.

With new resolve, I started to work. Writing longhand on yellow legal pads, I scrawled and crawled. It was a long, hard, and cathartic process. Finally I had something on paper.

The next day, while I was at the hospital listening to troubled teens, Scott called our house.

This was enough to strike me as proof of Goethe's advice: "Action has magic, grace, and power in it." Something had shifted.

"Happy birthday," Julia told Scott. "Mark's at work. Can I have a number for him to call you back?"

Julia reached me at the hospital.

"Scott called you," she said. "He sounds just like you. He asked for Mark from Virginia! Here's his number. Call him."

I called Scott but didn't get him. It was three long days before we reached each other. By then I had prepared myself: the call might be a false alarm; he might be calling to say it was just too traumatic for him to continue contact. But then we talked.

"What did he say?" Julia asked, eager for details.

"Well . . . he invited me to his wedding this summer. In July. I suggested he come out here to visit first. I told him I'd send him a ticket."

Scott came for a visit in June.

To meet him, I had to drive from our home in Taos, three hours through the winding mountain passes to Albuquerque. I would have to leave early–but I couldn't seem to get out the door that morning. I was very nervous and worried; I wanted everything to be just right. I started cleaning like a madman.

"Get out of here," Julia said.

"But–"

"Get out. You'll be late."

"But damn it! You call this a clean house?"

Julia refused to take the bait. She just smiled and told me, "Just go. You'll be late."

I nearly was. I got to the airport, parked, went into the terminal and settled near the edge of the waiting area–conspicuous enough so that Scott would see me but far enough away so that he wouldn't be embarrassed if he failed to recognize me, or I him. And what if he didn't show?

I watched intently as people got off the plane–daughters, grandparents, lovers, friends, strangers meeting for the first time. All with stories of their own. No Scott. My heart sank.

Then I spotted him, *much* older and taller than four years before–six-three to my six feet–but still thin in that before-thirty way. At twenty-two, he was still more boy than man, but he carried himself with an air of worldly confidence.

I remember having the overwhelming urge to grab him and pick him up and toss him in the air as one would a small child. Instead, we hugged and made small talk about his height, the flight, his baggage, and lunch.

I told him I was so nervous that I had tried to start an argument with Julia just before I left. He said he was very nervous too and that his fiancée, Elizabeth, expected him to throw up on the way to the airport. We had a nice chuckle over our nerves.

I was conscious of my desire to hug him, to make him feel loved, or maybe to make me feel loved, but I restrained myself. I had learned from working with teens that you have to take your time before making physical contact. So I just guided him to the baggage claim area.

We ate lunch in a cafeteria that I love for its fried fish, pies, and family atmosphere. No pretensions, I had promised myself, consciously working to counteract my desire to impress Scott with some grandiose gesture. I settled for Furr's Cafeteria, not Il Pranzo or some other posh eatery. I had vowed I would show myself to my son as I was and my life as it was.

During that visit, Scott and I repaired the irrigation ditches along our land. We rode horses and hiked a nearby mountain. We toured the surrounding country, exploring the great rift of the Rio Grande Gorge. It felt like a healing time.

An odd and symbolic moment occurred the first night. I was restless. Throughout the night I had to fight the impulse to get up and check on Scott as though he were a toddler. Only once, in the early morning, did I yield to it. My six-foot-plus son was sleeping soundly—or so it seemed.

That morning at breakfast Scott told me of his own restless night and a dream he'd had: "I saw myself as a small child and watched as you and I played together. Later, during the night, I felt as if there were old people all around me, standing and sitting in the room, I couldn't quite see them but knew they were there. I felt they were protecting me. I could not tell whether they were male or female or how old they were. Just that they were real and that I was safe. This seemed to go on all night long. When I finally woke up I had the sense of being home."

Over the next few days, over our work in the muddy

ditches, over the breakfast table, we began what has become a deep and respectful friendship.

Although we didn't talk of it in such terms until much later, on some deep level, both my son and I felt more complete.

Many parents I have worked with say that their relationship with their children developed on some deep level of consciousness that affected their sleep patterns and their dreams.

A few nights later, I had my own fitful sleep and vivid dream that echoed Scott's: I was driving when suddenly I saw a kid standing by the roadside. As I watched, he sank into a hole in the asphalt. I swerved my car to the shoulder, leaped out, and raced to help him. An older man watched from a distance. I rescued the boy, got back in my car, and drove on.

Then it happened again. Another boy, older this time, fell into a hole filled with water. I raced to save him, and as he sank beneath the surface, I leaned way in, put my arm into the ooze of deep water, and circled my hand around and around until I felt his hand touch mine. We locked wrists, and I pulled him out. When we came up, the same old man was standing nearby. He did not move, and I did not know who he was. I felt that he was ready to help, but the boy was safe and so was I.

Looking back, I now see this as a dream about my own capacity as a father. Would I be able to save my boy? Would I have help if I needed it? Many parents have doubts and dreams like this. It is the unconscious working to assimilate the reality of reunion—a reality so powerful that it will also affect their serenity when awake.

Throughout Scott's visit I was conscious of a desire somehow to make time stand still, to make our reunion permanent and set in stone. I was afraid I would lose him again. I had to fight the urge to make him promise me that this would never happen.

What accounted for Scott's four-year absence and his sudden return? The answer, it turns out, is as complicated and irrational as it is familiar.

SCOTT'S STORY

"That first visit was pretty good," Scott said, "but it was too short for me to form much of an opinion. I did not know why, but I cut off contact with my father and didn't talk to him for almost four years. I do recall being grateful at how open he was with me then, though at the time I wasn't sure what to believe and what to toss out as b.s. I had to learn to trust him. Maybe that was part of it. My breaking contact involved my fear of actually reestablishing a relationship with a father I didn't know.

"He existed outside my comfort zone. I was too immature at the time to take the challenge. Although he was still a mystery to me, all I could think about was how much I looked like him. I couldn't believe it. I then understood, I think, some of the hostility I had felt from my mom since I was a kid.

"Four more years of questions and wondering went by. On my twenty-second birthday I called his house. I still don't know what made me call, especially on that particular day. I remember his new wife answered the phone and I hung up.

"What was I doing? I thought. Was I crazy? Then a cooler head prevailed, and I dialed again. This time his stepdaughter answered and I suddenly felt like an intruder. I introduced myself anyway and asked to talk to her mother, my father's new wife. Julia seemed as shocked as I was, but she obviously knew a lot about me because she wished me a happy birthday. I remember thinking how strange it was that she knew it was my birthday when I knew absolutely zero about her.

"Julia explained that my father was at work and would love

to hear from me. My heart was pounding so hard in my throat and my hands were sweating so profusely that I thought leaving the message was enough. Yet I somehow picked up the phone again and reached Mark. I was in a haze during the conversation, so it wasn't until some time later that I realized I had agreed to fly west to meet him and his new family.

"Suddenly I was five years old again. I was scared to death, as excited as if I were going to meet Santa. I couldn't sleep for weeks. The day finally arrived; I was relatively calm until the plane landed. Then I started to shake. I walked off the plane and couldn't believe it when I saw the same man I had met years ago–a man who looked exactly like me, but older–waiting to pick me up.

"It was an awkward two-and-a-half-hour drive to his house. We talked a little, shared a few details, stared out the window, and went to a restaurant and stuffed ourselves. We had a great week together. We didn't sleep much. We talked a lot.

"I learned a lot about my father during that visit, and I told him a lot about myself. I went home feeling that a missing piece had been replaced. It was and still is hard to explain that feeling. I was determined not to break contact again, so we talked and wrote occasionally.

"It is becoming more like a friendship because I am older and independent, but a great relationship just the same. I still get embarrassed when he talks about presents he would like to have given me and when we talk about the future. Sometimes I feel he is trying to make up for the years of missed fatherhood all at one time, and that puts me in a corner.

"But my intent in writing my feelings for this book was never to hurt or blame one side or the other for what has happened in my life. I wanted to express my innermost feelings, as much as it hurt sometimes, so that other children and young adults can learn that they are not alone in their hopes and fears. I also wanted to help mothers and fathers in similar situations understand what their children may be feeling, because the children's thoughts are often forgotten or not considered at all. I hope this book helps everyone reestablish that all-important *contact*.

"Our relationship is all trial and error, but I'm determined to make it work. It has taught me a lot about where I came from and who I am now."

REUNION REACTIONS

My return four years earlier had prompted a reaction in Scott that left him in a place somewhere between exaltation and panic—unable to process or understand his tumultuous emotions. Therefore, self-protectively, he withdrew.

Subsequently I have seen my own son's physical and emotional retreat played out to varying degrees in the stories of many of the families I counsel. This retreat can be a setback, a major disappointment that can smack down your confidence.

Following the anxious planning and excitement of the initial reunion, it is not unusual, for example, for both the father and the child to feel unsure of their roiling emotions, uncertain how to act with each other and even how to be together. One father I know has dubbed this the "Now what?" feeling.

Some of the "now whats" can be hard to handle. But not impossible.

BRACE YOURSELF FOR REALITY

It is not unusual for a child to shed tears or express distrust or anger toward the father; and it is not unnatural for the father to feel confused about his role or to feel sad once the initial thrill of the reunion is over.

Preparing ahead of time, anticipating the inevitable confusion reunion brings, and knowing exactly how to behave will prevent another estrangement. Being able to listen closely and attend to the signals your child is sending—however loud, direct, hurtful, or silent—and to respond with the same patience and maturity that have carried you this far will allow you both to build a relationship that will last and be fulfilling.

Suppose your child says, "I don't know if I want to see you this Saturday, Dad." Should you take this as a literal statement of fact?

Probably not. Often a child needs to be reassured that you, in fact, do want to see him.

"I'm really looking forward to seeing you," followed by silence, is a good response.

The cautious but heartfelt answer will probably be "Yeah, I guess we could go to a movie or something."

PREPARE YOURSELF FOR THE FANTASY FACTOR

Just about every reunion scenario includes an element of fantasy. The expectations that father and child have of each other are usually unrealistic and often unspoken, even unconscious; therefore the actual relationship may at first fall short of the dream.

While no two relationships can ever be the same, I have found that with prodigal fathers and their children, the longer the period of absence, the higher the expectations. And, unfortunately, the longer the absence, the more awkward and difficult the building of trust will be.

> A *merry heart doeth good like a medicine, but a broken spirit drieth the bones.*
>
> —PROVERBS

At best, early visits are highly charged and people tend to be hypersensitive, so it can be helpful to take all reactions, yours and your child's, with a grain of salt. Remember, the longer the separation has been, the less you know about each other.

"When my daughter and I went to dinner at a restaurant, I was appalled by her behavior—elbows on the table, leaning into her soup, hair in her face. What had her mother taught her about manners?"

And on the child's part.

"I don't think Dad gets what I'm talking about when I tell him about my teachers. He seems to think they're always right."

What's new and fresh and exciting about your reunion and the act of mutual discovery inevitably gives way to the ordinary sameness that is the stuff of everyday life. There's laundry to do and meals to prepare and work to go to, and on and on.

Our children do have to deal with the everyday reality of homework, discipline, and school schedules. Despite their busy schedules, however, they often do not want to be told what to do by anyone, let alone a returning father. For this reason it is sometimes hard to find a balance between active parenting and simple friendship.

"My daughter says she never gets any homework. Is that possible? When I was a kid, I was buried half the time."

"My son tells me that all the kids smoke—and not just cigarettes. I say pot is still illegal, but he says his mother is relieved it's not hard drugs, and besides, she smokes dope every weekend with her boyfriend. Should I ask her if that's true, or would I be betraying a confidence from my son?"

Just when you want to reclaim your parental authority, your children may feel you gave away your right to discipline them. They may test you to see if you have the courage to discipline.

"I caught my daughter—she's thirteen—hanging out with a much older boy. She's flattered by his attention. I wanted to break his legs. I dropped by the spot where they hang out. I thought it would do him good just to know I was very much in her life."

Conversely, if they are starved for masculine direction and firm boundaries—with a mother who is too lenient due to her guilt at being a single parent—they may look to you to make *all* the decisions. This is flattering but highly dangerous, and it will not endear you to the ex who is your partner in raising these children. Be alert for flattery that might mask an attempt at manipulation.

Whatever your situation, listening is the magic word.

Often children can self-regulate if given choices. Good parenting is about teaching limits and boundaries by word and by deed. But children can be overly sensitive and resent even the gentlest direction.

A request as simple as "Take your dishes to the kitchen"—with or with out a "please"—can incite rebellion if the child hears it as a criticism. When emotions are running high your patience can be truly tested. But remember this is stage one. As a rule of thumb, balance constructive criticism with an equal amount of heartfelt praise. Then double the praise.

Some fathers I have worked with have found that with hypersensitive kids allowing the children to figure out *how* to help is better.

"This place is really getting messy. How can you help me?" or "I could really use your help. The trash needs to be taken out, the dishes need to be done, and the floor needs to be swept. Do you have a favorite, or should we just flip a coin?"

You may, on the other hand, have a child who does not rebel and instead seems far too eager to curry your favor. These children are equally insecure, but are masking it differently. They are the do-bees. They will try to do everything in an attempt to win your favor and hopefully ensure themselves a continuing place in your life. Like the rebellious kids, these children need careful handling. Make it clear that their presence in your life is not conditional upon their behavior.

As children tend to react differently to reunion, finding a balance between fun, communication about important matters, everyday chores, and hang-out time tends to be a trial-and-error process.

"I kept having these huge heart-to-hearts," Jack remembers. "I finally realized we were all exhausted."

"I thought my job was homework sergeant," Alan remembers. "Their mother said she was having trouble in that area. I finally realized I had to be the one to define what my role should be. I had to consider her but not just cater to her needs."

> A *soft answer turneth away wrath but grievous words stir up anger.*
>
> —PROVERBS

Regardless of how well you have settled your working relationship with the child's mother—and stepfather, if there is one—regardless of how aware you are of the fantasy element, you must find a flexible routine that works for all of you. This means compromise.

If you were raised in a home where one or both parents ruled with an iron fist, you may find that compromise has a tendency to stick in your throat. Keep remembering that this is about the rest of your life with your child or children—and with your ex and her significant other. Take the long view whenever possible.

There are many ways that you can cue kids into knowing you consider them a permanent part of your life:

- Ask them for their pictures. Frame them and hang them.
- Get them a magazine subscription—delivered to your home.
- Clear drawers and closet space for their use.
- Buy them their own breakfast mugs.

Add your own idea to this list.

STRUCTURE FOR SAFETY AND SECURITY

I suggest that you try to keep a regular schedule of contact from the very beginning, striving to see your children at least once a week, if only for a few moments. If you live far away from them, set a weekly phone date.

It is not necessary that the visit be a big thing. Hanging out together is usually better, in fact, than trying for too official a visit. Visits with your child are not therapy and should be treated as a time to get to know each other.

"I was tongue-tied," Charles remembers, "so I used to take my daughter to the movies. This gave us something concrete to talk about at dinner."

Some fathers, extremely shy in the presence of their offspring, find themselves overcompensating by talking their heads off. Unfortunately, I was one of those. ("Boy, were you ever," my son says.)

Scott would have been happier just to sit and watch television than talk about what he was feeling, what I was feeling, what we were feeling, what the dog was feeling. I could have allowed conversations to meander and make the focus an activity at hand, not some agenda of "healing."

> D*irect yourself to one thing only, to put yourself in motion and to check yourself at all times.*
>
> –MARCUS AURELIUS

For me, one of the ironies of this work has been the realization of how many things my own father did right: we built model airplanes together, played football and basketball, and did household projects–talking casually all the while.

Try to create a safe atmosphere for your children during visits, one where your child will feel loved and secure. The other side of this safe atmosphere is that your children will one day feel free to open up and express their anger over your absence.

No matter how grateful they are that you're back, they may also be mad–hurt–that you were gone. Accept this, and accept what it brings with it. Your job here is to respond with empathy, not react with anger of your own. So think of this as an exercise in spiritual aikido: let the anger flow by you like wind as you step aside.

The child's anger may come out sideways as snipes at you,

friendly teasing with a certain edge to it, or it may be as overt as "f– you, Dad."

Anger can also come out in the children's behavior: suddenly they will not want to see you for a while. They may cancel visits, act up, or pout.

The anger may reveal itself as blame or as silence.

Again, avoid reacting with anger of your own. Instead, listen. Listen. Then listen some more. Listen to your gut when something doesn't feel quite right about the interaction between you and your child. Talk it over with your mentors. And remember, compassion for others and yourself is the key here. Avoid being defensive.

These attacks can be especially hard to take, because they are rarely voiced directly, as in "Dad, I'm really mad." Instead, your son might tell you he hates all three of the breakfast cereals you bought.

It is important to let him know that you don't believe he's really mad about the cereal, that you can tell he is bothered by something else, and that you will listen to what he has to say. These attacks are usually about fear–fear that you don't love him, fear that you'll go away again, fear that you really are the failure his mother may have said you are, fear that he is just like you in a negative way, fear that you don't really like him.

It is usually the older children who are most likely to disguise how they really feel; they may not even know how they really feel. Younger children can sometimes tell you more honestly what they think. Regardless of how old they are, you need to remember that they are the children and you are the adult. When you feel overwhelmed, take time out, go into another room, and pray.

Never shame them or threaten to withdraw your love, and never strike back at them physically or verbally to defend yourself. Remember that this is your child's way of saying she feels safe enough to test you a little. It is a good sign of a deepening relationship. Remember that when the going gets tough.

Remember also to admit that sometimes what they are saying is *true*. What they may be pointing out to you is something you could have done better. There will be times when all you can do is say, "I'm sorry." Then you can change the behavior that is causing the pain.

Sometimes safety will bring with it disclosures about what they don't like that you are doing right now.

Scott told me that it made him feel uncomfortable when I introduced him as my son and patted him on the back. I had to start asking him if it was okay to introduce him or not. It was a delicate negotiation for a while.

Shifts like this require a give-and-take that you will have to remain alert to. Remember that children have a right to their feelings and that it is all right for those feelings to change, sometimes quickly. Yes, I know this sounds like a roller-coaster ride; that's what it is. Let your children have their emotions, whatever they are. Let them have their say. Listen with your heart, not just your ears.

Even though it's easier said than done, do not: tell them they shouldn't feel that way or that they shouldn't cry.

Hold to your emotional center and remember the emotion will pass.

NEITHER BLAME NOR ACCEPT BLAME

It's especially important during these times to avoid the tendency to blame someone: It's their mother's fault, it's the damn in-laws, it's the court system, and so on. Don't blame yourself for the past, either: If only I hadn't left. If only I'd gotten here sooner. Blame of any sort solves nothing

Children are quick to pick up on tension. They are also quick to manipulate tensions to their own perceived advantage.

Andrea, for example, loved to alarm her father, Jim, with

horror stories about how strict her stepfather was, how harsh he was, how he didn't understand her. For a while, she managed to get her father seething with anger—until Jim checked out Andrea's stories.

"I discovered that I agreed with a lot of what Andrea's live-in dad was doing," Jim said. "I thought the rules he laid down were pretty sensible. I saw that Andrea was trying to play us off against each other. She wanted to run with a faster crowd than her stepfather approved of—and I didn't approve of them either."

Although we may wish it were otherwise, the reality is that children always carry the weight of one parent's disrespect for the other as shame, depression, or anger. A child's self-image is formed by the image carried of both or all parental figures, particularly both sides of the genetic lineage. For this reason, it is critical that you not be provoked into criticizing the other parents. Anything you say about your child's mother will be internalized by that child as criticism of him or her.

> When you are offended at anyone's fault, turn to yourself and study your own failings. By attending to them, you will forget your anger and learn to live wisely.
>
> —MARCUS AURELIUS

Therefore, it is very important that you not take a child's hostility personally. Much of it will not be coming from the child alone but will arise out of the child's fear or out of the disrespect shown by one parent for the other.

Try to remember that all people under stress will regress to earlier methods of coping. You may catch yourself feeling like the young man you once were, reacting angrily to your ex, who will also suddenly act the way she did long ago. Have a little compassion here for both of you. Think of these bouts as *emotional flashbacks.* They happen to all of us—and they happen to our children.

Your child, too, may regress to an earlier stage of development when overwhelmed, so that a three-year-old may act two, a five-year-old three, a ten-year-old seven, a fourteen-year-old ten. Let them have their feelings. They will need reassurance and comfort during these times; not judgment.

STAY IN THE PRESENT

Deal with what is happening now and let blame go by the wayside. This will help you avoid power struggles with your children or their mother, because when you stop blaming others you also stop accepting blame for past behavior and proceed into the present.

Focus on the solution not the problem.

My child is upset, *what can I do now to comfort her?*

I am upset by not feeling appreciated by her. What can I do to comfort me?

Call your support team and let them appreciate you and remind you that what you are doing may be hard but it is important and they are proud of you for doing it. Never worry about getting too much support—that isn't possible. Support is important, because you are in this for the long haul.

Watch for any signs of emotional shutdown when you are with your child. Responses to emotions vary at different times for different children. Sometimes your children will want to express their feelings or talk about them. Sometimes they may just need some time alone.

"I sleep," says twelve-year-old Elizabeth. "When things get emotional, I just crash."

"Sometimes I just need to veg," says Marc. "I don't want to do anything but watch some dumb TV."

Your children may be very sensitive to any perceived slight. A broken promise will seem very big to them, seeming to threaten the stability of your newly developing friendship.

If your agenda does not put them first or first behind your work schedule, you will have to think real hard about your priorities. They will hear every invitation to dinner, every promise you make, every side conversation that you have about other plans.

Kids are very smart and will not be fooled for long. If you break promises and fail to be consistent, they may suddenly surprise you by breaking off all contact before you even know anything is wrong.

You are a parent, not a therapist. Your love is the medicine your children need. You do not have to fix their feelings. Just let them have their emotions and show your support. Try not to be afraid of emotions, though they may be confusing—yours and theirs. And *be* there.

On Tom's fourth visit with Kimberly, his eight-year-old daughter, she kept asking him to buy her things. This upset Tom, who was not in good financial shape at the time, and though he had said yes to a few things, he finally could not take it anymore.

"Kimberly, I need to talk to you for a minute," Tom said, squatting down so he and Kimberly were at eye level.

"What?" His daughter looked a little guilty.

"I need to tell you that my feelings are starting to be hurt. All day long you have said, 'Buy me this,' buy me that, and I'm starting to feel like all you want me here for is to buy you things. And that if I don't buy them you'll think I don't love you."

Kimberly stood quietly for a moment and then started to tear up.

"What is it?" Tom asked. "Tell me."

"I'm afraid you are going to go away again," Kimberly said softly. Tom held her as her emotion swept over them both. He sat on the floor at the side of the aisle in the drugstore. Kimberly climbed into his lap, and they had a good father-daughter cry. In her eight-year-old mind she was having trouble with the concept that he loved her and yet could still go away after their visits. If he bought her what she wanted, it meant he loved her.

"I am going to go away again each time I visit," he explained. "But I will be back again and again and again. And I will be here when you need me. Do you understand?"

"I think so."

"Are you sure?"

"Maybe."

As the months have gone by, Kimberly has gotten more secure with the knowledge that her daddy is still her daddy, will always be her daddy, and will be there when she needs him.

Tom has demonstrated this in deed as well as word.

On one occasion, Kimberly's mother was going on a trip. She had arranged for Kimberly to stay with a neighbor whom Kimberly liked. But Tom decided it was too soon for Kimberly to be without both of her parents at the same time and arranged to spend the five days with Kimberly at her mom's house. He was there when she needed him.

YOUR CRITICAL ROLE: EDUCATION

You may not be aware of this, but your very presence as a father will help your child with their intellectual development. Some scientists believe that fathers parent in a unique way—one that is different from that of mothers. Fathers tend to stress competition, initiative, and independence; their way of playing with their children is more physical and exciting and helps prepare children for competition and achievement.

David Popenoe in his book *Life Without Father* states that a number of studies have uncovered a strong relationship between father involvement and the quantitative and mathematical abilities of their sons. Others have found a relationship between paternal nurturing and the verbal intelligence of boys. Similar results have been found with girls. Popenoe attributes this to "the male sense of play, reasoning, challenge, and problem solving and the traditional male association with achievement and occupational advancement."

Whatever the reason for these results, the rewards are real, and when you return to the lives of your children, you will be participating in their intellectual development in ways that will pay off for everyone.

The presence of a father AND mother allows each parent to make their individual contributions to their child. Just as depth perception takes binocular vision, it takes two pairs of eyes (father's and mother's) to properly focus on a child's development. Any increase in parental *attention* from either parent makes for a child's enhanced educational development.

There are specific things you can do to support your child's education. The first step is to discuss schooling with your child's mother; ask her how your child is doing and what you can do to help. Ask what the school's policy is regarding visiting parents; is there an orientation day when parents meet all of the child's teachers? Are there special events where parents are invited? Tell the mother of your children that you want to be involved. If it is awkward for you to attend events together, attend separately, *but attend.*

I find it is better to have established your new relationship with your child and maintained that relationship for a period of several months before you attempt to offer your support regarding their schooling and homework. Otherwise they may feel "put on the spot," or threatened. Just let the relationship build naturally from personal contact, and the emphasis on schooling evolve out of genuine concern for your child's well-being.

Show interest in your child's day, their plans for study, the names of their courses and teachers. This attention to detail will remind them that you care. What are their favorite subjects? Which ones could you help with? Your assistance will require a balance between listening to them and offering them active help.

You are not back in their lives to be the boss or judge. They may be hypersensitive to any criticism from you. Your job is to help them schedule their time, and applaud their efforts. It can be as simple as sitting quietly together at a table, both of you working, your children on their homework, you on something you need to do. One night a week to help with homework is a good start. You are there to help the child, not embarrass him, to believe in him, not berate him. You can be the cheerleader and coach. You are not there to do the work or demand perfection.

You will be providing for your child the most important support you can give them—high expectations, and the personal loving attention of a father who cares for them. They will benefit from this attention for the rest of their lives. So will you.

You can be a great encourager for children who are older as well, whether it be college, beauty school, nursing, mechanics, technical, electronics . . . whatever. All school is learning, and learning needs to be appreciated by the parent.

> Nothing decreases the rate of crime and violence as powerfully and effectively as does education.
>
> —JAMES GILLIGAN

Education is the key to your children's future, and success at school is often their most powerful source of self-esteem. Failure at school is also the earliest warning sign of trouble of all kinds. School failure, particularly early school failure, is a very strong predictor for later problems in life. Do your part to make schooling a focus of your work with your child. This has long been a part of a father's traditional role. Remember that education is a secret weapon that the rich would like to keep to themselves.

We must help our children get a good education, and if they are failing to live up to their potential, we must intervene in any way that works—tutors, therapy, support groups—for them (and for you, if needed). Never ask something of your child you would not do yourself.

Be careful when you go to their school to talk with their teachers, that you do this in a respectful, caring way. You are not there to blame the teacher or make excuses for your child. You are there to ask the teacher how you might help your child do better. Show your honest interest in your child's success. Teachers appreciate this, and are often pleasantly surprised to find more fathers involved in school activities. Make yourself a positive presence on your child's behalf. Just knowing you are interested and believe in your children's ability to learn can make a tremendous difference in their grades and even how they are perceived and treated by their teachers.

If your child is doing poorly in all subjects, you will need to take a delicate but active approach. Have the school test your child for learning disabilities that may not be apparent, or for emotional problems. Do not hesitate to seek professional psychotherapy for ANY child who is not doing well. *If a child is failing at school, something is wrong and must be addressed.*

> *Schools need to greatly expand their efforts to involve noncustodial parents in their children's education, by, for example, inviting them to parent-teacher conferences and school assemblies, sending them report cards, extending the school day, and offering evening activities that expand opportunities for working parents to interact with their children.*
>
> —RICHARD WEISSBOURD

Many parents make the mistake of blaming the teacher or punishing the child. Or they do nothing, convincing themselves that the child's problems are "just a phase." This is almost never the case. School failure is a red flag signaling trouble and should be treated as an *emotional emergency*. Talk to the school, get tutors, counselors, or clergy involved—whatever it takes—but *do not let your child's failure in school go unnoticed.*

School failure is something that parents are often in denial about, because it threatens their sense of self-esteem and their image of themselves as a "good" parent. They may also do nothing about it because they are confused about what to do. Without judging the child or the mother, stay focused on the goal of working with the school and the child to ensure your child's success. There is no reason that the average child in America should not finish high school.

Education can make children happier and help stabilize their relationships as well as increase their income as adults. Make sure you have just as high an expectation and offer just as much support to your girls as to the boys. They deserve it; make sure they get it. Work with (or without) the mother's cooperation to make sure your daughter gets the support she needs to succeed in tomorrow's world.

Helping with your children's education will not only allow you to help provide a vital service to them, it will give you a defining role in which you can focus your love and energy. It will strengthen the bond between the two of you and take away any confusion you may have about *why* you are in your children's lives and what you are supposed to do when you get there. You and your children will be happier (and richer) for it.

Keep in mind that many parents who did not do well in school or did not finish their education may not place a high emphasis on "book learning." This is a tragic mistake that will hurt the child's future job possibilities and self-esteem.

If you did not do well in school or have dreams of finishing your education, then I strongly urge you to do so. You can study for the GED (the high school equivalency test) at any local high school, and all cities have community colleges or universities you might attend. There are also more than 100 college and graduate degrees you can earn by mail or over the internet, and over 1,200 colleges that give credits for life experience. Even just taking a computer class can raise your self-esteem and your earning potential. Kids are influenced more by what they see than what they are told, and there is no better way to encourage your child's education than to continue to go to school yourself. School is the best investment you can make.

If your former experience with education was not fulfilling, or was traumatic for you, seeing your child through some of the problems you faced will not only help them, but will help you to reframe that experience and see yourself from a new vantage point. I flunked out of Ohio State when I was an eighteen-year-old father, working full-time, struggling to figure out what to do. I was too ashamed to ever talk about it or ask for help.

Once in therapy, I faced my dream of an education and was able to talk my early failure. I was able to go back to college. I found myself excited (and scared) to be learning again, going to school at night while I worked a construction job. I graduated from DePaul University's School of New Learning in 1986. It is never too late to get an education, even if that education has to start in a therapist's office. Attending school yourself will send a direct message to your child that school is important.

HANGING IN THERE

Yes, you have reunited with your child, but now after every visit you and your child must once again experience the pain of separation. This is especially tough if you live in a different state and your visits are less frequent than those of a local dad.

For those of us who have known the terrible isolation of The Haunting, the separation after visits can be hard, but never as hard as the time in exile. That deep pain of separation need never come again. There will be small hurts, though, like the good-byes to your children every time you visit. Just keep in mind that you are going to stay the course, and you will.

Tom was divorced after a decade of marriage to Linda and moved to Idaho from Los Angeles to take a job there. Since he had been working from home for much of his daughter's life, she had been with him almost every day. He left his daughter behind in L.A., and although their separation was brief, only a few months, he found the pain of parting very intense.

"It was early evening," he recalls. "I had not seen my daughter in three months and our first visit was coming to a close. She was seven at the time. I dropped her off at her girl-friend's house where she was going to spend the night.

"I could feel the pain and tears building in my chest long before we got to her friend's house. I dropped her off and was barely able to manage any words with the girl's mother.

"I drove halfway down the block, pulled over, and wept from a place inside of me that I didn't even know existed. It was as if firemen were using white-hot Jaws of Life to rip open my chest and kill me.

"After about twenty minutes I was able to drive back to where I was staying. On the drive back, I thought I would have to call one of the psychiatrists I knew. When I walked into the house where I was staying, one of the doctors was actually sitting in the living room, visiting. I told him I desperately needed to talk.

"We went downstairs to the little apartment I was staying in, and I spent the next hour and a half weeping about the pain of being separated from my daughter. I spoke about how hard it was not to be there in the morning when she woke up, to not be at the events at school, not to be there to read to her at night or if she woke afraid in the dark.

"When I finished, the doctor told me about the terrible pain he had felt years earlier when he dropped off his eight-year-old son after visits. His son is now twenty-five, and they have a deep relationship. He said he used to drive back to his apartment after a visit and throw up.

"Hearing the doctor's experience and telling him mine helped me feel better. I had gotten my feelings out, and I knew I wasn't alone."

Tom's story supports my belief that you must acknowledge and feel your pain about separation in order to stay connected to your child. You must be alert, because for some fathers the pain of repeated separations is so great that without help they find a way to sabotage their visits, returning to what in their unconscious mind is the less painful role of absentee father.

Fred was a teenage father who lost touch with his son. He did the work of reunion when he was forty and his boy was nearly twenty-one. The two of them bonded over a summer-long visit, and all looked good—until they separated again.

"I wasn't prepared for how much I would miss him after he left," Fred told me. I really hurt when I drove back from the airport. Then I buried myself in work until I thought I'd kill myself. What I was trying to do was kill the feelings of loss by making myself out to be busy and important. I delayed answering his letters and his calls and even began postponing visits we'd planned. Fortunately, my support team busted me on this and I got back on track."

One of the many services your mentors will provide during this period is to share your joy with you and listen to you over coffee when it's painful.

Barry lived in the city, and his daughter, Annie, lived in the suburbs with his ex-wife. For the first few years after his divorce, Barry lost touch with his daughter, drifting into alcoholism and despair. When he got sober after joining a twelve-step program, Barry reached for reunion. He and Annie became father and daughter again.

"I had really missed her. I missed everything about parenting, even when she was a real pain in the ass. I missed the driving her to ice-skating, taking her and her friends to the movies and picking them up afterward. I missed trying to answer her questions about math. It was great to have her back—and really hard every time we had to say good-bye."

After Annie's weekend visits with him, Barry made a regular Monday-night beeline to his mentor's house for dinner.

"I don't know how many times I went over and just sat there like a stone through dinner. It felt good to me just to be in a family circle."

The mother and the child are also in pain during separation, and you need to be compassionate about their feelings, always assuring them you will be back and saying when. If you are on a regular visitation schedule, it will be important to acknowledge the feelings everyone will have that accompany the separations.

Janet, the mother of an eleven-year-old boy, said that every Sunday night when her son returned from his weekend with his father he would go to bed and cry. "I miss Dad," he would say. "Why can't I stay with him?" Janet reassured him that in just five days he and his father would be together again, but the transitions—leaving and returning—are especially hard for young children. They need extra comfort at these times.

During the hard times of establishing a relationship—and all relationships go through hard times—remember that comfort and compassion and a listening ear are important.

Don't cut down on your visits. Many parents rationalize that they will make up for missed time with their children with "quality time." In their brilliant book *Reclaiming Youth at Risk,* Brendtro, Brokenleg, and Bockern explain that there is no such thing as "quality time"—convenient, planned, set-aside time for children. They believe quality time is a facile, unrealistic invention: "We cannot care for children in convenient time; we can't learn from our elders in convenient time; we can't maintain marriages in convenient time. The result of adjusting our lives to the fiction of time will inevitably be empty adults, lonely elders, and neglected children."

TELLING YOUR STORY

Once there is a degree of comfort between you and your children, it will be time to tell them your story. They will begin to ask you many questions—some direct, some indirect.

"How old was I when you and Mom got divorced?"
"Did you love Mom?"
"Was it weird for you when you left?"

Many children do not know the pain and frustration you suffered over them and the separation. As a result, they have no framework in which to judge the circumstances that surrounded your departure. Remember this: it is a blunt clinical fact that children often do blame themselves for divorce.

YOUR STORY BECOMES THEIR OWN

Hearing you tell your story is an essential step in the reunion process. Use your Narrative Time Line and the answers to earlier questions as a reference point to tell your story to your children. It should focus on pleasant memories, and it can unfold naturally over several months if need be, one memory at a time, or in small blocks of time together. The goal is to let your children internalize some of what you have experienced. They need to know their dad's story.

> *Admit your faults to one another and pray for each other so that you may be healed.*
>
> –SAINT JAMES

This history will provide a serious healing for many children, particularly those old enough to identify with the father's feelings. Again, be sure to ground your story in as many happy experiences and feelings as you can recall. This should not be a bitching session.

You might say, for example, "I remember that when you were born–your mother was so brave–the first thing I did was count your fingers and your toes. We wanted to make sure you were all right."

This is the place where much of your earlier work will pay off in unexpected dividends. Your Narrative Time Line, your answers to the questions–all of this will have helped you recall specific memories and modify dangerously high emotional responses to the bleaker incidents. It should also have triggered your memory of pleasant experiences that you can now share with your child.

"I remember the first time I saw your mother. This may sound corny, but she was in a white dress going to church. I thought, She is the most beautiful girl I have ever seen."

"When you were two you had your own headphones and you would lie on my stomach and listen to rock and roll."

Many children grow up not knowing a remarkable number of things about their father, some of them so basic you will be astounded, and if you were separated before they were five, they may have no memory of the years when you were with them. They may not know how you and their mother met, what sort of work you do, or what your strengths and good qualities are. The mother's own pain over the separation may have made it too stressful for her to talk about you, their father.

> It is one of the most beautiful compensations of this life that no man can sincerely try to help another without helping himself.
>
> –RALPH WALDO EMERSON

"It wasn't until I remarried that I was able to tell my kids about their dad," recalls Janet. "I wasn't exactly trying to keep them in the dark. It was just so painful to think about how much we had loved each other and how it hadn't worked out."

As you hang in with your kids during the early stages of reunion, you will be slowly giving them the bricks and mortar to rebuild a sense of continuity and trust in the life process. Yes, there was a separation, but it is mended now and they do have you back. Over time, you and they will come to trust that.

SOUL TIME

Once you have been reunited with your children and have become more available emotionally to them, they will be on your mind and in your heart very often.

Love exists in what I call soul time. It is the positive side of The Haunting–the connection that is unbreakable, that exists through time and distance. Soul time, like dream time, is a space-time warp in which connection is both real and psychic.

It will not be uncommon for them to pop into your head at various times of the day or night.

- "Boy, that kid looks like Davie."
- "I should take Carrie to the planetarium."
- "I wonder if Leo could take care of a puppy. His mother loves dogs."
- "Should I get him a ball or a mitt?"
- "I wonder if she has an ice-skating outfit or if kids just wear regular stuff these days?"
- "What is Johnny going to need for school this year?"
- "I wonder if Sally needs a ride to dance class?"
- "Maybe I can take Freddy to have his braces removed.

> *It is this intangible thing, love, love in many forms, which enters into every therapeutic relationship. It is an element of which the physician may be the carrier, the vessel. And it is an element which binds and heals, which comforts and restores, which works what we have to call— for now—miracles.*
>
> —KARL MENNINGER

You may develop a sudden interest in the Disney Channel or in the neighborhood bookstore that has a weekend story hour. Welcome to the soul time of parenthood. Watch how your discussions about children increase. Are you talking more about your kids with others?

Many parents speak of receiving mental and emotional telegrams from their children: a sense that they should call their child and touch base, if only for a few minutes. How many times have you called and heard your child say, "Dad! I was just thinking about you . . ." followed by some pressing youthful question?

When you get these messages from soul time, you should

act on them. A postcard from you, a T-shirt from the city you visited on business, a photo of the child's report card attached to your refrigerator by a magnet—all of these small concrete actions spell love to your child. Remember that children do not inherently "know" that you love them. You must show them and tell them they are in your thoughts. A brief call from an airport pay phone can mean the world to them. Act on your impulses to reach them.

It is a privilege to get to live in soul time. The payoffs are continual gifts of connection.

One day far into our reunited relationship, during a time when Scott was living nearby, he dropped by unannounced just to hang out at my house. I did not want to make a big deal about how thrilled I was by it. I acted as if I didn't notice that he had never done that before. He just came over in the middle of the day, walked in, grabbed a chair in the dining room, and started talking, as if he and I had hung out together all his life. I could not help but grin inwardly at the casual way he now claimed his space in my life.

Shortly after that day, he dropped by to have a heart-to-heart talk with me about how he felt—another milestone in our relationship. He didn't come to ask me for advice or to have me fix anything. What mattered was that Scott finally felt safe enough to come over and truly tell me what was going on in his life, his head, his heart.

FROM THE HORSE'S MOUTH

Below are some thoughts from the children of prodigal fathers. These kids were all teens who either had been reunited with an absent father or had a visiting father after a divorce.

Chelsea: I wanted to see my dad on a regular schedule so that it wasn't just every Christmas and Easter. Seeing him just on holidays was too much pressure. I had to be the "good daughter," and that was just too hard. It would have been better if we could have had some casual time together to get to know each other.

Erin: I wanted my dad to come and see where I lived. My relationship with him really changed when he started coming to visit me and hanging out. I wanted him to see what my room looked like. I wanted him to have some of my stuff at his house, too, so I felt like I lived there instead of just visiting. I used to fly in to see him and take my stuffed animal so that I wouldn't be alone there. It would have been nice if I'd had my own room.

Jason: I wanted my father to be with me when I visited. To do things with me. My father still talks about the only class trip he ever went on when I was six, and I'm almost thirteen now. I wish we would have done more stuff together like that. Also, I wanted him to talk to me and not around me when we were out with other people.

Mike: I have had a great relationship with my father. But not with my stepfather. My stepfather drank a lot and was always negative and put us down. I couldn't stand how he would call my mother stupid. I used to want to beat his ass for that. I wish I could have had my bio father to talk to about it. Maybe he could have influenced my stepfather. I think if my bio dad had been more friendly with my mom, she wouldn't have taken that shit from my stepfather.

Jason: I didn't want my dad's new wife to treat me like she was my mother, but I didn't want her to ignore me either. I've had two stepmoms; one acted like I didn't exist, and the other one acted like she was my mother. I *have* a mother, but I could have used a friend. I think all the parents—and some of us have lots of them—have to be aware that *we* have to adjust to everybody too.

Mike: I wanted to do things that were fun part of the time. My father was always working, so he'd "fit me in." I never felt like I had his attention. Even a walk around the block would have felt good if I'd had his whole attention.

Chelsea: My father used to take me out for ice cream after school, and I loved that. Or we would go to the planetarium or a museum, that kind of stuff. It was interesting and didn't feel like such a big deal. It got easier that way.

Erin: I like to talk to my father on the phone now, because we've talked enough that he remembers who my friends are and what my schedule is, that kind of thing, so I can really ask him about stuff.

Jason: My mom has a fax and my father faxes me notes and sends cards sometimes. It's always great to get mail.

Chelsea: It hurt me a lot when my father criticized me or corrected me for anything because I hardly ever saw him, so I was really sensitive when he found fault with me. Even though I knew it was perfectly normal for him to correct me, like my table manners, when he did it, it really hurt.

Mike: I wanted my stepdad and my father to get along. I always felt like they didn't like each other or something. It would have been nice to think they could at least have had dinner. I mean, they married the same woman. They are both in my life. Why couldn't they be more in each other's?

Chelsea: I wanted to have the right not to talk about how I was feeling. Sometimes when my stepdad asked me how a visit with my father went, I didn't want to tell him, just because I didn't know how I was feeling. I wanted time to think about things.

Mike: I think my stepfather should remember that I had a relationship with my father first and that, good or bad, it is part of who I am. I was grateful when my mom and stepdad and bio father got together and did some therapy. My father started to come to visit, and everybody was less critical of each other. It's hard to be a kid in the middle.

Erin: I want my dad to remember that my mom is the most important person in my life, because I haven't lived with him. I don't want him cutting her down when she's all I've got most of the time. It would be nice to know they like each other.

Chelsea: I got to know my dad as a friend after he came back in my life and we'd be talking and all of a sudden I'd realize how similar we were. That was fun.

Mike: I want to be forgiven for all the stuff I did when I was real little and visiting my dad. I couldn't stand our visits at first. I would paint on the walls or be so angry that I wouldn't talk and just sit there. I wish someone had gotten me help. I still feel like that sometimes. I can't think about that time without feeling a big lump in my throat. It would have been nice to have had a place to talk about it. I think parents have to get the kid help if the kid's not happy.

MAINTENANCE REMINDERS

1. Set aside a separate room or part of a room for your children. Have them keep a change of clothes, pajamas, and toothbrushes there, so they will feel they have a home with you.

2. Do not try to buy your kid's affection. Gifts are all right in moderation, but you don't have to exceed your financial resources to persuade your children to love you or to demonstrate your love for them. Money can't buy love. Also, it can be really harmful to the reunion process to buy elaborate gifts for your children when you are not making regular child-support payments, attempting to catch up on back payments, or are not visiting regularly.

3. Set up a consistent visitation schedule and contact your children often by phone or letter to allay their fear of abandonment. If you call, say, every Friday evening at seven o'clock, they will feel certain that they can count on you. Work out a schedule with your children and their mother. Weekly or twice-weekly contact is often best. Do be careful not to overwhelm them, though. Children need time during the week to adjust to your

being back. Whatever your schedule, work hard to stay current and not get behind.

4. Establish routines together to deal with everyday things like homework, laundry, and grooming. If you live in the same city, take over some of the mainte- nance tasks of your child's life: doctor's appointments, shopping for clothes, shuttling them to dance class and soccer games. Again the same caution: be careful not to overwhelm them, and work these plans out with their mother.

5. Do not force the children to be more affectionate than they want to be. Think of your child as a scared kitten you are trying to coax out from under the bed. A kitten is best allowed to come out when it is ready. Do not rely on them to meet your emotional needs with hugs or kisses. And—most important—*never* compare one child's style of affection with another.

6. Don't endeavor to make every visit a big event. Plan time to just hang out. Strike a balance between activity and just plain being together. This is important in the development of trust. Some of the old standbys—doing chores, cooking, building model airplanes, playing board games, doing jigsaw puzzles together—are good ways to gently connect.

7. Keep your sense of humor. Your child will follow your lead. Humor is an important element of optimism, which helps us succeed in the world. I've found Pola- roid pictures of our adventures and misadventures—the hike, the work on the land, the horseback riding—to be a source of much humor and many fond memories for Scott and me.

8. Listen when your children tell you about their day-to- day activities. Who are their friends? Where do they meet? What are their favorite movies? What's going on at school? Record names and facts in your Reunion

Notebook. Your children will love it when you mention their friends by name or ask about what they did at their hangout. Be aware of what's important to them at school and what events they are going to participate in. Hang a calendar in your kitchen with the important dates penciled in.

9. Whether you like it or not, your ex-wife is the gatekeeper to your child. Keep that in the forefront of your mind. When you deal with her you are dealing with your child's future. Set up a regular meeting where you listen as well as talk.

10. Where possible, be flexible. Children often change their minds. You may have a day all planned, but they may want to do something else. This is where negotiations start. This is one of the reasons it pays to find out what your child enjoys and make plans accordingly.

11. The going can get very tough in the beginning. Do not hesitate to get help from a professional counselor, therapist, or pastor.

12. Make sure your child's photographs are displayed and make a space for the gifts they give you. Richard has a gallery of photos of his daughter taken every summer. Paul has an "inch-by-inch" wall in his kitchen to measure his child's growth.

13. Remember that music and videos are powerful playthings for children. Keep a collection of their favorites at your house that you can share with them.

REUNION REDO

Use your Reunion Notebook to answer these questions:

1. What will you do differently on the next visit? Why?
2. What could you do every week to maintain a closer connection with your child? Visit? Send a card? Call?

3. Have you noticed any positive changes in yourself?
4. Has your work life changed? Have your co-workers mentioned anything to you about your attitude? Are you more confident?
5. Have you found yourself talking about your children more with others?

9

EMBRACING
YOUR CHILD'S
EXTENDED FAMILY

THE RETURN HOME

Scott was married in July 1992. He and I both knew my presence at the wedding might cause some waves. Nonetheless, he wanted me there, and I wanted to attend.

Julia and I flew into Washington, D.C., rented a car, spent a day with my father in Charlestown, West Virginia, then drove down to Virginia for Scott's wedding. I drove straight to my old neighborhood to show Julia the house I had lived in as a teenager, twenty-five years earlier.

Two blocks from my house two boys were folding newspapers for delivery, just as I had done. They looked to be about sixteen, the age I was when I got Betsy pregnant and our world changed forever. These boys were happily chatting as they worked. I stopped the car and shouted at them through Julia's window.

"Hey! How many papers do you have on your route?"

"Fifty-five," the older-looking boy answered.

"I had this route twenty-five years ago!" Both of the boys smiled politely. I knew what they were thinking. They would never be as old as I was now.

When Julia and I drove by my old high school, which Scott had also attended, she began to cry as she realized how young Betsy and I had been.

I decided to show Julia where my friends and I used to surf, a stretch of once deserted beach that now is crowded with summer visitors. At the far end there is an old restaurant called the Sand Dollar, still unchanged some quarter century later. We went in for dinner, then watched the ocean before checking into our hotel. There was no call from Scott and Elizabeth, and we knew there might not be. We decided to play tourist.

As we walked back into the room hours later, the phone rang. It was my brother, Jim, calling to say that my mother and eldest niece were coming to the wedding despite the fact that they had definitely *not* been invited. Julia suggested I call Betsy, lest the surprise upset her arrangements. Nervous, I dialed the number.

Betsy answered the phone. I said, "Hello? Betsy? This is Mark."

"How are you?" she said, cool but friendly.

"Fine, but I just learned my mother is driving down to the wedding. I thought you should know so you won't go into shock when you see her. I know how much careful planning you've done."

Silence.

Outside the plate-glass windows of our hotel, a sudden nor'easter whirled into town. The sky turned liquid as a terrible wind whipped the trees flat and raised the waves to a frenzy. The weather matched my own emotions. Betsy's silence seemed louder than the storm.

I continued, "My mom told my brother that your brother invited her."

"I can't believe my brother would do that. I'm sure that isn't true." Betsy sounded hurt and exasperated.

"Betsy, I don't know what the truth is. I just didn't want you to be angry at me, since I had nothing to do with it. That's all."

"Well, I'll have the guards out looking," she huffed.

The guards? I couldn't help chuckling. I knew she was just nervous.

"Well, good luck today," I said. " I'm sure it will be a beautiful wedding."

As I hung up, Julia laughed and said, "Well, it looks as if everyone is going to act like they are four years old."

We dressed and headed for the church. I wore a dark blue gabardine suit; Julia wore a dress of rich green silk and low heels. We were determined to look impeccable despite the storm, despite our emotions. We planned to get to the church early and quietly take our seats.

The rain was coming in great gray sheets. Water was standing a foot deep at some intersections. Traffic was snarled. I wanted to wait for the rain to stop.

Julia, who insisted on getting there early because there would be a large crowd, said, "Mark, just because everyone else is acting angry and put out doesn't mean you can't act calm. What would normal people do? They would go to the church and sit down. So let's do that."

Arriving at church, we passed an open side door where my former in-laws were standing, obviously nervous. Betsy's mom stepped toward me and offered me her hand. I shook it and said, "Congratulations."

"Thank you," she said. "It's a big day for us."

Betsy's father did not acknowledge me in any way. Julia and I went to the church entrance and waited to be seated with everyone else.

Betsy's sister, Scott's aunt who had accompanied him to that first meeting, leaned across, said hello, and introduced us to her new baby. Betsy's brother, an usher today, was friendly as he led us down the aisle. We asked to sit halfway back, groom's side, not wanting to be intrusive. He said my mother was in the parking lot. He had invited her to come in, but she had refused, asking him instead to just take a few pictures with her camera.

"Don't get into any drama," Julia whispered.

At last, Betsy and John entered. Betsy looked the same as I remembered—still very beautiful. The princess was now a queen. She wore a slender white beaded dress. John was tall, proud, and handsome in his tuxedo.

Scott came in, looking pale and a bit harried. He winked at me when he saw us and took up his position at the front of the church. Elizabeth, radiant and calm in an old-fashioned gown, was escorted down the aisle by her father.

After the vows, when the minister announced them as Mr. and Mrs., using Scott's adopted name, sadness washed through me. Scott was my son and yet my family name was gone. It was both a proud and difficult moment for me.

Julia and I attended the reception after the ceremony, as we had promised Scott we would. Immediately inside the grand ballroom was a bandstand surrounded by large tables set with place cards, crystal, silver, and extravagant flower arrangements. In an adjacent room a pianist accompanied a torch singer while guests grabbed hors d'oeuvres.

Betsy and John walked by me as I tried to say hello. Julia grabbed my arm and steered me toward the other room. We passed Betsy and John several more times that afternoon, never with any acknowledgment. I had been so hopeful of a reconciliation or at least a hello."

At last Betsy's mother walked up to us. She extended a friendly greeting and we chatted for a while. I asked her if she got my letter. (I had written my former in-laws a letter making amends and telling them I would be at the wedding.) She said, "Yes, thank you."

I said, "I've missed you in my life." We both began to cry a little and we hugged. I said to her that I might even try to shake my ex-father-in-law's hand.

"No," she said. "I don't think that would be a good idea."

"Okay, don't worry," I said. Julia and I walked on to congratulate the bride and groom.

Elizabeth was a happy and radiant bride. Scott, elegant and tall, looked relieved. We hugged them, kissed them, wished them well. Their friends and well-wishers swarmed around. It was obvious to everyone who I was since we look so much alike.

Then Betsy's dad walked over to us and spoke not to me but to Julia: "I don't mean to be rude, but I guess I just hold grudges."

"Oh?" Julia was carefully neutral.

I felt a little bit as if it were not only a fairy-tale wedding but a fairy tale, period. Julia and I were in a kingdom where we were not really welcome and did not really belong.

He paused for a moment and then said, pointing to Scott, "We got the best end of that deal."

Our eyes met.

He and I looked at each other across twenty-five years.

"Thank you for all you have done," I said, stepping forward. He nodded, but we did not shake hands.

I knew Betsy's father had never moved past his anger at me. Projecting how I might have felt had I been in his shoes, I understood his anger. Still, it stung.

Julia took me by the hand, and we quietly made our way to the door.

DIGGING OUT

I am not sure that my work over the years quite prepared me for the emotional repercussions of that visit.

I felt the urge to run away, to dodge the feelings. I felt so sick and feverish that I had to go to bed. I was conscious only of the old shameful sensation that I was nothing and had even less to offer. I wanted to cover my head and sleep, sleep, sleep. I denigrated myself for my failures. I forgot to be grateful for my successes.

I kept seeing Betsy and John, the proud parents. Had they snubbed me or was I just imagining it? Were the feelings I was experiencing left over from twenty-five years ago? I will probably never know for sure.

Gradually, as the fever cleared and the adult I am now came back into focus, I realized that the most important thing was that I had *shown up for my son's wedding.* I was able to be there to support him because *he asked me to be.* I did not hide from anyone. I had the courage to stay for the reception and the good sense to know when it was time to go. All this was a gift from God, the wisdom and guidance of my friends and my mentors, and the work on my own. I was very grateful.

DIGGING IN

As prodigal fathers, many of you will have to deal with the wreckage of the relationships you left behind. As your relationship with your child deepens, you may find yourself additionally dealing with new family members who appeared during your absence.

I refer to the stepfather as "the second father," because I believe that there are too many genetic factors at work for the biological parent to be forgotten.

> Nothing on earth consumes a man more completely than the passion of resentment.
>
> —Friedrich Nietzsche

No matter what you choose to call your child's new parent, you should try in every way to respect him and others who are in your child's life; any loving person is an important ally not only for your child but for you. Avoid scarcity thinking. If your child's heart must be big enough to include them and you, then your heart is big enough to include all those your child has found to love. There is enough love to go around.

It is critical that you acknowledge the efforts they have made on the child's behalf, as you may expect to see those people with some regularity. Remember that your reappearance in your child's life may upset the equilibrium of the stepfamily. It is imperative that you make the child feel safe in loving both or all of his parental figures—his mother, his stepfather, and you. It is important that you help make the adults feel safe as well.

Whenever possible, a three-way line of communication should be established between the two fathers and the mother, so that all are in the loop about decisions for the child. I call this building a corral. The object is to keep your child safe and sound in the middle of a circle of loving adults.

The more people who genuinely love your child, the better that child will do in the world. It does take a whole village to raise a child, and this is never more true than when referring to those closest to the child. Trying to earn your way to your child's heart by disrespecting the mother or her mate or friends will backfire and you will lose your children by causing a loyalty conflict that will force them to choose.

It is often valuable to think of a family unit in terms of a mobile, as John Bradshaw says. Each family member is one part of the mobile, and the whole family hangs together in relationship to each part. Your entrance adds a new and weighty piece to your child's family mobile. All of the other pieces will jiggle and joggle and juggle in response and come to a new equilibrium. Realizing this will help you to be aware of and compassionate about the reactions of others.

For the stepfather, disturbing questions will arise: Will my

> *We all carry it within us: supreme strength, the fullness of wisdom, unquenchable joy. It is never thwarted and cannot be destroyed. But it is hidden deep, which is what makes life a problem.*
>
> —HUSTON SMITH

children love him more than me? Will he take them away? Will they have more fun with him? What does this mean to me? It is critical that you be sensitive to this man's love and commitment as well as your own.

SHARING THE MASCULINE MENTORING

Men in our society are raised to think territorially and competitively: we win or lose, and all too often we think of women as spoils of war. This thinking can extend to our children as well. In order to do the work necessary to reconnect to our children, we must do a few "spiritual sit-ups," as Julia would say.

On the one hand, this is a book about fathers' rights and, by extension, ancestral rights—that is, the right of our entire paternal family to continue and to claim our lineage. On the other hand—and this must be the focus for now—we are not our children's owners. They are not our property. We are their guardians, their custodial adults. It is in this spirit that we must approach and regard their stepparents.

Dennis found himself bristling because whenever he phoned his son, the boy's stepfather seemed brusque with him.

Finally Dennis asked himself, "Am I the one, like—brusque?" The answer was yes. He says, "I never asked the guy how he was or how it was going. I was like 'Let me talk to my kid.' So the next time I called, I said, 'How's the big construction contract going? That project sounds like a bear.' Suddenly we were talking one to one. He just needed to be acknowledged as a parent and appreciated."

Chris, a stepfather, remembers the shock of his stepdaughter's biological father's reappearance. "For five years I had been Carrie's dad," he says. "I drove her to school. I painted her room. I went to parent-teacher meetings, listened to her talk about her fights at school, advised her about first boyfriends. Then suddenly her dad comes back and he's the big deal.

"She'd get on the phone with him and have these long talks. Then she'd say, *'Dad says...'* and repeat something that never sounded like the height of Apollonian wisdom to me. I felt shut out. I guess I really was scared I'd lose her, like I'd just been a stand-in and now the real McCoy was back. Frankly I hated the guy's guts, but he was her father and I knew how much he meant to her. So I finally wrote the s.o.b. a letter and established a rapport with him. The next year we celebrated Christmas together."

> *Shared joy is doubled joy, and shared sorrow is half-sorrow.*
>
> —SWEDISH PROVERB

Our lives are a continuum; we are moving either toward love and union or toward fear and separation. Try to always move toward the love. Ask yourself, What is the compassionate thing to do? Most often it is to take a moment, step back from your own emotions, and consider what it would feel like for you to be in the other man's shoes.

This heightened perspective is important in overcoming the tendency of the ego to play one-upmanship. Divided loyalties that can occur in mixed families are dangerous for children and unpleasant for adults. It is important that you use your best people skills for nurturing—or at least tolerating—the many new relationships that need to be built.

Anthony had been separated from his daughter by both time and distance. He had allowed the coolness of his second wife to influence his decisions, and when she professed to be uncomfortable with his visits with his child, he retreated into his new marriage, leaving his daughter behind, although he did continue to send child support. After nearly three years he made his way slowly back into her life, first with phone calls, then with visits, and finally with a commitment to family counseling.

"In the long run, I have to say I did what I felt I had to do," Anthony says. "The right thing was to be friendly. Since then her stepdad and I've shared her high school years, graduation, college years, and I imagine someday we'll all be there when she gets married. I want to be the one to walk her down the aisle, but I suppose we could both do it. The important thing is that when she didn't have me, she had him and now she's got us both."

Trying to earn your way to your child's heart by disrespecting the mother's mate will backfire.

> By means of radical thought, deep intuition, or exemplary actions, men and women throughout the ages challenged the idea that the exemplary life necessitates supporting a flawed world.
>
> —GIL NOAM

Tammy was the only child of her parents' short-lived marriage. When her parents divorced, her father moved across the country and her mother remarried. All questions about her father were off limits. He was part of a painful past, and her mother did not want to talk about him.

When Tammy was fourteen, her father resurfaced. His work had brought him back across the country, and his heart had brought him to seek reunion with his daughter. Tammy's stepfather reacted as if he were being betrayed. Tammy's mother took the lid off a decade of silence and said every poisonous thing she could think of. Tammy rebelled against both of them by continuing to seek interaction with her birth father.

"It was very volatile," he remembers. "While I wanted a bond with my daughter, I did not want it at her expense. I began a letter campaign assuring her mother and stepfather that theirs was the primary household and that I wanted to be a part of my daughter's life but not a disruptive part. This seemed to calm everybody down. Over time we have developed a distant but cordial relationship."

Tammy's father walked a delicate line, one that you may be

walking now. The first father must respect the second father because the second father is living in the house with the child; and the second father must respect the first father because the child received half of her genetic heritage from him.

THE FULL FAMILY

Sometimes these mixed family situations can be confusing for children. Angie is the seventeen-year-old daughter of a man who has married repeatedly. Although she herself was the only child in her mother's marriage to her father, she has a half sister, Andrea, whom she hardly knows.

"It's weird," Angie says. "Sometimes I go to visit my dad at Christmas and Andrea's there and she even brings her other half sister with her, from her mom's marriage now. I don't think I'm related to her. Am I?"

Elizabeth was reunited with her biological father and built a close relationship, getting to know not only him but his parents as well. Elizabeth started seeing her grandparents occasionally and taking them presents on the holidays. She talked with them by phone regularly. Recently, though, she has spent more time there, even though she says they are old and "always want to know who I'm dating." She is seventeen.

This year her grandfather began to fail. He had worked his whole life as a tailor in the garment district in New York City and had put his children through college while staying married to the same woman for fifty-four years. He had several surgeries involving long stretches in the hospital, and Elizabeth was there. She visited him often and took him gifts of food he liked. She listened to family stories from her grandmother as they sat in the hospital cafeteria and waiting rooms. She was present at his death. The funeral was a traditional Italian one with stories of the past and a funeral march through Little Italy.

I cannot calculate what this meant to Elizabeth and to her family. I know that she probably learned more than she realizes. It may be years before she knows what this experience taught her or what it meant to her soul.

I still remember the walk to the Hatfield cemetery in a tiny mountain village in West Virginia, when I was twelve years old, to bury my father's father, my grandpa Frank. My father talked about his dad, and the clan gathered, but he and I walked alone, for I was his eldest son. He told me of our strengths and our weaknesses. Now, thirty years later, that talk is still a palpable presence in my memory bank.

In mythology, the last part of the hero's journey is often the journey home. You have faced yourself, your responsibility to and reunion with your children, and have made peace with your child's mother and her family. Now it is time to reestablish or rejuvenate your relationship with your own family.

Like many prodigal fathers, I was estranged from my own father for many years. And like the men I've counseled, I entered into therapy to look for cause and effect in my life, to understand the mistakes I made, the roads I did not take. It was in therapy that I first faced the fact that my mistakes had a price for many people other than myself. The same may be true for you.

José and Lydia are estranged grandparents. Their daughter-in-law is estranged from their son, who is so bitter he has left the state and is no longer in touch with his child—the daughter José and Lydia helped raise until she was two years old.

Since the divorce, they have spent over $10,000 in legal fees striving to reestablish contact with their grandchild. On a wintry Tuesday night they have come to a men's meeting to seek counsel. Disillusioned by their experience in the court system, they are hoping to find others who feel as they do—that they have a right to see their grandchild and that the custody laws should be changed to reflect that.

At many men's meetings, the grandparents are there with, or standing in for, a son who is an estranged father. Their grief attests to the fact that it is not the father alone who loses contact with his children but his entire lineage.

Although they never would speak in such terms, what José and Lydia are arguing is genetic or tribal dominion, or you might prefer to call it ancestors' rights. Across America many grandparents like José and Lydia have spent dollars and years trying to get the right to see their grandchild. This tug-of-war is grounded in love, not property. For many people, beloved grandchildren are their one tangible link with the future. Even when they do not believe in an afterlife, they do believe in life after, and that life is embodied in their children's children.

> As my fathers planted for me, so do I plant for my children.
>
> —THE TALMUD

At this fathers meeting, José and Lydia were delighted to find a second pair of grandparents with similar aims. They too had welcomed the child's mother into their family, only to lose both her and their grandchild when the union with their son dissolved.

In order to put yourself in closer touch with the emotional realities of your extended family, you may want to ask your parents to join you on your journey by writing out their Narrative Time Lines and using their stories to help fill in the gaps of your own.

I asked my mother and father to write their stories of how they met, what they loved about each other, and what happened to them during the first four years of my life. I am grateful that they both did it, and reading their words had a profound impact on me.

I heard my mother's story of being a nineteen-year-old college freshman in West Virginia in 1951, going to classes and living in a dorm, getting letters from her sailor boyfriend whom she had known in high school. I heard of my father's many love letters and his overseas phone calls from some port to his sweetheart in the States. All of it was new to me. Reading stories of my parents as young lovers, with hopes and dreams and fears, helped me to let go of judgment about what I thought they did wrong so that I could focus on the many things they did right and well. It helped me to love them more fully again and to pass that love, rather than bitterness, on to my son, Scott.

> *Victory is not won in miles but in inches. Win a little now, hold your ground, and later win a little more.*
>
> –Louis L'Amour

As a returning father, the fullness of your acceptance *by* your family depends in large part on the fullness of your acceptance *of* your family. Again, I urge you to open your heart. As men, capable of loving many people, the determination to love our child's extended family as our own will create an atmosphere of respect that is instantly felt, if not articulated.

When James reunited with his son, he had to walk back into his ex-wife's large Greek family, whose sheer size had thrown him as a young man. "It was like I was one guy and they were more like a town than a family. Talk about intimidated."

Intimidated or not, James walked back. It took a full year of his showing up at family events–christenings, Christmas Eve parties, Fourth of July picnics–before the family grudgingly accepted the fact that he was really back.

"I really had to tough it out," James recalls, "the family being so protective of my ex-wife, I became the enemy. But it meant a lot to my daughter that I didn't let the family chase me off. After a while–and I had to be really stubborn with myself about staying positive–they finally sort of shrugged and said, "He's back." Now they joke about how there's no getting rid of me. My daughter hears that joke and she grins."

Once you have a rapport with the custodial family, you can begin to discuss your child's well-being together. You need to remember they were present in your child's life in your absence. Have the humility to let them tell you what they think.

Remember, this is about the child.

Parenting means loving your child and helping that child be all that he or she can be. You and the child's other parents are the management team. Viewed that way, what is the best way for you to use your various talents and abilities together to help that child?

Eleanor's biological father was an intellectual, her mother was an artist, and her stepfather was in the construction business. Each of these adults brought to her a richness of experience. Together they offered her a deep pool of guidance and possibility.

When Eleanor's mother was hospitalized with a nervous breakdown while on a work project abroad, both her stepfather and her father were concerned. Eleanor wanted to get on a plane and fly to her mother's aid.

> *Never doubt that a small group of thoughtful, committed citizens can change the world; indeed it is the only thing that ever does.*
>
> –MARGARET MEAD

"She's too young," her stepfather insisted.

"I don't know. She really wants to go," said her father, "but I can't go with her."

"I'd go," answered her stepfather, "but I can't afford to take the time off from work. We're really strapped right now."

"What if I pay for your missed salary and flights so that you can go? I could keep Eleanor with me until you think it's appropriate for her to follow."

"That sounds good. I'll fly over. I think it's important we keep Eleanor out of the loop until we see how scary the situation really is."

While powwowing about a transatlantic rescue may seem pretty dramatic, your combined efforts can provide a safety net neither of you could have provided alone.

The work you do to build your relationship with the adults around your child will pay off tenfold for you and a hundredfold for your child.

You will know when it begins to pay off for the child, because he will regain his sense of humor.

Peter remembers, "My daughter started teasing me about my bald spot. At first I didn't laugh. She'd say, 'Dad, even though you comb your hair sideways, I still know you've got that spot, and so does everybody else.' Finally I lightened up, decided she was right, and got a short haircut—no more weird long strands combed across the dome."

John says, "My son started teasing me about my taste in music, how un-hip it was. At first I was indignant. Then I said, 'Okay. Give me some of the music you like to listen to.' This opened up a whole new area of communication between us. Now I take him to hear the blues, and he takes me to grunge concerts."

BRINGING YOUR CHILD INTO YOUR FAMILY

While you are becoming a part of your child's extended family, your child will become a part of yours. Many of you may have remarried, and your new wives will be taking on the role of stepmother—some happily, some reluctantly.

"I married my husband for better or for worse," Caroline recalls. "But I was thinking in terms of the two of us. Suddenly there was this new kid and all the stuff from an entire other family to deal with. I was committed to supporting my husband in his reunion, but it was a lot to handle. We not only got the kid back, we got his first wife back, too. When she started calling for 'parent talks,' I felt threatened."

Issues like jealousy, fear of abandonment, and monetary concerns will arise. Be sensitive to your new family as well as to your child and his family.

"My husband began making financial commitments to his reunited daughter that he didn't clear with me first. I began to wonder, 'What about us?' and 'There goes our vacation in Yosemite.' I felt like a spiritual midget, and it took me a while to work it through.

Sheila remembers, "When Tom reunited with his son, our family was the one that needed therapy to handle the shift. We did half a dozen family counseling sessions to talk through our feelings about our new family situation."

Remember that at the root of anger, you will nearly always find an unspoken fear. If you and your new wife have children, they may fear the reentry of your child into your family unit.

"I got really jealous," Victoria remembers. "I felt like my Dad was suddenly obsessed with this other kid, my new stepbrother. I got real clingy for a while. I don't know how I acted, but I sure felt hostile toward my new half brother."

Annie, a teenager, remembers, "First I lost my birth dad. Then I got my stepdad. Then my stepdad got back with his birth daughter and I got real scared that I was going to lose him. I didn't know if it was my imagination, but he seemed to lose interest in me for a while. I got really angry."

You may need to lean heavily on your support group for help in working through these family dynamics. Often we are insensitive in ways we do not see.

Annie's second father admits, "I kept asking my stepdaughter for her opinion on how things were going in reunion with my son. It never occurred to me that she might feel threatened or think I loved her any less. I thought we were one big happy family."

With the help of mentoring, the support of parent groups, and, yes, prayer, happily reunited extended families often can and do evolve.

Two years ago Scott was reunited with my father, Jim, his paternal grandfather. It was a quiet meeting with little fanfare, but it was important for what it said about how far we all had come as a family.

I still remember my father, years ago, pushing his motorcycle around the yard with then two-year-old Scott, gripping the handlebars and gleefully shouting, "Vroom, vroom."

Dad had held Scott within an hour of his birth and now, twenty-five years later, he was meeting him for the first time as a man. My exile had in turn caused an exile for my father and mother from Scott, their first grandchild.

My father and his second wife were touring the West in their motor home. Scott and his wife, Elizabeth, were living in Santa Fe, and Scott was a student at the college where I taught. All of us got together for a family dinner, and this time we did go to the posh eatery Il Pranzo. Dad paid the tab.

The conversation was warm, if not easy. I was struck by the similarities between my father and my son. Each has a sharp wit and a quiet laugh. Both of them are married to women who pride themselves on keeping a beautiful home. Both my father and my son are sports enthusiasts, and both are meticulously knowledgeable about every car on the road. (I am not.)

At that dinner, sitting between the two of them, I felt a sense of comfort and continuity: this is how it should be. They both ribbed me a little. I am a Democrat and they are both Republicans, so they had something in common to tease me about. What I felt as they both zeroed in on me was, "Whew. At least we're only fighting about *politics!*"

Ever since that time, it has been a great joy to me to fill my father in on Scott's activities and to tell Scott about my dad. I have the feeling that each of them quietly takes pleasure in the bond between them—and they still enjoy kidding me.

TASK: SHARED FATHERING

Have you thanked the stepfather for all he has done and for his contribution to your child's well-being? If not, write him a letter. Ask your mentors to go over it with you, and if they approve, mail it. If you decide instead to meet the stepfather for a talk, rehearse the conversation with your mentors so you'll be comfortable with what you want to say.

1. What other family members have been affected by your return?
2. What can you do to make peace with them?
3. Do your children know your parents? If not, what can you do to bring them together?
4. How can you let your children know you are glad they have a stepfather who loves them?
5. Do you have a strained or nonexistent relationship with your child's maternal grandparents? How can you improve it?
6. In what ways can you include your child's other siblings in your relationship?

Dealing with former in-laws can be difficult, but remember that this is about cleaning up *your* side of the street, whether or not they clean up theirs.

TASK: GRANDPARENTING

Your child's heritage does not begin and end with you and his mother. Your full lineage courses through your child's veins, as does that of his mother. Make it your business to acquaint your child with your family history. Reuniting him with his grandparents, if only for a moment, should be a top priority once your relationship is on solid ground. If that is impossible or impractical, acquaint him with your parents through photos and stories. You may wish to make for him, or with him, a photo album of your side of the family. If your parents are no longer living, perhaps there are other people in your life who could act as surrogate grandparents for your child.

EPILOGUE

My reunion with my son and the friendship we have forged is the most important thing in my life. Scott tells me that he too feels more connected than he did before. We talk weekly on the phone, he from Virginia, where he is working and Elizabeth is teaching, and I from Cambridge, Massachusetts, where I am attending graduate school. We keep track of each other's busy, peripatetic lives in a loving way. I look forward to our visits, grateful for the time we have ahead of us, no longer grieving for the time we lost.

Two years ago at Saint Vincent's Hospital in Santa Fe, New Mexico, I waited for the birth of my first grandchild, just as my father had in 1970. Scott was in the delivery room with Elizabeth; they'd been married for two years.

He had called me when it was time. I was directed to a little room with a Coke machine and six chairs. When I introduced myself at the nurses' station as the grandfather, they all giggled a little—I was only forty-one years old—but I didn't mind the teasing, and the nurses promised to come and get me when it was time to see the baby.

Sitting there, I found it impossible not to remember myself as a skinny seventeen-year-old father-to-be, anxiously pacing the maternity ward of Saint Ann's Hospital in Columbus, Ohio.

I am humbled by the grace in my life that allowed me to sit with my son as his first child was born. When I arrived at the delivery room feeling a little nervous, wanting to do it right, I said to Scott, "Be happy." What I meant to say was, "I love you, I am proud of you. Thank you for letting me be part of your life."

On the day of the birth of our grandchild, sad to say, much of the distance between Betsy and me remained unbridged. But in conversations since, I have been able to tell her how very much I had loved her and how I wish I had known better what to do as a father and husband. She recently told me that she had indeed loved me very much back then, all those years ago.

Now I send greetings and ask her about her and John and their other children. We talk about Scott. Scott says his mother now asks about me. That makes me smile.

Our granddaughter, Caroline, was born at 12:11 P.M. Mountain Standard Time. She weighed 9 pounds and was 22 inches long. When I walked into the delivery room, Elizabeth was nestling the new baby and Scott was on the phone to his mother, first on his list to be told the good news: "It's a girl. Mother and baby are doing fine."

Scott held Caroline for a moment and then gave her to me. I took my grandchild in my arms and held her close. In that instant I realized that I had not held a newborn baby since Scott's birth twenty-four years before. On that day the nurses had wheeled Betsy, my beautiful seventeen-year-old wife, out of the delivery room, her eyes so tired she could only stare and smile, her lips so dry and chapped that I had to swab them with lemon twists before she could whisper that she was all right and that she loved me. That moment, touching Betsy's face with my hand as she lay on the gurney, remains to this day the deepest feeling of love I have ever experienced. The smell of Scott's newborn hair is forever mingled with that memory.

This deeply felt moment of soul connection between Betsy and me on the day of Scott's birth was what I had drowned out for years. I remembered my nervous call to Betsy's mom, both of us weeping, when Scott was born.

And now I held Caroline. The look in her eyes seemed to say that she still felt connected to the other side but would resign herself to life on this one. She had long fingers, a full head of wispy blond hair, and a little smushed-up nose. She and I just looked at each other for a long time as I spoke to her in silly, hushed rhymes.

In this moment I was in fact happy. Happy for Scott and Elizabeth. Happy for Caroline. I was happy thinking of shopping for little baby gifts, doing some baby-sitting so that Scott and Elizabeth could get out a bit, teaching Caroline to count to 100, watching her grow up, watching my son grow up with her. Looking forward to growing up more myself.

I gave a quiet sigh when I saw the name tag on Caroline's wrist that did not carry my family name, a part of the damage from my exile that could not be undone. In my workshops for young fathers, I ask them to look five, ten, twenty years into the future and imagine what they want their life to be. How they want to be known by their child. How they want their child to be known by them. It always makes a big impression on them, some never having considered next week, let alone the next decade. I urge them to know their children, claim their fatherhood.

In the background I could hear Scott happily telling the story of Caroline's birth over and over again to family and friends. Rocking my grandchild in my arms, I was happy for the grace of having come full circle. Happy for the friends I had who would be over later to see the baby. Friends I wanted my grandchild to know.

It takes a whole village to raise a child. I am grateful that you and I get to be a part of it.

FOR MOTHERS

I asked Annie, a single mother whose ex has not seen their children in two years, if she was angry with him.

"No, I rarely think about him," she said.

"You don't have any deeply felt resentment or sadness about it? Is there nothing he could have done better?"

"Sure, there was plenty he could have done better. But I don't think about it. I don't have time to think about it."

"Susan Jeffers, in her book *Opening Our Hearts to Men,* says, 'To love requires that we let go of many preconceived notions and begin to see men, as well as ourselves, with new eyes,'" I told Annie.

"And what the hell does that mean?" she asked me.

"It means look at yourself and see what you're willing to do to help bridge the gap."

"I can't stand one more self-righteous man talking down to me," Annie snapped.

"Well, it didn't take long to get to the anger, I see." Annie and I both laughed.

"Well, all right. I wish my kids' dad would get it together. They want to know him."

"What might you do to help?" I pressed.

"God, you're pushy." Annie laughed.

"That's right. This is important. What do you think is in this for your kids?"

"Well . . ." Annie took a deep breath. "I may not like their father, but they may actually need him. To tell you the truth, sometimes I think I need him myself–not remarriage. God, no! Just another set of hands."

"Annie," I said, "if that's all you need, another set of hands, why don't you just hire them or borrow them?"

"All right," she conceded, "maybe I secretly feel they should be his hands. I can tell the kids feel that way."

"What does that mean?"

"It means I'm a good mother–a great mother–but they still want to know their father. Maybe it's just biology."

"Maybe."

"Or conditioning."

"Maybe."

"Maybe it doesn't matter what it is."

"Maybe not, Annie."

"Maybe I hate his guts?"

"Maybe. Want to change that?"

"NO." We both laughed again.

"How would you feel if you could put away that anger you said you didn't have?" I asked.

Annie laughed again. "Okay, you got me. I wish it were that easy."

> *Laughter is a tranquilizer with no side effects.*
>
> –ARNOLD GLASOW

Then I asked Annie to think about how she might help get the father back into her children's life.

"When you first asked me that question, Mark, I wanted to answer, 'What will I do? Not one damn thing.' Then I thought about it for a while.

"Yeah, it would be nice to be able to say that the kids' dad had them for the weekend, or that he was taking them to school. I even had to laugh as I imagined complaining about him to my girlfriends: 'He wants to take them for the weekend and I have plans for them,' or 'He always keeps Bobby up past his bedtime and then he's cranky with me.' You know, I almost began to cry when I realized how much I *have* missed not having his help.

"*I* could have a fuller life, too. Not just the kids. A reunion could help me. I would have more time for myself and *my* interests.

"The problem is, I just don't know how to help, and I can tell you this, I am NOT going to do it alone."

"I am not asking you to do it all," I answered. "Just wanting your children to be reunited with their father is a huge step."

Although Annie, a fireball, would hate to hear me say this, she is like many of the mothers with whom I have worked. Most mothers care passionately about their children. *You* must or you would not have this book in your hands.

I have listened to enough mothers to say with confidence that most of them, at the deepest levels of their heart, want their children to have everything, including the love of their father. [I also want to note here that there are some men (and women) who are so abusive that contact with them constitutes reopening a psychological wound rather than effecting a healing. Such men and women, however, are far fewer in number than our media or our anger might suggest. There are relatively few who could not be helped.]

> *Love, love, love, that is the soul of genius.*
>
> —WOLFGANG AMADEUS MOZART

In the years since Betsy and I divorced so painfully, I have often wished I could hug her and that we could mourn together, forgiving our younger selves for their broken dreams. This may never happen, and that fact makes me sad. Many of you may be in this situation. It is important that you know that a reunion between a father and child can still be a positive change for the child, even if it must happen in an atmosphere of less than ideal feelings between the mother and father.

You know the pain of your children who are estranged from their father as no one else does. Some of you may feel too angry at past trespasses to want that man in your child's life, some of you will feel too guilty at your own wrongs to let down your guard and accept help. But it is also the children we must consider here.

Most mothers believe their children need their fathers, but they are baffled about how to help achieve a reunion, and they ask, "Is that really *my* job?"

Good question.

I never recommend that anyone—father or mother—be near their children if they are harmful or abusive physically, emotionally, or spiritually. But I am asking that we all keep our hearts open to forgive when forgiveness is warranted and to know that redemption is possible. I have asked as much of the father, and I ask the same of you. For it is the relationship between you and the father that determines the quality and quantity of visitation.

Remember that the degree of your anger might be a measure of the sadness that you feel at the loss. Many of us hold anger or sadness for years without knowing how much of our energy it consumes. This haunting can take a huge emotional toll over time.

Many women think that because their ex is gone he no longer remembers her or the children. It is painful to think we can be forgotten. But I know only too well that men do not forget their wives and children. They often carry the same anger, sadness, or confusion as you do over the loss of your relationship. It haunts most men at a visceral level.

This is what I told Annie. And *knowing* this is the first step toward reunion.

ANNE OF A THOUSAND FACES

I have heard Annie's story from many women: first the indifference and then the anger; under that, the sense that their kids may need their dads and that they, as mothers, should listen to that need; and under that, the sense that maybe they are carrying a cross they would like to put down.

Let's talk first about the anger. It's often justified and it has probably been useful. Maybe there were times when you needed anger to get tough enough to set your boundaries and act as the man traditionally did, to bring home the paycheck and to steel yourself for the world. It was simply a survival mechanism. But anger is an emotion that kills. It is useful only in small doses or in short bursts.

As one mother said, "I was so mad for so long it damaged my ability to be open to another marriage. Had I been able to grieve and lighten up, my child might have had a stepfather and I a new mate."

Reading this, you may say, "Who needs a new mate? Who wants one?" But many women do.

> H*elp thy brother's boat across and lo! thine own has reached shore.*
>
> —HINDU PROVERB

"I'm very aware that my child deserves more support than I can give by myself, and I deserve support too, by which I don't mean just the money," says Julie.

THE MONEY

Okay, what about the money?

"He owes me money," many women tell me.

"I want the money and then we'll talk."

This isn't only anger speaking. It is also pragmatism. Mothers know all too well the financial costs of raising a child. Certainly the father should help financially, and I have told them to do that—and a whole lot more. Of course you need the money for the rent, the food, the Nikes, the telephone bill, the electric bill, the Halloween costumes, the Little League, the ice skates. You should not have to bear these costs alone. If you read this book, and I hope you do, you will see that I have said exactly that to men. I have also said I am a pragmatist and what matters to me is what works in helping to heal the relationship between you and

> T*he principal thing in this world is to keep one's soul aloft.*
>
> —GUSTAVE FLAUBERT

your children's father so that everyone—especially the kids—benefits.

I want to talk about money further and ask you to take a few deep breaths and read on. It is important that you know that money is the most volatile issue in the reunion process. Perhaps because of its crucial role in everyday life it becomes a symbol, particularly for the man, of his value. Men in our society are often judged by what they earn, not who they are. They resent handing over money to women without any say in how it is spent or without any regard for the less tangible but important contributions they make in raising their children. Think about it—would you want to be treated as if you could be replaced in your children's life by a check every month? How would you feel if your children lived with their father and you paid child support and had circumscribed visiting days? (For the record, women in this situation do not pay court-ordered child support with any better regularity than men.) Do you see how your child's father might feel discounted? This is why money is the most highly charged area of conflict during a separation.

> Learning is discovering that something is possible.
>
> —FRITZ PERLS

To the ex-husband, demands for money make him feel he was never loved for who he was but only for what he earned. To the ex-wife, consistent financial support shows her that he cares for her welfare and the needs of their children. In other words, money means completely different things emotionally to each parent. When these feelings get miscommunicated, they cause many of the post-divorce battles.

"Money talks," Beth reminds me. "When my ex ponied up a more reasonable amount toward helping out, I began to think maybe he was serious about being a real parent. Maybe that's being hard-hearted. I thought of it as being hardheaded."

Like Beth, you may want to ask for some money as a show of faith if your ex is behind in his child support. Most prodigal fathers will be. Other women choose not to make money the first issue.

"I had to really think about this one," Judith, a divorced single mother of two, told me. "In my case—and I'm not saying this is right for everybody—I decided it was more important that the kids see their dad. Over the years since he's been back, he's *never* contributed on a you-can-count-on-it-monthly basis. What he has done is helped with their education, taken them on trips, done a lot to broaden their horizons. Several times our son has lived with his dad instead of with me, and that's been good for him. Yes, I'd have liked more money that I could count on, but I think what the kids got was worth my compromising."

The danger in demanding that financial debts be satisfied before the father attempts to effect a reunion is that the issues of guilt and abandonment may be so volatile as to blow up the bridge being built toward one another.

Charles Ballard, who has reunited many inner-city fathers, has proven that even under these difficult conditions, when a father is given a chance to know his children, he is motivated to get a job. Ballard found that these men will help financially 90 percent of the time, even when their earning power is minimal.

It will take a lot of forgiveness, acceptance, and patience to build this important bridge. I suggest to mothers that they let the father connect from his heart. The money will follow. I always suggest returning fathers pay something, no matter how little, as a show of good faith. I ask that mothers accept the money, seeing it as a beginning. When there is no money, begin anyway. It will pay many dividends in the long run that can't be counted.

> I*f you judge people, you have no time to love them.*
>
> —MOTHER TERESA

Despite—or maybe because of—the financial struggles with your child's father, your compassion will pave the way for reunion.

Deborah, a nurse at a Los Angeles hospital, recently

cleared the way for the return of her thirteen-year-old son's prodigal father.

"I knew Jack didn't have any money," she explains, "so I decided to forget about the money for a while, and we concentrated on building Jack's connection with Kenny, our son.

"I told Jack, 'You have to grow on him. You have to earn his respect and love, because Kenny loved you unconditionally at age seven, and then he was hurt by your leaving. Now you have to make up for all that. Kenny is very guarded. It's going to take a lot for him to do a turnaround.'"

Deborah says Jack seemed to be at a loss as to what to do with Kenny when he took him for the weekend. "I told Jack that half of being a parent is just being bored together at home. Sitting there, talking to him, listening when he needs to talk, getting out the Band-Aids if he scrapes his knee, or doing nothing. Just putting in time together.

"Jack finally realized that the money he sends me is for his *SON*. He stopped blaming me. This was a big thing, because a man's relationship with his child is his own. It really has nothing to do with me—that is, beyond a certain amount of compromise."

When I ask Deborah what she would tell other mothers, she says, "It's necessary to avoid making up a fantasy relationship between your child's father and the child just because you want your child to be happy. Let it be the father's responsibility to make a relationship and to pay the money he owes. Then just step back for a while." You have to keep your relationship with the father totally separate from the kid's relationship with his dad.

MAKING IT WORK

Barbara, a thirty-eight-year-old mother of three children, ages six, nine, and twelve, made it through her divorce with a solid working relationship with both her children and their father.

"When I left my husband, my daughter was two and a half; she was a baby, and I felt that she needed to see both of us all the time. So he keeps the kids half the week and I keep the kids half the week."

When I ask Barbara how she has managed to stay so friendly, she laughs. "Sometimes we're friendly, and sometimes we're not. It's still a touch-and-go thing. For example, I had a fight with my boyfriend one night, and the kids told their father about it. He called me up right away and said, 'I don't want my kids around this.'

> I*t is extraordinary how extraordinary the ordinary person is.*
>
> —GEORGE F. WILL

"I said, 'That's really interesting. First of all, you have absolutely no business . . .' et cetera, et cetera. When the kids are with him, I expect him to be a responsible person, just as I am a responsible person when they're with me."

Barbara says she sometimes still regrets the failure of her marriage: "All he had to do was call and say, 'I'm sorry.' But he never would."

Barbara got help for herself, and that made all the difference, she says. "He always loved the kids; I never doubted that." Counseling helped her and her children work through their anger over losing their father.

"I'm proud of the way we handled our divorce. The judge said, in front of everybody, 'I want to say I'm really impressed with the effort these two people made to work out a plan that really seems best for their kids.'"

Barbara beams with pride as she finishes the story: "And I was happy that their father wanted the kids in his life and that he felt love from them. I knew we had really tried, and after all else had failed between us, we at least did what was best for the kids. The kids are thriving."

Remember, we are working for a better future with your child. The trick in most reunions is for everyone to stretch their comfort zone without violating their own integrity. You can expect that your children's father (who has read this book and is reaching for reunion) will listen to your comments, compromise in areas of disagreement, and commit to consistent involvement in the future of your children.

> We blame little things in others and pass over great things in ourselves; we are quick enough to perceiving and weighing what we suffer from others but we mind not what others suffer from us.
>
> —THOMAS À KEMPIS

Listen very carefully first to yourself and then to the prodigal father who is seeking to return. You must satisfy yourself that he is earnest. This may take compassion on your part and a considerable effort on his.

This book contains a workable plan for the reunion of fathers and children, a tested campaign for changing a man's life, and therefore the lives of those to whom he owes, and wants to give, his allegiance. If the father of your children, a man you once loved, has worked with this book or chooses to when you give it to him, he will be a better father.

I hope with all my heart that you give him the chance.

A QUIZ FOR MOTHERS

1. Which of their father's good traits do you see in your children? Write about them: physical, emotional, mental (for example, the way they approach a challenge, etc.), scholastic, the way they walk, and so forth.

2. Have you told the children about these traits and qualities? You might want to set aside an afternoon to do this, perhaps while you're doing a family project. Very often, the best conversations occur while hiking, painting bookshelves, or raking leaves.

3. What did you like about their father? Do the children know this? You might want to write about this before sharing with the children. Writing might bring up some strong emotions, both bad and good.

4. What did you enjoy doing with their father? Have you told the kids or done the same things with them?
5. Plan an outing that will include some of the activities you and their father enjoyed together. Write about it afterward. What things did the kids seem to take to and what things did they shy away from?
6. What were their father's negative traits? If strong feelings of anger begin to nag at you, power-write for five minutes without stopping. This may help you deal with these feelings.

> *This above all, to refuse to be a victim. Unless I can do that I can do nothing.*
>
> —MARGARET ATWOOD

7. In what ways are you bitter toward or contemptuous of their father? Have you communicated this to your kids? In what ways have you softened toward him? Write about it.
8. Write about ways in which you have offered your children a more balanced perspective now than you used to. (Congratulate yourself, too.)
9. Write about ways in which you might offer an even more positive perspective.
10. How do you feel about this man now? (Again, the five-minute power-writing exercise may be cathartic for you.) Are you willing to allow that feeling to change? Put your ideal down on paper. Are you willing to forgive him now? Write about why or why not. Are you willing to forgive yourself now? Write about that.

SPIRITUAL SIT-UPS

Read through this book if you have not already done so. Allow yourself to answer the questions at the end each chapter, rewording them to fit your situation. What would your Narrative Time Line say? How would your inventory read? Can you remember to do the same self-care that I ask of the fathers?

Are you doing any daily prayer? Writing? Exercise? Who are your supportive friends? Take as good care of yourself as you do of your children.

Reading this book in its entirety will give you a new insight into fathers and children and may help you feel better along the way. I ask you to read it with an open mind and an open heart.

ONE LAST WORD

We are the product of a thousand generations of evolution—of births and deaths and joy and laughter and kindness and cruelty and lust and forgiveness. We have come too far to let our society break down, our children become disenfranchised.

The price children are paying across America today is too high.

It is time to remember the power of our national dream of honor and freedom, a dream that still inspires men and women to make their way to our country over deserts, rivers, and oceans. We must not let this light of freedom be dimmed from the inside.

Now is the time to stand again with gratitude and joy for what we have built and, despite our individual differences, to work together to lend a hand to our aged, our fathers, mothers, and especially our children.

A GUIDE TO STARTING
A STUDY GROUP

BEGINNING

This guide will help you get started with a support team. I recommend that you find several people, fathers if possible, and meet weekly to discuss with each other your reunion or ongoing parenting. Just one other person will do, more is better. Set a date, and start with whoever shows up.

You can meet one week at your house, the next week at another member's house, and so on, or rent an empty room in a church or a school if the group gets too big. I like the circle as a form: Put the chairs in a circle in the living room, or around a big dining room table, whatever is convenient. If the group becomes too big, then break into groups of four, so you will have more time to talk.

USE A TWELVE-WEEK SCHEDULE

An initial commitment of one weekly meeting for a minimum of twelve weeks is a good time frame. If it takes longer, it's all right. Many groups stay together for a year or more; that is up to the group. Be as democratic as possible, voting on all decisions that affect the group.

Group meetings need not take more than an hour or two–time for everyone to "check in." You'll be checking in about your journal writing (do not read your personal journals–they are private), tasks from the book, your general mood and any insights, problems or successes you may have had since the last meeting. Be sure to focus on the positive; reframe your failures by reflecting on what you learned from the experience.

You can use the exercises in the book as a starting point. Write your answers to all the questions in a notebook you will keep. Each week, answer several questions in group and then share your answers with each other, going around the circle one by one. Those fathers who are living with or visiting their children will be surprised at how much this work can provide insight into their parenting, and their experiences will be very helpful to those fathers working toward reunion.

There may be teachers, therapists, or facilitators who will use the book to guide others. This is good, but not required. This is meant to be a group process rather than a teaching situation, egalitarian rather than hierarchical. Most groups work fine. Most often, the group will be a collective composed of all who wish to walk the path to reunion where each person is equally a part, no one more than another.

LISTEN

We each get what we need from the group process by sharing our own material and by *listening* to others. We do not need to comment on another person's contribution in order to help that person. We must refrain from trying to "fix" someone else. Each group has a unique blend of individuals, and will therefore have a unique cooperative "voice."

When listening, go around the circle, without commenting unduly on what is heard. The circle, as a form, is very important. We are intended to witness, not control, one another. When sharing answers with the group, take your time and try not to be ashamed to talk about your mistakes—everyone has made them. A behavior is an action, it is not a person. Your mistakes are behaviors you can change, they are *not* who you are.

Remember to share your successes, too. Many men are as shy about revealing their good points as their problem areas. The important thing to remember is that the meeting is sacred and what is shared there among the members is *not* to be shared with anyone outside that room. You are there to give each other support—not to judge each other, or to "therapize each other."

It is important that others hear you speak your truth, and that you give them the chance to speak theirs, without shaming anyone. Shame is a very destructive force. Try to see everyone as "God's children," and work to accept them unconditionally. Keep your communication worded in the "I" statements: "I think," "I was," "I did," "I felt."

RESPECT EACH OTHER

Be certain that respect as well as compassion is accorded equally to every member. Each person must be able to speak about his own sadness, anger, hopes, and dreams. This is a deep and powerful internal process. There is no one "right way" to do this. Love is important. Be kind to yourself. Be kind to one another.

When members of the group express their emotions, give them the dignity of experiencing the emotion without touching them. Any communication takes them out of the moment. The best way to react to another's strong feelings or tears is to just sit quietly, respecting the other person's right to express them. As men, we have been trained to suppress our emotions, and it may take some practice for you to know how to accept the feelings of others, as well as your own. Try to experience your emotions when they happen without stuffing or denying them, and sense what feelings another person's emotions cause you. (If someone in your group expresses strong emotions, you may wish to reassure them quietly after the meeting is over.)

Often, after strong emotions have been expressed and released, laughter or joy will fill the room. This is why I call this work not "grief work," but "Joy Work." Learning to experience emotions in ourselves and others is one of the most important things this process will teach us.

EXPECT CHANGE IN THE GROUP MAKEUP

Many people will–and some will not–fulfill the 12-week commitment. Know that there is often a rebellious period within the initial 12 weeks, or even afterward, and that some people will return to the process later. When they do, they often find that the process has continued to unfold internally for them.

Many groups drift apart at about the tenth week because of feelings of loss associated with the group's approaching end. Face that truth as a fellowship by talking about it. You may decide to stay together. If your group breaks up, and you want to continue, find another group. You can find group members by posting a notice in bookstores, contacting a therapist or member of the clergy, or asking friends to help.

BE AUTONOMOUS

Know that you cannot control your own process, let alone anyone else's. You may feel stubborn at times: you won't want to work on your Narrative Time Line, or write in your journal. This is common. You cannot do this process perfectly, so relax, be kind to yourself, and hold on to your hat. This is a deepening into your true self, your own intuition, your "higher purpose." This process will take you across the bridge toward your biggest self–and to your children and the future.

BE SELF-LOVING

You may tend to judge yourself or others harshly. This is the "old you" trying to stay disconnected–putting up more resistance. It need not stop the process. Lighten up and keep a sense of humor and self-love.

If there is a facilitator in your group and he feels somehow "wrong" to you, be alert to the possibility that this may also be resistance. And remember that you can always change clusters or start your own. Continually seek other guidance, *and* listen to your own inner wisdom. You have many of your own answers within you; use your time of journaling, solitude, and prayer to find them.

A WORD TO THERAPISTS AND MEMBERS OF THE CLERGY

Thank you for the wonderful work you do in important and often difficult professions. Men and women like you helped save my life and taught me how to build a new one. I will be eternally grateful.

While many of you will use this book with your clients, or use it in facilitating groups of your own, I would like to ask that you work through the exercises yourself—so that you might explore your own feelings about parenting issues and your relationship with your children or father. This will keep the group process clear and add to your own growth.

Many therapists and members of the clergy I know have a hard time taking care of themselves and forget how emotionally challenging the work of counseling can be. Find good supervision and a place to recharge your batteries. You have a sacred trust. Thank you for keeping it.

PASS IT ON

It is my hope that you will send me stories of your reunions, let me hear of your problems and your successes. You may write to me, care of The Father Project, P.O. Box 38-26-66, Cambridge, MA 02238-2666, (617) 547-6726. Or contact *The Prodigal Father* web page on the internet at http://www.randomhouse.com/. Either way, allow me some time to answer.

To those of you running peer group clusters, if you follow the spiritual practice of tithing, I recommend you work to reunite an estranged father, comfort a single mother, or lighten a sad child's burden. Buy someone the book, and pass it on.

BIBLIOGRAPHY

Though I have found all of the following books helpful, I have marked the *must-read* books with an asterisk.

Amneus, Daniel. *The Garbage Generation.* Alhambra, Ca.: Primrose Press, 1990.

Arterburn, Stephen, and Jack Felton. *Toxic Faith.* Nashville: Oliver-Nelson Books, 1991.

Aziz, Robert. *C. G. Jung's Psychology of Religion and Synchronicity.* Albany, N.Y.: New York University Press, 1990.

* Bachrach, Arthur. *Psychological Research.* New York: Random House, 1962.

* Blankenhorn, David. *Fatherless America.* New York: BasicBooks, 1995.

* Bly, Robert. *Iron John.* Boston: Addison-Wesley Publishing, 1990.

Bowlby, John. *A Secure Base.* New York: BasicBooks, 1988.

Brazelton, T. Berry, M.D. *Touchpoints.* Boston: Addison-Wesley Publishing, 1992.

Brendtro, Larry K. Martin Brokenleg, and Steve Van Bockern. *Reclaiming Youth at Risk.* Bloomington, In.: National Educational Service, 1990.

Bryan, Mark, and Julia Cameron. *The Money Drunk.* New York: Ballantine Books, 1992.

Burns, E. Timothy. *From Risk to Resilience.* Dallas: Marco Polo Publishers, 1994.

* Cameron, Julia. *The Artist's Way.* New York: Tarcher, 1992.

Cameron, Julia. *The Vein of Gold.* New York: Tarcher, 1992.

Carnoy, Martin, and David Carnoy. *Fathers of a Certain Age.* Winchester, Ma.: Faber and Faber, 1995.

Chomsky, Noam, and Edward Herman. *Manufacturing Consent: The Political Economy of the Mass Media.* New York: Pantheon Books, 1988.

Clinton, Hillary Rodham. *It Takes a Village.* New York: Simon & Schuster, 1996.

Corneau, Guy. *Absent Fathers, Lost Sons.* Boston: Shambhala Publications, Inc. 1991.

Ducey, Charles. *Basic Techniques of Psychodynamic Psychotherapy,* "Suggestion: History and Theory." 1986.

Edelman, Hope. *Motherless Daughters*. Boston: Addison-Wesley Publishing Company, 1994.

Erikson, Erik H. *Childhood and Society*. New York: W. W. Norton & Company, 1950, rep. 1963.

* Farrell, Warren, Ph.D. *The Myth of Male Power*. New York: Berkley Publishing, 1994.

Fisher, Helen E. *Anatomy of Love*. New York: W. W. Norton & Company, Inc., 1992.

Gaylin, Willard, M.D. *Male Ego*. New York: Penguin Books, 1992.

Gardner, Howard. *Frames of Mind*. New York: BasicBooks, 1983.

* Gilligan, Carol, and Lyn Mikel Brown. *Meeting at the Crossroads: Women's Psychology and Girl's Development*. Cambridge, Mass.: Harvard University Press, 1992.

* Gilligan, Carol. *In a Different Voice*. Cambridge, Mass.: Harvard University Press, 1993.

* Gilligan, James. *Violence: Our Deadly Epidemic and Its Causes*. New York: G. P. Putnam and Sons, 1996.

Glazner, Greg. *From the Iron Chair*. New York: W. W. Norton, 1992.

Goldstein, Joseph, Anna Freud, and J. Albert Solnit. *Before the Best Interests of the Child*. New York: The Free Press, 1979.

Goldstein, Joseph, Anna Freud, and J. Albert Solnit. *Beyond the Best Interests of the Child*. New York: The Free Press, 1979.

Goldstein, Joseph, Anna Freud, and J. Albert Solnit. *In the Best Interests of the Child*. New York: The Free Press, 1986.

Griswold, Robert L. *Fatherhood in America*. New York: BasicBooks, 1993.

* Havens, L. *Making Contact: Uses of Language in Psychotherapy*. Cambridge, Mass.: Harvard University Press, 1986.

James, John W., and Frank Cherry. *The Grief Recovery Handbook*. New York: Harper & Row, 1988.

Johnson, Spencer, M.D. *The One Minute Father*. New York: Candle Communications Corp., 1993.

Keen, Sam. *Fire in the Belly*. New York: Bantam Books, 1991.

Kegan, Robert. *The Evolving Ego*. Cambridge, Mass.: Harvard University Press, 1982.

Kimbrell, Andrew. *The Masculine Mystique*. New York: Ballantine, 1995.

Kozol, Jonathan. *Savage Inequalities*. New York: Crown Publishers, Inc., 1991.

Lewis, C. S. *Miracles.* New York: Macmillan Publishing Company, 1947, rep. 1960.

* Masterson, James. *The Search for the Real Self.* New York: BasicBooks, 1992.

* Meade, Michael. *Men and the Water of Life.* San Francisco: HarperSan-Francisco, 1993.

Medved, Michael. *Hollywood vs. America.* New York: Harper Collins, 1992.

O'Hagan, Kieran. *Emotional and Psychological Abuse of Children.* Toronto & Buffalo: University of Toronto Press, 1993.

Osherson, Samuel. *Finding Our Fathers.* New York: Ballantine, 1983.

* Peck, Scott M., M.D. *The Road Less Traveled.* New York: Touchstone, 1978.

Reiss, Albert J., Jeffrey A. Roth. *Understanding and Preventing Violence.* Washington, D.C.: National Academy Press, 1993.

* Ricci, Isolina, Ph.D. *Mom's House, Dad's House.* New York: Macmillan Publishing, 1980.

Schenk, Roy U., and John Everingham. *Men Healing Shame.* New York: Springer Publishing Company, 1995.

Sloan, Bob. *Dad's Own CookBook.* New York: Workman Publishing, 1993.

Smith, Huston. *The World's Religions.* New York: HarperCollins Publishing, 1991.

Smith, Huston. *Forgotten Truth.* New York: HarperCollins Publishers, 1992.

Stettbacher, Konrad J. *Making Sense of Suffering.* New York: Penguin Books, 1993.

Wallerstein, Judith S., and Sandra Blakeslee. *Second Chances.* New York: Ticknor & Fields, 1989.

* Vaillant, George. *The Wisdom of the Ego.* Cambridge, Mass.: Harvard University Press, 1995.

* Weissbourd, Richard. *The Vulnerable Child.* Boston: Addison-Wesley Publishing, 1996.

Yalom, Irvin D. *The Theory and Practice of Group Psychotherapy,* 3rd Edition. New York: BasicBooks, 1985.

RESEARCH SOURCES

I have used more than 150 journal articles, dissertations, and books in my research for *The Prodigal Father*. Below is a partial list. A complete list is available from:

The Father Project
P.O. Box 38-26-66
Cambridge, MA 02238-2666

Abarbanel, A. (1979). *Shared parenting after separation and divorce: A study of joint custody*. American Journal of Orthopsychiatry, Apr., Vol. 49(2), 320–329.

Ahrons, Constance R. (1983). *Predictors of paternal involvement postdivorce: Mothers' and fathers' perceptions*. U. Wisconsin, Madison. Journal of Divorce, Spr., Vol. 6(3), 55–69.

Amato, Paul R. (1987). *Family processes in one-parent, stepparent, and intact families: The child's point of view*. Australian Inst. of Family Studies, Melbourne, Victoria, Australia. Journal of Marriage & the Family, May, Vol. 49(2), 327–337.

Ames, Laurie A. (1992). *Open adoptions: Truth and consequences*. U. Alabama School of Law, Law & Psychology Review, Tuscaloosa. Law & Psychology Review, Spr., Vol. 16, 137–152.

Arditti, Joyce A. (1992). *Differences between fathers with joint custody and non-custodial fathers*. Virginia Polytechnic Inst. & State U., Blacksburg. American Journal of Orthopsychiatry, Apr., Vol. 62(2), 186–195.

Arditti, Joyce A. (1992). *Factors related to custody, visitation, and child support for divorced fathers: An exploratory analysis*. Virginia Polytechnic Inst. & State U., Blacksburg. Journal of Divorce & Remarriage, Vol. 17(3–4), 23–42.

Barling, J. (1986). *Fathers' work experiences, the father-child relationship and children's behaviour*. Queen's U., Kingston, Canada. Journal of Occupational Behaviour, Jan., Vol. 7(1), 61–66.

Berman, Barbara G. (1983). *Parents' perceptions of the non-custodial father's post-divorce influence on children*. Michigan State U. Dissertation Abstracts International, Mar., Vol. 43(9–B), 2867.

Bertrand, Jeanne A. (1984). *What might have been–what could be: Working with the grief of children in long-term care*. Keele Conference: Children: Loss and growth (1984, Keele, England). Columbia U. Journal of Social Work Practice, Nov., Vol. 1(3), 23–41.

Borduin, Charles M.; Henggeler, Scott W. (1987). *Post-divorce mother-son relations of delinquent and well-adjusted adolescents.* U. Missouri, Columbia. Journal of Applied Developmental Psychology, July-Sep., Vol. 8(3), 273–88.

Bowlby, J. (1982). *Attachment and loss: Retrospect and prospect.* Tavistock Clinic, London, England. American Journal of Orthopsychiatry, Oct., Vol. 52(4), 664–78.

Boyd, Donald A.; Parish, Thomas S. (1984). *An investigation of father loss and college students' androgyny scores.* Journal of Genetic Psychology. Kansas State U., Office of Educational Resources, Manhattan. Dec.

Bruce, Martha L.; Kim, Kathleen M. (1992). *Differences in the effects of divorce on major depression in men and women.* Yale U. School of Medicine, New Haven, CT. American Journal of Psychiatry, July, Vol. 149(7), 914–17.

Colburn, Kenneth; Lin, Phylis L.; Moore, Mary C. (1992). *Gender and the divorce experience.* Butler U., IN. Journal of Divorce & Remarriage, Vol. 17(3–4), 87–108.

Counts, Robert M. (1991). *Second and third divorces: The flood to come.* New York U. Medical Ctr. School of Medicine, Family Therapy Program. Journal of Divorce & Remarriage, Vol. 17(1–2), 193–200.

Darden, Ellen C.; Zimmerman, Toni S. (1992). *Blended families: A decade review, 1979 to 1990.* Virginia Polytechnic Inst. & State U., Marriage & Family Therapy Program, Blacksburg. Family Therapy, Vol. 19(1), 25–31.

Dixon, Samuel L. (1991). *Contributions of cultural, social and psychological factors to the etiology of alcoholism in African Americans.* Ohio State U., Coll. of Social Work. Western Journal of Black Studies, Fall, Vol. 15(3), 133–37.

Dupree, Deborah J. (1984). *The effects of changes in the family structure on the development of adolescents.* U. South Carolina. Dissertation Abstracts International, Mar., Vol. 44 (9–A), 2898.

Duryee, Mary (1992). *Mandatory court mediation: Demographic summary and consumer evaluation of one court service: Executive summary.* Alameda County Superior Court, Family Court Services, Oakland, CA. Family & Conciliation Courts Review, Apr., Vol. 30(2), 260–67.

Elliot, Faith R. (1978). *Occupational commitments and paternal deprivation.* Lanchester Polytechnic, Coventry, England. Child Care, Health & Development, Sep.–Oct., Vol. 4(5), 305–15.

Elster, Arthur B.; Lamb, Michael E. (1982). *Adolescent fathers: A group potentially at risk for parenting failure.* U. Utah Medical Ctr., Dept. of Pediatrics, Salt Lake City. Infant Mental Health Journal, Fall, Vol. 3(3), 148–54.

Friedman, Henry J. (1980). *The father's parenting experience in divorce.* Tufts U. School of Medicine, American Journal of Psychiatry, Oct., Vol. 137(10), 1177–82.

Friedman, Henry J. (1982). *The challenge of divorce to adequate fathering: The peripheral father in marriage and divorce.* Harvard Medical School, Boston. Psychiatric Clinics of North America, Dec., Vol. 5(3), 565–80.

Gale, Jerry; Newfield, N. (1992). *A conversation analysis of a solution-focused marital therapy session.* U. Georgia, Athens. Journal of Marital & Family Therapy, Apr., Vol. 18(2), 153–65.

Gerasch, Johna C. (1984). *Adolescent female adjustment: Is it family type or family functioning?* U. Wisconsin, Madison. Dissertation Abstracts International, Sep., Vol. 45(3–B), 1037.

Goldstein, Harris S. (1984). *Parental composition, supervision, and conduct problems in youths 12 to 17 years old.* U. of Medicine & Dentistry of New Jersey–Rutgers Medical School, Piscataway. Journal of the American Academy of Child Psychiatry, Nov., Vol. 23(6), 679–84.

Greif, Judith B. (1982). *Therapy with remarriage families: IV. The father-child relationship subsequent to divorce.* Yeshiva U., Albert Einstein Coll. of Medicine, Div. of Child & Adolescent Psychiatry. Family Therapy Collections, Vol. 2, 47–57.

Grisso, Thomas (1990). *Evolving guidelines for divorce/custody evaluations.* Meeting of the Southwest Region of the Association of Family and Conciliation Courts (1988, Phoenix, Arizona). U. Massachusetts Medical Ctr. Family & Conciliation Courts Review, June, Vol. 28(1), 35–41.

Hingst, Ann G.; Hyman, Bruce M.; Salmon, Joy L. (1985). *Male children of divorce grown up: Parental bonding, relationship satisfaction, commitment and sex role identification.* Florida State U. Australian Journal of Sex, Marriage & Family, Feb., Vol. 6(1), 15–32.

Huttunen, Matti O.; Niskanen, P. (1979). *Prenatal loss of father and psychiatric disorders.* U. Helsinki, Finland. Annual Progress in Child Psychiatry & Child Development, 331–38.

Imbrogno, S. (1991). *A transcultural analysis of families in complex systems.* Ohio State U., Coll. of Social Work, Columbus. International Social Work, Jan., Vol. 34(1), 69–82.

Isaacs, Marla B.; Leon, George H.; Kline, M. (1987). *When is a parent out of the picture? Different custody, different perceptions.* Philadelphia Child Guidance Clinic, Families of Divorce Project, PA. Family Process, Mar., Vol. 26(1), 101–10.

Jacobs, John W. (1982). *The effect of divorce on fathers: An overview of the literature.* Montefiore Hosp. & Medical Ctr., Dept. of Psychiatry Outpatient Div., Bronx, NY. American Journal of Psychiatry, Oct., Vol. 139(10), 1235–41.

Kelly, Joan B. (1989). *Mediated and adversarial divorce: Respondents' perceptions of their processes and outcomes.* Norhtern California Mediation Ctr., Corte Madera. Mediation Quarterly, Sum., No. 24, 71–88.

Koch, Mary A.; Lowery, Carol R. (1984). *Visitation and the noncustodial father.* Journal of Divorce, Win., Vol. 8(2), 47–65.

Kressel, Kenneth; Butler-DeFreitas, Frances; Forlenza, Samuel G.; Wilcox, Cynthia (1989). *Research in contested custody mediations: An illustration of the case study method.* Rutgers U., Newark, NJ. Mediation Quarterly, Sum., No. 24, 55–70.

Kruk, E. (1992). *Psychological and structural factors contributing to the disengagement of noncustodial fathers after divorce.* Special Issue: Gender. U. British Columbia, Vancouver, Canada. Family & Conciliation Courts Review, Jan., Vol. 30(1), 81–101.

Lange, Linda D. (1991). *The achievement patterns of early adolescents in intact, remarried, and divorced families.* U. Michigan. Dissertation Abstracts International, Sep., Vol. 52(3–A), 850–51.

Little, Margaret A. (1992). *The impact of the custody plan on the family: A five-year follow-up: Executive summary.* Los Angeles County Superior Court, CA. Family & Conciliation Courts Review, Apr., Vol. 30(2), 243–51.

MacKinnon, Kenneth R. (1984). *Factors relevant to child adjustment in single parent families.* York U., Toronto, Canada. Dissertation Abstracts International, Feb., Vol. 44(8–B).

Maida, Peter R. (1991). *Child support guidelines: A conflict analysis.* Council of Better Business Bureaus, Alternative Dispute Resolution Div. Family & Conciliation Courts Review, Oct., Vol. 29(4), 429–47.

Maier, Karen V. (1985). *Children of divorce: Adolescent female self-concept, attitudes, counseling needs, and father-daughter relationships.* U. Michigan. Dissertation Abstracts International, Jan., Vol. 45(7–A).

Mendonca, M. M. (1977). *Pedopsychiatric study of the children of alcoholic parents.* Hosp. Sobral Cid, Coimbra, Portugal. Revue de Neuropsychiatrie Infantile et d'Hygiene Mentale de l'Enfance, July, Vol. 25(7), 411–28.

March, Karen A. (1992). *The stranger who bore me: Adoptee-birth mother interactions.* McMaster U., Hamilton, ON, Canada. Dissertation Abstracts International, Apr., Vol. 52(10–A), 3738.

Moberly, Elizabeth R. (1986). *Attachment and separation: The implications for gender identity and for the structuralization of the self: A theoretical model for transsexualism, and homosexuality.* Psychiatric Journal of the University of Ottawa, Dec., Vol. 11(4), 205–08.

Moran, Patricia; Barclay, A. (1988). *Effect of fathers' absence on deliquent boys: Dependency and hypermasculinity.* St. Louis U., MO. Psychological Reports, Feb., Vol. 62(1), 115–21.

Mulkey, Lynn M.; Crain, Robert L.; Harrington, Alexander J. (1992). *One-parent households and achievement: Economic and behavioral explanations of a small effect.* Hofstra U., Hempstead, NY. Sociology of Education, Jan., Vol. 65(1), 48–65.

Nelson, Geoffrey B. (1980). *Families coping with the loss of father by death or divorce.* U. Manitoba, Winnipeg, Canada. Dissertation Abstracts International, Feb., Vol. 40(8–B), 3956–57.

Paasch, Kathleen M.; Teachman, Jay D. (1991). *Gender of children and receipt of assistance from absent fathers.* Special Issue: Families, poverty, and public policies. U. Maryland. Journal of Family Issues, Dec., Vol. 12(4), 450–66.

Peat, Barbara J.; Winfree, L. (1992). *Reducing the intrainstitutional effects of "prisonization": A study of a therapeutic community for drug-using inmates.*

Annual Meetings of the American Society of Criminology (1980, Baltimore, Maryland). New Mexico State U. Criminal Justice & Behavior, June, Vol. 19(2), 206–25.

Peele, Stanton (1992). *Alcoholism, politics and bureaucracy: The consensus against controlled-drinking therapy in America.* Addictive Behaviors, Vol. 17(1), 49–62.

Persons, Suzanne P. (1990). *The adult daughter's experience of abandonment by the father: A phenomenological investigation.* Union Inst., OH. Dissertation Abstracts International, Sep., Vol. 51(3-B), 1480.

Peters, Donald L.; Stewart, Robert B. (1991). *Father-child interactions in a shopping mall: A naturalistic study of father role behavior.* Pennsylvania State U., Div. of Individual & Family Studies, University Park. Journal of Genetic Psychology, June, Vol. 138(2), 269–78.

Ruffin, Wilma J. (1991). *Paternal involvement of divorced fathers related to marital status, custody arrangements, and beliefs about the amount of child support paid.* U. Minnesota. Dissertation Abstracts International, Nov., Vol. 52(5-A), 1910.

Santrock, John W. (1987). *The effects of divorce on adolescents: Needed research perspectives.* U. Texas-Dallas, Richardson. Family Therapy, Vol. 14(2), 147–59.

Schalin, Lars-Johan. (1983). *Phallic integration and male identity development: Aspects on the importance of the father relation to boys in the latency period.* Scandinavian Psychoanalytic Review, Vol. 6(1), 21–42.

Serovich, Julianne M.; Price, Sharon J.; Chapman, Steven F.; Wright, David W. (1992). *Attachment between former spouses: Impact on co-parental communication and parental involvement.* Annual Conference on Family Relations (1988, Philadelphia, Pennsylvania). U. Georgia. Journal of Divorce & Remarriage, Vol. 17(3-4), 109–19.

Sevér, Aysan; Pirie, M. (1991). *Factors that enhance or curtail the social functioning of female single parents: A path analysis.* U. Toronto, Scarborough Coll., ON, Canada. Family & Conciliation Courts Review, July, Vol. 29(3), 318–37.

Smollar, Jacqueline; Youniss, James (1985). *Parent-adolescent relations in adolescents whose parents are divorced. Special Issue: Contemporary approaches to the study of families with adolescents.* Catholic U. of America, Ctr. for the Study of Youth Development. Journal of Early Adolescence, Spr., Vol. 5(1), 129–44.

Soth, Nancy; Levy, Daniel I.; Wilson, M. Robert; Gimse, Jackie Constance Bultman. (1987). *Borderline daughters: An optimal configuration for their growth.* American Association of Psychiatric Services for Children (1986, Las Vegas, Nevada). Ctr. for Adolescent Psychiatry, Faribault, MN. Child & Adolescent Social Work Journal, Sum., Vol. 4(2), 105–22.

Stevens, Constance J.; Puchtell, Laura A.; Ryu, Seongryeol; Mortimer, Jeylan T. (1992). *Adolescent work and boys' and girls' orientations to the future.* Federal Bureau of Prisons, WI. Sociological Quarterly, Sum., Vol. 33(2), 153–69.

Teachman, Jay D. (1991). *Contributions to children by divorced fathers.* U. Maryland, Ctr. on Population, Gender, & Social Inequality, College Park. Social Problems, Aug., Vol. 38(3), 358–71.

Tepp, Alan V. (1983). *Divorced fathers: Predictors of continued paternal involvement.* American Journal of Psychiatry, Nov., Vol. 140(11), 1465–69.

Tierney, Carol W. (1984). *Visitation patterns and adjustment of preschool children of divorce.* U. Colorado, Boulder. Dissertation Abstracts International, May, Vol. 44(11–B).

Tropf, Walter D. (1984). *An exploratory examination of the effect of remarriage on child support and personal contacts.* U. Central Florida. Journal of Divorce, Spr., Vol. 7(3), 57–73.

Trunnell, Thomas L. (1968). *The absent father's children's emotional disturbances.* 8001 Frost St., San Diego, Calif. Archives of General Psychiatry, Vol. 19(2), 180–88.

Wallerstein, Judith S.; Kelly, Joan B. (1980). *Effects of divorce on the visiting father-child relationship.* Marin Community Mental Health Services, San Rafael, CA. American Journal of Psychiatry, Dec., Vol. 137(12), 1534–39.

Wallerstein, Judith S.; Kelly, Joan B. (1981). *Effects of divorce on the visiting father-child relationship.* Ctr. for the Family in Transition, Corte Medera, CA. Annual Progress in Child Psychiatry & Child Development, 380–91.

Warshak, Richard A. (1979). *The effects of father-custody and mother-custody on children's personality development.* U. Texas Health Science Ctr., Dallas. Dissertation Abstracts International, Aug., Vol. 40(2–B), 940.

Wigle, Stanley E. (1983). *A longitudinal study of the relationship between father absence subsequent to divorce and children's evaluations of themselves and their parents.* Kansas State U. Dissertation Abstracts International, Nov., Vol. 44(5–A), 1396–97.

Yamazaki, T. (1984). *Achievement of true ego identity: Psychotherapeutic process of a college graduate male.* Ichiyoukai Hosp., Fukushima, Japan. Tohoku Psychologica Folia, Vol. 43(1–4), 105–11.

ACKNOWLEDGMENTS

To the men, women, and children who share
their stories and journey with me. God Bless.

The following list contains the names of the people who have been dearest in my life. First, for the book:

Julia Cameron, for her brilliant insights, writing, and intuitive teaching; for sharing her stage; for being my believing mirror; for the last-minute saves; and for saying YES. Without her this book would not exist.

Bob Earll, for his stories, editing, sense of humor, endless patience, and walking his talk.

My agent, Susan Schulman, for her guidance, patience, and humor in the face of adversity.

My editor, Carol Southern, for her faith and trust; my Publisher, Chip Gibson, and Potter's Editorial Director, Lauren Shakely, for their confidence and support; the great Crown/Potter team: Eliza Scott, Steve Magnuson, Andrew Martin, Tina Constable, Elke Villa, Robbin Gourley, Paula Cohen, Susan DeStaebler, Jane Searle, Laurie Stark, Mark McCauslin, and all the others working behind the scenes.

Dr. Sheila Flaherty, for loving guidance and healing.

Carl Fritz, for the steps of manhood, his fierce defense, and his love.

My research assistants (and friends): Colleen Cline, for being the "can do" woman; Kizziah Burton, for the laughter and pastoral counseling; Genevieve Strother, Kate and Joss Black, Snow Anderson, and Erik Herman, for handling the deadlines; Suzanne Brussard and Kelly Morgan, for teaching The Artist's Way with humor; Camille Denton, for sanity.

Susan Leon, for her editing help and kindness; Larry Sugar, Janice Gallagher, Bill Patrick, Marcy Posner, Art

Bachrach, and Dr. Richard Hendren, for their original faith in the project and in me.

In their time and way, many of the following people helped save my life and make my life. Their contributions include a good word at the right time, a hand proffered in friendship, an expectation to live up to. I love them more than I can show.

Gary Soloman, Dina Petrakis, Matt Brandebur, Bill Holler, Michelle Lowrance, Peter George, Phyllis Estes, Anton Ursini, Dennis Minogue, Vicki Hubley, Bruce Houston, Ann Foster, Mark Pearson, Maggie Gautier, Mitchell Canoff, Sophy Burnam, Peter Ziminsky, Dori Vanelli, Hank Evans, Cokey Evans, Bob Morgan, and Charles Simmons, for their humor and kindheartedness; Michael Cotter, for being my eskimo. Barry Cecconi, Ted Gluck, Laura Lashever, Dr. Richard Rosen, and Dr. Arnold Jones, for their patience.

Dan Craig, Jeff Crosthwaite, Gordon Dia'Chenko, Dan McNamara, Patrick Dragon, Michelle Lowrance, Doug O'Donahue, and Greg Stevens, for being friends no matter what and watching my back.

Jim Miller, Jamie Frankfurt, and Gaven de Becker, for showing me what it is like to be a man, and Thursday-night dinners.

Carol Gilligan and Rick Weissbourd—for their brilliant work and for taking an interest in mine.

Gene "Merlin" Woody for the music. Katie Hemmeter, for all that talent; Ellen Longo and Jenny Trindel, for their eye on the bottom line; Elizabeth McLeod and the Bay Area Girls Center; Kim Whitelock, for hiring me in the wilderness; Brian Gill, for letting me pound nails with him when times were tough; Chris Cameron, for the music; the Parent Assistance Center, Santa Fe; Loren Basch, Michelle Menendez, Gilbert Ramos, Thiery, Ezra, Selina, Greg, and Rebecca; Stan and Phil and the Bodhi Tree Bookstore; Kirk Ladine and Phillip Lamb, for their example and their music.

Brenda M., Gracie H., Stewart H., Amanda, Ezra, and Erin;

Toby Berlin and Paul Adamo of the Learning Annex; Dini Petty; Elizabeth Lesser of the Omega Institute; Barbara Zirl from Bozell; the officials and employees at Amtrak; Adele Heyman and Sandy Levine of the Open Center, Arielle Ford, Marianne Williamson, Matthew Fox, Brian Weiss, Andy Weil; David Thorn, Gail Hunt, Joan Oliver, Greta Biegle of *New Age Journal;* Interface in Cambridge; Nancy Lunney and Esalen; Jeremy Tarcher, Joel Fotinos, John and Karen Baca, Keith Rudman, Joyce Rey, Lori Henry, Mimi Fleischman, Phil Dunbar, Sarah Koph, Robin Jacobowitz, Skip Pettus, Sherry and David McConghie, Peg Moulden, Lila and Rubio Padilla, Jose and Lydia, Linda, Pamela, Carolyn Cook, ML, from New Mexico.

For being there beyond the call of duty—Theda Real, for her courage; Nick Joost; Mary Fichter; Teresea Delucio; Doug Vogel; Scott Brown; Neal Handler; Susan Golds; Carol Shaw, for her sparkling intelligence; Mary Cirillo, for her grace; Babette Ison, for unconditional love; Cathy Allen, for her faith and courage; Howard Sherman, for that big brain; Ron Schultz; Neal Romaneck, for getting famous and giving me a job; David Seligman; Jamie Lulu and Kristen Spear, for the big voice and letting me backstage; Michael Iskra; Peter Stein, for the racing; Nancy F., for the sunshine; Todd Shapiro; Karen V., for the laughter; Nate and Carolyn; Shirley K., for her courage; my brothers, Jon and Jim, and sister, Paula.

Eddie, G.B., Lisa, Francis, Scott, and Donny, who didn't make it and died before their time.

My faithful friends and believing mirrors: Colleen M.C.; Marvin R.; Deb Morgan; Debbie Field; Dan Pomerantz; Jeannie Teutsch; Maureen Miller; Vail Lopez; Marie Leaner, for erudition and kindness; Sweet November; John Isham; Marci; my grandmothers, Minnie and Elizabeth; Grandpas Arnie and Frank; Marcella, Tom, Norma, Bill, Brenda, Harry, and Ruth, all the cousins; Mandy, Matthew, Sarah, April and her recovery; Emma and Brandi and Little Jon; Barbara, Gerry, and Glenn, for doing such a good job; Sharon Fried, Bonnie, Phil,

Guy, Greg, Barbara Bixby, Katie and Lucy Burton, and Barbara
Laird, for her excellent treatise on the autobiographical novel;
Shelley Scott, for her lesson in commitment and honor; Pat
Ryan and Martin Block, for guiding my return to college; Ira
Gonzales and the First State Bank of Taos for their trust;
Colleen O'Rourke at Citibank; Mike and Sara Matoin; Unity
Church Chicago; Susan and the librarians at the Harwood
Library, Taos; Mark and the librarians in Santa Fe. Jeannette
Woodward and my teaching colleagues at the College of Santa
Fe. To JAA, for reawakening the dream.

I would especially like to acknowledge the researchers. Many
of the people listed below are already famous; the others
should be. So many people do the hard work of looking for the
answers, sorting out the truth, often without the pay or recognition that such a sacred duty deserves. I would like to thank
them for teaching me through their writings, their lectures, or
the interviews they granted me. (For the record, however, the
opinions in my books are mine—not necessarily theirs.) Over
183 journal articles and books went into the research for *The
Prodigal Father*. I want to thank the following people.

Vice President Al Gore, Jr., and the Father to Father Initiative; Jim Levine of the Fatherhood Project, N.Y.C.; Charles Ballard and Joe Jones for their commitment and success—and
doing what no one thought possible; Dr. Carol Gilligan, for her
book *In a Different Voice*, and for her kindness in reading the
manuscript and fighting the good fight; the Harvard Project on
Women's Psychology, Boys' Development, and the Culture of
Manhood.

Dr. Richard Weissbourd, for his generous time, notes on
the manuscript, and his brilliant book *The Vulnerable Child*.

Dr. Linda Powell, for her wit, humor, and vision. Dr.
William Velez for a conversation on a train.

Terry Hunt at the Center for Psychology and Social Change.

My other professors at Harvard, particularly Dean Murphy,

Gil Noam, Kurt Fischer, Charles Ducey, Howard Gardner, Robert Kegan; Rev. Claudia Highbaugh, Rev. Thomas Mikelson, Rev. Peter Goans, and Ron David, M.D. They proved to me why Harvard is Harvard and taught me as fast as I could learn. (I will eventually catch up on the reading.)

Jamie Young, Tim Collins, Gwendolyn Atwood, Ruben Alvarez, and Jill Jeffer; John Bradshaw, for his guidance; Robert Bly; Michael Mead; Andrew Kimbrell; bell hooks; Sam Keen; T. Berry Brazelton, for the interview and his books; David Blankenhorn; Isolina Ricci, for *Mom's House, Dad's House*; Richard Louv, for his time and *Fatherlove*; Warren Farrell, for *The Myth of Male Power*; Dr. John Livingstone, for the encouragement; Geoffrey Greif; Michael Lamb; Tom Pasch; Judith Wallerstein; Judith Greif; Joseph Weiss; Les Haven's *Making Contact*; George Vaillant's *Wisdom of the Ego*; James Masterson's *The Search for the Real Self*; James Gilligan and his book *Violence*; Joyce Arditti; Edward Kruk; Judge Michelle Lowrance; John Santrock; Ann D'Andrea; Faith Elliot; Thomas Trunnel; Barbara Peat; Tom Winfrey; Marion Jacobs; Gilbert Ramos; Harris Goldstein; Kyle Pruitt; Henry J. Friedman; Constance Ahrons; Arthur Elster; Patricia Gongla; John Jacobs; and many more I have probably left out. To all of you a salute.

And to all The Artist's Way students—for your courage and love, please give this book to a friend. Thanks.

INDEX